AF333581

Developing Software Applications in a Changing IT Environment

Other McGraw-Hill Books of Interest

0-07-000748-9	Aiken	*Data Reverse Engineering: Untying the Legacy Knot*
0-07-001974-6	Andriole	*Managing Systems Requirements: Methods, Tools, and Cases*
0-07-015840-1	Davis	*201 Principles of Software Development*
0-07-032826-9	Jones	*Applied Software Measurement: Assuring Productivity and Quality*
0-07-039400-8	Lyu	*The Handbook of Software Reliability Engineering*
0-07-042948-0	Modell	*A Professional's Guide to Systems Analysis, 2/e*
0-07-052229-4	Pressman	*A Manager's Guide to Software Engineering*

Developing Software Applications in a Changing IT Environment

Management Strategies and Techniques

John A. Stone

McGraw-Hill

New York   San Francisco   Washington, D.C.   Auckland   Bogotá
Caracas   Lisbon   London   Madrid   Mexico City   Milan
Montreal   New Delhi   San Juan   Singapore
Sydney   Tokyo   Toronto

Library of Congress Cataloging-in-Publication Data

Stone, John A.
    Developing software applications in a changing IT environment :
management strategies and techniques   /   John A. Stone
        p.   cm.
    Includes index.
    ISBN 0-07-061719-8
    1. Application software—Development.   I. Title.
QA76.76.A65S78   1996
005.1′068 — dc21   96-37128
                                                                CIP

McGraw-Hill 

A Division of The McGraw·Hill Companies

Copyright © 1997 by The McGraw-Hill Companies, Inc. All rights
reserved. Printed in the United States of America. Except as permitted
under the United States Copyright Act of 1976, no part of this publica-
tion may be reproduced or distributed in any form or by any means, or
stored in a data base or retrieval system, without the prior written per-
mission of the publisher.

1 2 3 4 5 6 7 8 9 0   DOC/DOC   9 0 1 0 9 8 7 6

ISBN 0-07-061719-8

*The sponsoring editor for this book was John Wyzalek, the editing
supervisor was Penny Linskey, and the production supervisor was Don
Schmidt. It was set in Century Schoolbook by Dina John of McGraw
Hill's Professional Book Group Composition Unit.
Printed and bound by R. R. Donnelley & Sons Company.*

*McGraw-Hill books are available at special quantity discounts to use
as premiums and sales promotions, or for use in corporate training
programs. For more information, please write to the Director of Special
Sales, McGraw-Hill, 11 West 19th Street, New York, NY 10011.
Or contact your local bookstore.*

*This book is printed on recycled, acid-free paper containing a
minimum of 50% recycled de-inked fiber.*

Information contained in this work has been obtained by The
McGraw-Hill Companies, Inc. ("McGraw-Hill") from sources
believed to be reliable. However, neither McGraw-Hill nor its
authors guarantee the accuracy or completeness of any information published herein, and neither McGraw-Hill nor its authors
shall be responsible for any errors, omissions, or damages aris-
ing out of use of this information. This work is published with
the understanding that McGraw-Hill and its authors are supply-
ing information, but are not attempting to render engineering or
other professional services. If such services are required, the
assistance of an appropriate professional should be sought.

To Barbara Schaefer, my wife

Contents

Part 2   Time Compression Management—A Framework of Strategies and Techniques for Developing Successful Applications in a Time Compressed Changing Technology Environment

Chapter 11. A Life Cycle Approach to Time Compression Management

Introduction

In the coming years, almost every aspect of application development as we know it will change. Driven by a combination of globalization, business reengineering empowerment, and an increasing abundance of new and promising technologies, the process of developing large-scale business applications will take on many more dimensions than have existed in the past. Our challenge as Information Technology (IT) professionals is to harness these changes to support the needs of our businesses, to satisfy their increasing dependence on the applications we develop, and to do so in an expeditious and cost-effective manner. But leveraging the barrage of new and changing technologies to produce better and more relevant business applications that are delivered more quickly and at lower costs has been an elusive goal that very few organizations have been able to achieve.

The objectives of this book are to explore the reasons why developing business applications in our increasingly dynamic technology environment has proved to be so difficult, and to provide a workable set of strategies and techniques for managing our changing technology environments to develop better applications.

To help readers get the most out of this book I've divided it into two parts. Part I explores the changes in our development and execution technology environments, along with the ways in which the changes impact our ability to develop large-scale applications to support our businesses. We can't fix the problem if we cannot understand it. Part II presents the changes that we'll have to make in our application development cultures, infrastructure, and processes in order to develop successful applications in our changing technology environments, along with practical strategies and techniques for implementing these changes.

I've written this book for the wide spectrum of IT professionals and knowledgeable business users who find themselves increasingly involved with large-scale business application development, but who are frustrated with their inability to harness the technologies we use to make things better than they are. To help such people, I've tried to provide a management perspective on why things happen the way they do, and what can be done to effect positive changes, along with examples from my experiences in large-scale application development. Although many of the book's examples are taken from object-oriented (OO) technology—the technology currently being adopted for wide-spread use in developing business applications—the principles hold for many of the development technologies used in the past, and should (hopefully) hold for many of our future technologies as well.

John A. Stone

Acknowledgments

During the two years that it took to write this book, I was fortunate to have had the assistance of many individuals. I want to take this opportunity to thank them and to acknowledge their contributions, without which this project wouldn't have been possible. Tom Gunn deserves special thanks for his ideas and encouragement, as does Jim Cash. Thanks to Steve Fogarty for his insights, and to Steve Rothman for his forward-thinking ideas and for not having a box. Thanks also to John Sifonis for his ideas and insights, and to Beverly Goldberg for her ideas and her help in turning my ideas into this book. I want to thank Marjorie Spencer for taking on this project, and John Wyzalek, my editor at McGraw-Hill, for his help in seeing the project through to a successful completion.

Finally, thanks to my sister and parents for their encouragement, and very special thanks to Barbara Schaefer, my wife, to whom this book is dedicated. Without her encouragement, advice, patience, understanding, and assistance, which went way beyond what anyone has a right to expect, I could not have written this book.

Time Compressed Technology Change—Proliferation and Evolution of Changes in Application Development, and How They Impact Our Organizations and Professional Lives

1

Introduction

The dimly lit face of Brian's bedroom clock registered 2:05 AM. Less than 15 minutes had passed since he had last rolled over and raised his troubled head to check it. This was going to be another sleepless night. As Brian slid back down into his pillow and closed his eyes to once again survey his company's application development landscape, what he didn't see was a smooth-running, well-integrated organization delivering quality computer applications to support the company's rapidly changing business. That was his vision 2 years ago, when he was promoted to Vice President (VP) of Information Systems. As the Chief Information Officer (CIO) of a Fortune 500 company, and a peer of the Vice Presidents of its major business units, he had looked forward to cleaning up the Information Technology (IT) problems of his company's past and leaving his mark as the officer who finally designed IT to fully meet their needs.

Now, as he pondered the reality of his company's application development projects, what he saw was a landscape marred by mayhem, confusion, late delivery—and in at least two cases—outright failure. The application developers in the Manufacturing and Sales Divisions had retrenched into two irreconcilable camps. The self-proclaimed "data bigots" in the Manufacturing Division took a rigorous information engineering (IE) approach utilizing IEF. The equally resolute developers in the Sales Division, convinced that object-oriented (OO) technology was the only way to go, were charging ahead with Smalltalk. When the VP of Manufacturing Operations disregarded the advice of his own developers and brought in a fast MRP system written in object-oriented C++, echoes of the Sales Division developers' cheers could be heard reverberating through the entire enterprise. The business people in Distribution had successfully implemented their own system—a series of PowerBuilder-based applications that they had purchased from an outside vendor for a third of the price quoted internally, and the CEO was upset because the information he received from each of his divisions wouldn't reconcile—with each other, or with his financial statements. And, as if that were not enough, the company's CFO, his boss, had just engaged a Big 6 consulting firm—the same firm that did their financial audits—to review his "application development business process" and to make recommendations for reengineering it.

Sound familiar? This kind of unfortunate situation is long way from the "good old days" when IBM mainframes dominated the market, COBOL, Customer Information Control Systems (CICS), and DB2 were the order of the day, and IT did the application development. Indeed, these problems are becoming an increasingly common 1990s phenomenon as business needs and the application development technologies available to address them evolve and change at an increasingly rapid rate.

The Late 1990s Applications Development Environment

The rapid globalization of our markets and business environment has created an abundance of new competitors, standards, expectations, and opportunities. Our business philosophies and practices, customer expectations, the standards by which our products are judged, our manufacturing processes, the way we approach markets, and the way we sell are subject to increased and rapid change.[1] (See Fig. 1.1.)

As our business practices undergo rapid and marked change, so must the computer applications that support them. In an integrated global economy, companies that do not have modern world-class com-

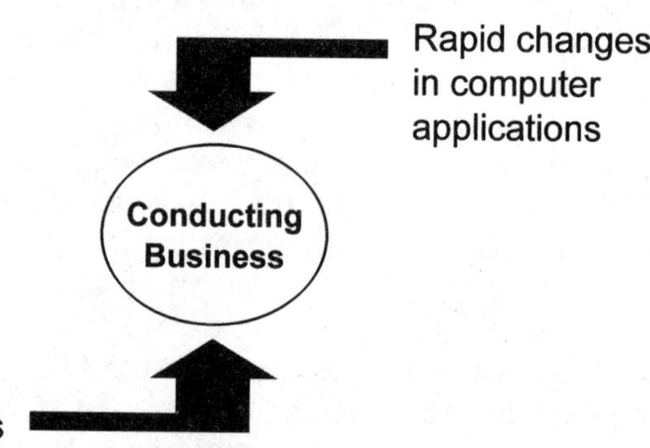

Figure 1.1 Productivity, nimbleness, and change are requirements for late 1990s business.

puter applications cannot effectively compete against those who do. To illustrate how important computer applications, delivered correctly and on time to support new business requirements, are to companies that wish to remain competitive into the 2000s, consider that they cannot:

- successfully implement just-in-time manufacturing or delivery without applications that make accurate inventory information available, when and where they are needed, on a just-in-time basis;
- bring inventory turns to world-class levels, with mainframe-based MRP (Manufacturing Resource Planning) systems that take weeks to assess the impact of changes that occur on a daily or hourly basis;
- effectively compete for business by taking days (of head office processing) to prepare a quote, after a major competitor implements a notebook-based application that supports real-time quotations and order processing right on the customer's premises;
- treat valued customers as the valued customers they are, if they cannot integrate data across business functions and geographic regions so that they can recognize a valued customer when they see one;
- empower employees and implement effective work groups, without applications through which they can quickly and easily communicate.

These business requirements, and others like them, demand more than modern up-to-date applications. The speed and flexibility needed to effectively support these business initiatives require that the applications that support them be based on current development technologies and techniques. Fast MRP systems, capable of performing an 8-hour MRP run in less than a minute, are quickly becoming an indispensable business tool among the world's leading manufacturers.[2] But as our unfortunate Manufacturing Division IT practitioners found out, successful fast MRP implementations are typically based on OO development technologies such as C++.

The IT problem, and a perennial business nemesis, is that consistent and reliable development of the applications required to support these kinds of business initiatives in today's business and IT environments, is itself a tricky and uncertain business. To understand why this is so, why application development technology innovations have so much trouble keeping up with the business changes that they have in many cases enabled, and to present some basic solutions to the problem, are the subjects of this book. But before we begin, we must first understand the late-1990s IT and business environments along with the pressures they exert on application development. Let's take a closer look.

Information Technology and Business Pressures on Application Development

"THE INFORMATION REVOLUTION: How digital technology is changing the way we work and live" read the front cover of a recent issue of *BusinessWeek*.[3] The feature article—and to a significant extent, the entire edition—went on to describe how developments in "digital technology" are reshaping every aspect of our 1990s personal and business lives. Behind every such development is of course an application, and behind each application was an application development project. Application development, in today's information-intensive business environment, is playing an increasingly pivotal role in determining the extent to which our businesses succeed—or fail. And with application development's increasingly important and visible role in business, comes increasing business pressure to succeed—pressures to deliver applications that are on time and correct, that provide up-to-date information when and where it is needed, that keep up with the dynamics of the 1990s business environment, and that are developed at lower incremental cost. Application development is also subject to IT pressures to produce applications that can be inexpensively changed, to improve the development process and lower software quality costs, to keep up with fast-moving information technologies, and at the same time, to manage a recalcitrant and slow-moving IT culture and infrastructure. It is within the confluence of these sets of pressures that today's application development takes place. (See Fig. 1.2.)

Delivering Information When and Where It's Needed

Although delivery of accurate information when and where needed, is a necessary, frequently articulated, and attainable late-1990s business goal, it can be deceptively difficult to achieve. The fact that the required data often reside in applications developed at different times, based on different assumptions, in different locations, and using different technologies, can turn even the basic job of knowing where the correct data are stored into an arduous task. While many companies have Data Administration (DA) organizations to address this problem, their DA functions are typically based on a bounded set

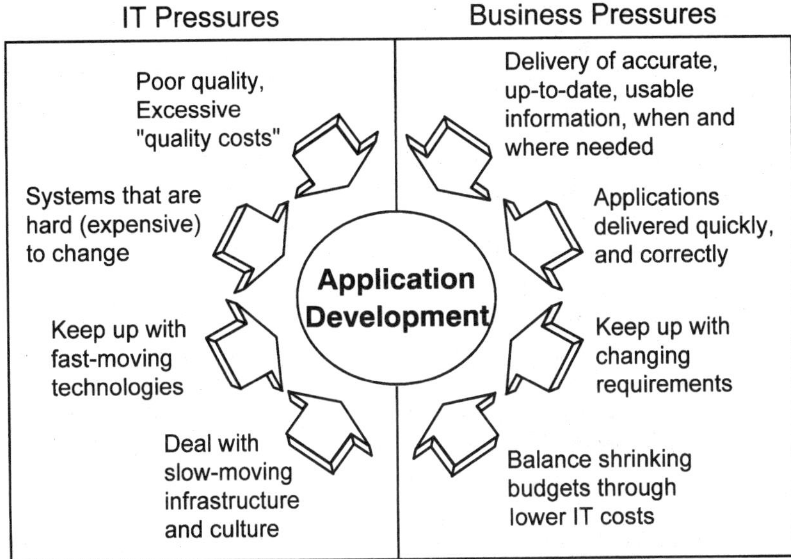

Figure 1.2   Late-1990s application development pressures.

of well-understood technologies—such as relational and hierarchical databases, flat files, and IE. In today's world of multiple and evolving information technologies, this is no longer sufficient. New technologies, such as distributed objects, Linda networks, and on-line analytical processing (OLAP) complicate the issue. How, for example, does an application provide correct and consistent information when and where it's needed when some parts of the information reside in relational databases that support open and unrestricted access from a variety of tools, and other parts of the information are encapsulated inside of "objects" that provide access only through the set of "methods" that are available to them? Or, how can information be provided when and where it's needed, when the information is needed on a range of multiple technologies—Intel PCs, Apple Macs, UNIX workstations, and notepads, for example—and when the tools utilized to develop and maintain the application that provide access to the information do not support the entire range? These kinds of problems would be daunting enough if the range of storage and delivery technologies involved in providing information was itself a stable target— something one could manage to. The fact that late 1990s information storage and delivery technologies are themselves diversifying and evolving at an accelerating rate can make this daunting task into one bordering on the impossible.[4] More about this later.

Rapid Development

Rapid development of correct applications—applications that are developed in time to meet current business needs upon initial delivery—has long been an IT goal that's as difficult to realize as it is important. So elusive is this goal that, looking back from the late 1990s, the Rapid Application Development (RAD) popularized by James Martin less than a decade ago seems more like a well-worn oxymoron than an achievable quest.[5] RAD technologies, in the form of fourth-generation languages (4GLs) and computer-aided software engineering (CASE) tools and methodologies have not produced rapid applications in a widespread, consistent, and repeatable manner. Nor have today's object-oriented graphical development tools and approaches. What these initiatives have produced, along with a handful of notable successes, is a legacy of computer application technology islands, with entrenched camps of enthusiastic followers and detractors.

But delivering applications quickly and correctly, is not sufficient. The dynamics of the late-1990s global business environment demand that applications, once delivered, be able to keep up with increasingly rapid changes in business requirements. External business pressures, from competitors halfway around the world, that sell into the same markets but by their own sets of rules, from new government regulations, from business initiatives for entering emerging markets, and from internal pressures from cost cutting, downsizing, and business reengineering efforts—to name just a few—are causing this to happen. The problem, and a source of considerable business-related IT pressure, is that many of our applications have trouble keeping up with the seemingly constant barrage of new business demands that result from these changes. While many specific examples of new approaches to application development are showing promise in this area, they fall short of the mark in two ways. The first is that much the reduction in maintenance effort often results, not from applications that can be more easily changed, but from applications that are more correct upon initial delivery. While reducing the gap between the time applications are initially delivered and the time when they fulfill their users' mission objectives is a worthy goal, and the consequent reduction in "quality costs" goes right to the company's bottom line, time reduction does little to ensure that the applications, once delivered, can be easily changed to meet changing business requirements.[6] The second problem is that, where the scope of the changes to business requirements covers applications and data that are implemented in different technologies, the changes can become significantly more difficult to implement. This kind of problem can result from

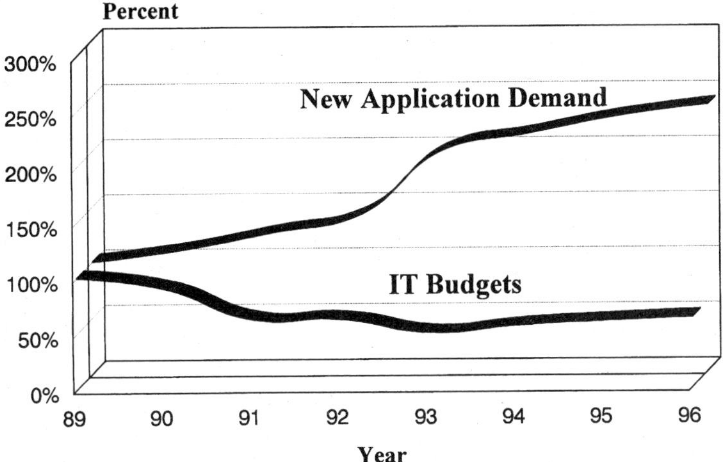

Figure 1.3 New application demand versus IT budgets.

business reengineering efforts that realign business processes to cut across former organizational boundaries—and consequently, former applications and technologies as well.

A final, and for many IT organizations, most immediate, business pressure is to reduce costs. In spite of the fact that demand for computer applications is increasing at an exponential rate, as the following figure shows, fewer and fewer companies are increasing IT budgets commensurate with the increased demand.[7] (See Fig. 1.3.)

Considering the basic orientation of most IT organizations toward technology, and the increasing pressure on IT to deliver more and more applications on a comparatively static budget, it should come as no surprise that many IT organizations look to new technologies as a means of addressing this gap. Indeed, many new application development technologies—OO frameworks and graphical development tools, for example—can, and do, provide more for less. Applications that took years to develop, only a half-decade ago, can now be developed in a matter of months utilizing these kinds of tools. The key word here is *can,* for as almost anyone currently associated with IT knows, many applications—especially those that are large, complex, and mission critical—still take an inordinately long time to develop. And the failure rate is still alarmingly high. In the following chapters, we will examine the reasons why, in spite of the prodigious advances in the technologies and tools we use, these problems continue to persist.

Of those applications that are successfully developed, many continue to be delivered to their users with relatively poor quality. Our quality costs—the costs that would not have been incurred if applications were precisely correct the first time and every time thereafter—are both visible and high.[8] It's not at all uncommon for large-scale applications to be delivered with only a fraction of the functionality required by their users, and for the IT organizations that developed them to spend substantial portions of their budgets on "maintaining" the delivered applications until their functionality is brought to an acceptable level. As with large and complex nonsoftware development projects, the occurrence of quality problems—and the quality costs in terms of the maintenance required to fix them when they do occur—increases with the number of new development technologies involved in the project. Although the reasons for the increase can be as varied as the projects themselves, where multiple and new development technologies are present, they typically include lack of application development fundamentals such as:

- a development infrastructure capable of supporting each of the development technologies,

- a consistent application process or approach that addresses the combined and individual needs of the suite of development technologies,

- a culture with a sufficiently broad outlook that more than a single development approach can be effectively embraced, and

- a life cycle for addressing new and changing developing technologies.

In my experience, failure to achieve this minimal set of requirements, when combined with the array of inappropriate expectations that almost always accompany new and not yet fully understood development technologies, leads—with 100 percent certainty—to a flawed application development process and a poor-quality result.

Problems with Maintenance

Applications that are brittle—difficult and expensive to maintain—have been a persistent and nettlesome problem for as long as companies have used computers. Indeed, many companies consistently spend 70 to 80 percent of their IT budgets on maintenance.[9] Given the number of new development technologies designed to make maintenance quicker and easier—OO development, 4GLs, I-CASE (Integrated CASE), for example—one would think that IT organizations would collectively be getting this problem under control, and that the percentage of IT budgets allocated to maintenance would decrease. But this isn't the case, and maintenance in 1997 continues to be as burdensome as it was in 1987 or 1977. Perhaps worse.

Although instances in which new development technologies have been instrumental in reducing maintenance are not an uncommon late-1990s phenomenon, a closer look reveals that they are usually limited to applications developed in a single technology. For mission-critical applications—applications that are typically large and complex, and that involve multiple development technologies—maintenance tends to be as costly as ever. A well-executed analysis—in IEF (Information Engineering Facility), for example—that provides a solid foundation for reducing maintenance for applications developed using some technologies, such as IEF or PowerBuilder, may not be much help for portions of the applications developed in other technologies, such as Java or Smalltalk. Problems, such as cultural incompatibilities, relevance of analysis to the implementation requirements and lack of traceability across technologies, get in the way. These problems are compounded when legacy systems written in older technologies are involved, or when the functionality to be changed involves applications written by different organizations.

Proliferation and Evolution of Information Technologies

At the heart of the problem of developing applications utilizing multiple technologies, is the technologies themselves—the accelerating pace at which new development technologies are coming on the scene, and the rate at which technologies already in use are evolving. Consider the startling array of application development technologies available to mid-1990s developers compared to the relatively narrow band of development technologies just 10 years before. (See Fig. 1.4.)

In the mid-1980s, most applications were developed utilizing a narrow and stable set of technologies. For large-scale mission-critical business applications, the most ubiquitous set of development technologies was hand-coded COBOL, CICS, and Structured Query Language (SQL) (for accessing DB2). Execution technologies, typical-

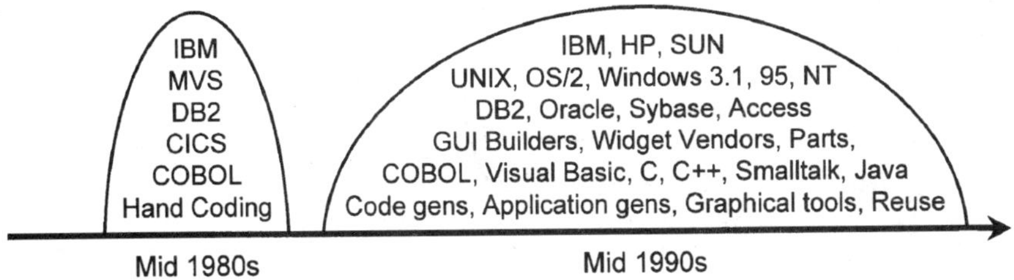

Figure 1.4 Mid-1980s versus mid-1990s application development technologies.

ly IBM mainframe, MVS, and 3270-style terminals, were correspondingly static.[10] By the mid-1990s, this was no longer true. The once stable set of mainframe technologies was rapidly giving way to Client/Server technologies that were at once broader and less stable. Client technologies could be Windows 95, NT (New Technology), OS/2 (Operating System 2), or any of a number of commercial flavors of UNIX. Server technologies included not only these, but mainframes and minicomputers as well, and business applications were being developed using technologies as diverse as IEF, PowerBuilder, VisualBasic, Java, Smalltalk, C, and C++.

To fully appreciate how profoundly this expansion of available information technologies affects application development, two important factors must be considered. The first is that application development is impacted by the execution technologies, on which the completed system will run, and by application development approaches, not just by application development technologies themselves. (See Fig. 1.5.) The second is that, as we shall see, application development is impacted by a "time compression" created by the combination of proliferation and evolution of development, execution, and approach technologies.

Execution, Approach, and Development Technology Interactions

Execution technology architectures, in terms of workstations, servers, fault tolerance, performance, interface, and interoperability require-

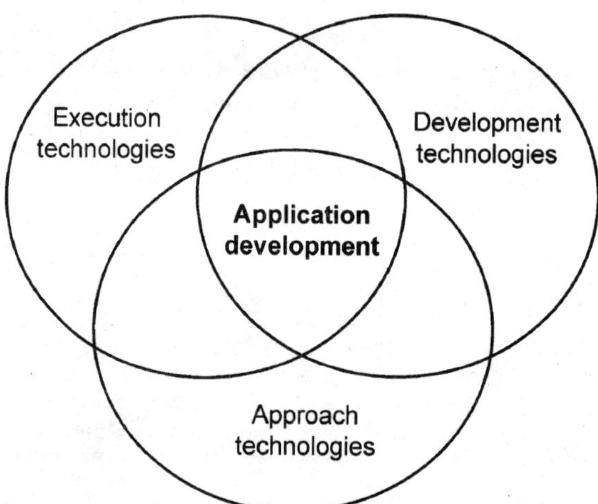

Figure 1.5 Development, execution, and approach technologies impact application development.

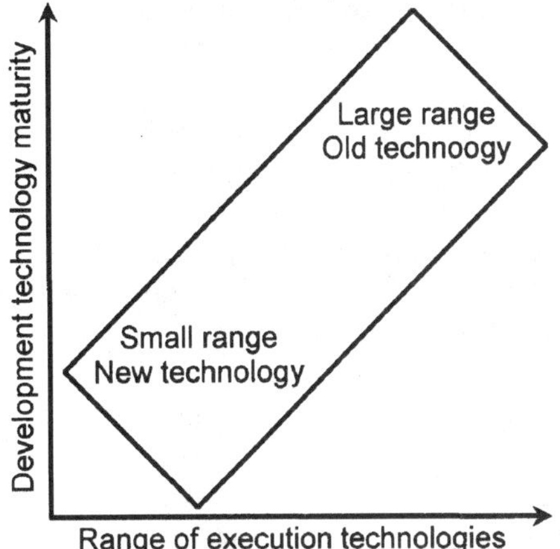

Figure 1.6 Execution technology range versus development technology maturity.

ments, for example, can profoundly affect application development. The execution technology architecture on which an application is to be deployed places limits on the range of technologies that can be utilized for its development. Although clearly not all development tools can be expected to support all technologies, this limitation can result in surprising and unwelcome consequences. The reason is that execution technology requirements also limit development technologies in terms of maturity: the wider the range of execution technologies, the higher will be the maturity requirements placed on the development technologies. (See Fig. 1.6.) The reason for this relationship is straightforward. Development technologies are themselves commercial applications, and the companies that develop and publish them almost universally prefer to release their new products on a narrow range of execution technologies, expanding the range only after their offerings are relatively mature. The problem is that where the new development technology represents a significant advance—something that is becoming increasingly common—a technology with a wide execution range requirement can result in a new application being developed in an older, less appropriate, technology.

While the business and IT impact of this problem may not be significant near the low maturity end of the curve—things are typically too risky down there for most businesses—it can be very significant near the high end of the curve, where it can cause new mission-critical applications to be developed in older technologies that place limits on important things like future functionality, maintainability, and interoperability. The underlying problem for business and IT, and an issue that we will directly address in this book, is that development and execution technology decisions are typically treated as parts of separate processes, under separate governance, and are therefore not engineered concurrently, as they should be.

Application development approach technologies, typically encountered in the form of development methodologies, can result in a different, but equally devastating, set of problems. The issue here is that approaches are not just closely coupled with development tools—which they have to be, in order to add significant value. They are also closely coupled with development support infrastructure and culture. As development technologies evolve and change, and as multiple development tools place conflicting demands on methodologies, the methodologies must change—and so must the infrastructure along with the IT, business, and management cultures that come into contact with application development. And while the latest whiz-bang high-tech application development tools can be acquired simply by cutting a purchase order, the methodology, infrastructure, and cultural changes required to get value from the newly purchased tools are much more difficult. They can take months, even years, to implement. All too often, the result is implementation of the new development technology without even the most basic kinds of foundation infrastructure required to make it work. When this happens, the consequences are as predictable as they are obvious.

Consider what happened when a major U.S. company decided to develop a new mission-critical application in Client/Server technology utilizing the IEF Upper CASE tool for analysis and PowerBuilder for implementation. For what they were trying to accomplish, IEF and PowerBuilder were a pretty good match. An IEF-based analysis produces a rock-solid data model that can be used by fast visual development tools, such as PowerBuilder, with up to a 100 percent productivity improvement.[11] But an IEF analysis, which yields a data model that's thorough and stable enough to support a high-performance PowerBuilder implementation, takes lots of resources and time—neither of which had been budgeted for the analysis portion of the project. Training in event-driven design and acquisition or development of a suitable library of PowerBuilder objects were also absent from the project's plan and budget, as was acquisition of a methodology to guide the developers through their first application development project utilizing these tools. The result was a 6-month project that took 18 months to complete! Because the company was basing their PowerBuilder implementation on an IEF data model that did not support all of the business requirements, this meant that the SQL code behind the PowerBuilder objects had to be continually updated as the database was changed to support newly discovered business requirements. The lack of training in event-driven design resulted in three

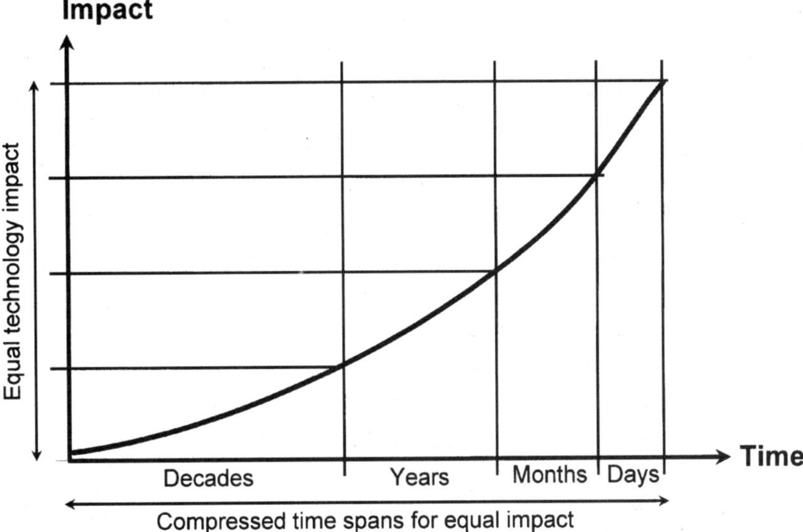

Figure 1.7 Time compression.

separate implementations of the same application before the developers figured things out and got the system's graphical interface right.

Time Compression

Time compression is the accelerating shrinkage—*compression*—of the amounts of time that IT professionals, especially those associated with application development, have for coming to terms with technology-based change. The time that it takes for current technologies to expand so that more of them become available, and for current technologies—those that are already available—to evolve and mature, is continuously being compressed. (See Fig. 1.7.) The degree of technology impact that took a decade to develop in the 1970s, is felt today in a matter of a year or two. If the trend continues—and for the next decade— and there is no reason why it should not—by the end of the 1990s, the same time interval may well compress down to months! At some point, it may be compressed all the way down to days.[12] For application developers, the two salient things about time compression are that:

■ The compression is not linear. The technologies with which we work are expanding and evolving at an *accelerating* rate, so that with each passing year, the time interval required for an equal degree of technology impact is *exponentially* compressed, and

- The results of the exponential compression are most acutely felt in terms of impact on individuals and their development projects.

Time compression for those associated with application development results from the confluence of two 1990s phenomena. The first is that, as we discussed, three sets of information technologies are involved in almost every sizable or complex 1990s application development project. They are:

- development technologies—the tools, languages and components that are utilized by developers to analyze requirements and build applications,

- execution technologies—the hardware, system software, network, and data management software that form the environment in which the completed application will run, and

- approach technologies—the technologies associated with the application development process, in terms of methodologies, standards, work products, participants, and support organizations involved in application development.

The second phenomenon is that, as we move through the 1990s, each of these technologies is subject to accelerating expansion and evolution. Take languages, for example. COBOL and C, the ubiquitous languages of the 1980s, have expanded to include C, C++, Java Smalltalk, and COBOL, along with a wide variety of CASE and graphical development tools, from a number of different vendors, each with its own proprietary language.[13] Many of these languages are available from an expanding variety of different development tool, package, database and consulting vendors, each with its own interpretation and agenda. Similar expansions are evident in execution and approach technologies. Indeed, a recent issue of *Application Development Trends* contained 46 Client/Server development tools and no less than 11 different methodologies currently in use just for OO development.[14]

If the technology challenge faced by late-1990s application developers, was limited to managing the accelerating rate at which development, execution, and approach technologies are diversifying, their task would be formidable enough. Developing mission-critical applications amid multiple—and in some cases conflicting—technologies is certainly not easy. But the reality is that the development, execution, and approach technologies are also evolving. And they are evolving at an accelerating rate.

Ability of Organizations to Cope

The accelerating pace at which development execution and approach technologies are expanding, and evolving and the time compression that results, stand in sharp contrast to the relatively static ability of most IT and business organizations to cope. Acquiring an OO CASE tool, for example, is far simpler than implementing the CASE tool, so that the company benefits from it. Getting real value from the CASE tool often requires changes in culture and infrastructure, such as:

- implementation of, and training in, the OO methodology that the new tool supports; business reorientation of IT personnel from technical to business;

- development of new support infrastructure components, such as standards, project management, reporting, and estimation metrics;

- organizational change to support acquisition, development, and reuse of OO classes (software components); and

- reorientation of business users so that they can work effectively with their IT counterparts in new and different ways, such as defining use cases or validating object models.

The problem, and the direct result of time compression, is that while these cultural and infrastructure changes are being implemented—a matter of a few months to several years for most organizations—time compressed technology expansion and evolution march on, at an accelerating pace, so that:

- the CASE tool, or the methodology it supports, may be substantially changed, or perhaps have been replaced by something newer and better,

- new and improved implementation technologies, based on the CASE tool, may enter the market, and

- alternate technologies, that are quicker and cheaper than those associated with the CASE tool may become available, and be successfully implemented on a newer execution technology, by business units who do so without even consulting IT. (See Fig. 1.8.)

Sound daunting? It is, but for those who can successfully manage the time-compressing confluence created by the expanding and evolving development, execution, and approach technologies that impact application development, the rewards can be substantial.

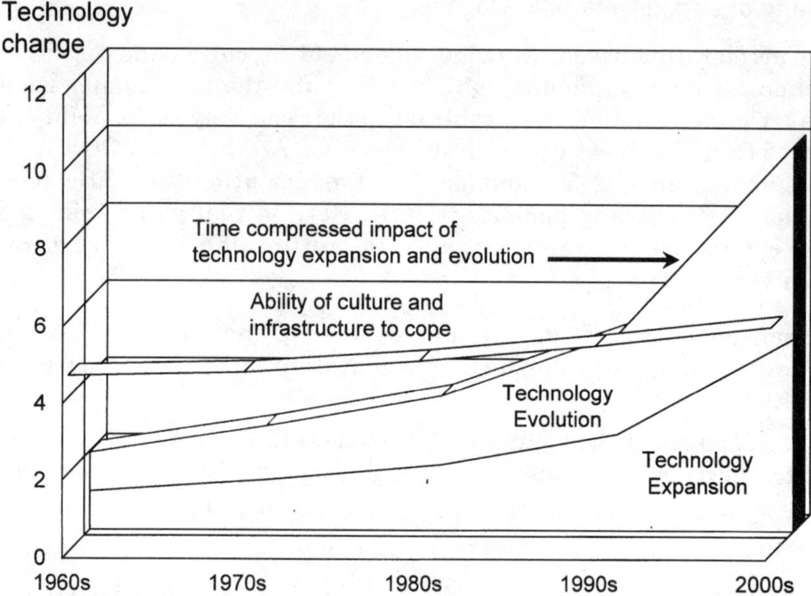

Figure 1.8   Technology change versus ability of IT organizations to cope.

To illustrate just how substantial, consider what happened a few years ago to a Midwest company that began a large-scale application development effort utilizing Texas Instruments' IEF CASE tool. One of the applications being developed was a decision-support system for planning and managing a billion-dollar worldwide inventory of capital assets. The time required to complete the system was estimated at 1 year, based on an implementation in IEF. As the analysis progressed, a decision was made to implement the system using Microsoft Excel, VisualBasic, and Access—the Microsoft database that had just hit the market. The system was implemented in these new technologies in just 6 months, half the time that would have been required using IEF. But the Excel, VisualBasic, and Access-based system, although successful, ran too slowly. The level of performance required by the system's business users could not be achieved. So the application was once more implemented, this time utilizing Essbase, a multidimensional database based on a newer, and more appropriate, technology. This time the implementation was completed in only 3 months. Although part of the decrease in implementation time can be attributed to the stability and correctness of the IEF models and to a better understanding of the business problem by the implementation team, much of the exponential decrease in implementation time was attributable to utilizing newer, faster, and more appropriate development and execution technologies.

A Canadian software company had a similar experience, although the application and the technologies used in its implementation could hardly have been more different. The system, an advanced manufacturing application for reduced instruction set computer (RISC) architecture UNIX workstations, was first implemented in ParkPlace Smalltalk. The development project represented a concentrated labor-intensive effort, in part because of the 6 staff-months that went into developing the custom widgets that were required for the system's unique graphical interface. When a second system was developed, by the same people a year later—with the similar graphical interface—but this time, utilizing Visual C++ along with a newly available library of graphical widgets—the effort required to implement the graphical interface required only 6 weeks! The business benefit derived from this kind of foreshortened development were important for each of these companies, as time was critical and a lot was at stake.

The idea here is not that Essbase is somehow better than Access, or that C++ is superior to Smalltalk. Depending on the circumstances, the opposite could just as easily be true. The idea is that the ability to switch to a newer and more appropriate suite of technologies for use by an application development project can pay off handsomely, as it did for these two companies.

The problem, and the late-1990s application development paradox, is that while technology change is accelerating, our IT organizations, strategies culture, and infrastructure, indeed our business institutions, as *users* of computer applications, have been developed around—and in many cases, painstakingly optimized to support—1980s-style static suites of development, execution, and approach technologies. Today, with time-compressed technologies advancing at an accelerating rate, and businesses dependent on delivery of new applications to the extent that the company's ultimate success or failure can hang in the balance, the static approaches of a decade ago are no longer adequate.

Time-Compressed Management

The problem is solvable. The impacts of time compressed change can be managed for organizations that have to deliver the fast, reliable, and relevant applications that will be required to support turn-of-the-century business. But for most organizations, solving the problem will be neither easy or quick. To illustrate the complexities involved in

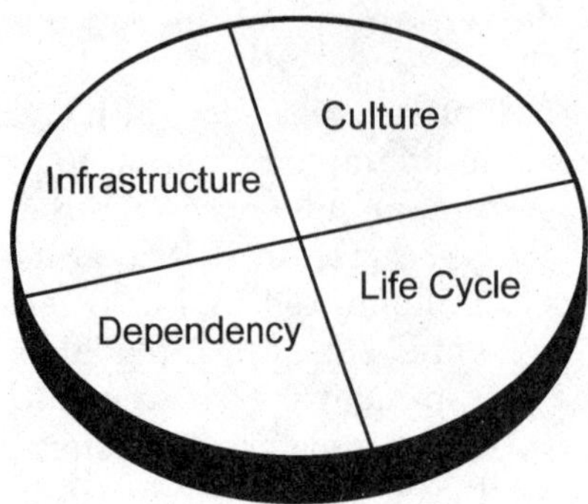

Figure 1.9 The four components of Time Compressed Management.

implementing a solution to this problem in real-world corporate environments, we'll use Time Compressed Management (TCM), a management framework that I've developed for exploring the problem and developing a set of solutions for it.

TCM consists of the following four components: (See Fig. 1.9.)

- *Culture Component:* A culture that's reoriented to anticipate and deal with time compressed change. As we shall see later in this book, to be effective, management, business, and IT cultures must be involved,

- *Infrastructure Component:* A dynamic information technology infrastructure, designed to cope with a time-compressed IT environment,

- *Dependency Component:* A set of initiatives that fortify application development dependencies against the ravages of time compressed change, and a

- *Life Cycle Component:* An information technology life cycle that's optimized, not for the stable suite of technologies of the past, but for today's multiple technologies that constantly evolve and change.

We'll present and explore TCM in Part II of this book. But before we dive into TCM, along with the culture, infrastructure, dependency, and life cycle components that real solutions to technology time compressed change must address, let's take a step backward and take a hard look at some basic misconceptions concerning time compressed technology change and application development.

References

1. For an excellent discussion of how our business practices are changing, along with the factors driving the changes, see Lester Thurow, *Head To Head,* William Morrow Co.,

1992; Tom Gunn, *Twenty First Century Manufacturing,* Harper Business, 1992; and Michael Hammer, *Reengineering The Corporation,* Harper Business, 1993.

2. Thomas Gunn, *In the Age of the Real-Time Enterprise,* Oliver Wight Publications, 1994.

3. "The Information Revolution," *BusinessWeek,* special 1994 bonus issue.

4. "Wonder Chips," *BusinessWeek,* July 4, 1994 provides insights on the accelerating rate at which computer hardware—especially chips—is developing, along with what might happen in the future.

5. James Martin, *Rapid Application Development,* Macmillan, 1991.

6. John Stone, *Inside ADW and IEF: The Promise and Reality of CASE,* McGraw-Hill, 1993.

7. Dr. Howard Rubin, Rubin Systems Inc.

8. Ronald M. Fortuna, "The Quality Imperative," in Ernest C. Hugh, ed., *Total Quality: An Executive's Guide for the 1990s,* Dow Jones-Irwin, IL 1990; Chap. 1. Also see John J. Heldt and Daniel J. Costa, *Quality Pays,* Hitchcock Publishing Company, Homewood, IL, 1988, pp. 1–24.

9. Roger Pressman, *Software Engineering: A Practitioner's Approach,* 3d ed., McGraw-Hill, 1992; Sec. 1.4. Also see Jerry Huchzermeyer, "What Can We Expect From Re-Engineering," *CEC Rapid Exchange,* Winter 1991.

10. Other static sets of development technologies were also put to use, during the same period, for other common types of business applications—C and UNIX for trading systems, Pascal for higher education, APL for certain kinds of analytics, to name just a few. The point is that, regardless of the particular technologies employed, for each type of business application—and especially for each development organization—the set was bounded and static.

11. John Stone, "CASE Plays a Role in Visual Development," *Application Development Trends,* January 1994.

12. For an insightful description of where development and execution technologies might be in the mid-2000s, see David Gelernter, *Mirror Worlds,* Oxford University Press, 1992. Also see "Wonder Chips," *BusinessWeek,* July 4, 1994. For a different, but just as fascinating and relevant perspective, see p.62, Microprocessors in 2020, David Patterson; p.68, Wireless Networks, George Zysuan; p.80 Artificial Intelligence, Douglas Lenat; p.84, Intelligent Software, Pattie Maes; p.90 Commentary: Virtual Reality, Brenda Laurel; p.192, Technology Infrastructure, Arati Prabhakar; p.198, Digital Literacy, Richard Lanham; p.200 The Information Economy, Hal Varian—"Key Technologies For The 21st Century," *Scientific American,* 150th Anniversary Issue, September 1995.

13. Although Lower CASE tools may generate code in standard languages, the diagrams and constructs that form the input to the code generators—and that are therefore the languages that developers must deal with—cover a wide range of vender-specific languages. Widget usage and scripting languages for graphical development tools also tend to be vendor-specific and therefore represent a wide range of languages.

14. *Application Development Trends,* March 1994.

Critical Success Factors for Application Development— How They're Impacted by Technology change

"Throw it out! No more object-oriented Smalltalk! No more object-oriented anything! I want you to write my system in COBOL," roared the Wall Street trader, who's Smalltalk-based application development project was 6 months behind schedule with no completion in sight. The trader, who ran an immensely profitable operation and needed the new application to stay ahead of her competitors, didn't know much about Smalltalk. She didn't know much about COBOL either, or the vastly different approaches that these two languages represent. What she did know was that her development project was headed for certain failure, that she was going to cut her losses, and that she wanted her application to be built using something that she "knew would work."

Her application development project was indeed behind schedule, and it probably was headed for failure. But the problems that the project was experiencing were only peripherally related to OO and Smalltalk. The real culprits were a lack of project management, a team that didn't have the right skill set, and worst of all, an amount of work that could not have been completed within the project's time frame—regardless of the technology or approach. And the real shame of the situation was that with the aid of appropriate estimation metrics backed by the right team and good project management, the problem would have been identified early and dealt with, the project would have been a success, and her application would have been delivered in Smalltalk—the language that was, in fact, the most appropriate for her needs.

Lack of good project management—along with our inability to accurately estimate development effort, control scope, assemble a correctly staffed team, rely on an appropriate development support infrastructure, even report progress in an understandable manner—have been constant and nettlesome thorns in the side of application development.[1] One would think that, with the time compressed proliferation of new application development technologies and approaches, we would also be improving our ability to managing the projects that utilize our new technologies. The reality is that while many new technologies successfully address specific application development problems, they do not fix many of the fundamental flaws that continue to plague our application development projects. Indeed, they can make them worse.

Six CSFs for Application Development

Although there are many well-documented factors that contribute to successful application development, I've found the following critical success factors (CSFs) to be particularly difficult for those developing applications in a time compressed environment to achieve. (See Fig. 2.1.) In time compressed environments, their achievement remains very much the exception rather than the norm.

Accurate Estimation and Scope Control

From a management perspective, accurate estimation and scope control of development projects is among the most important of the CSFs. (See Fig. 2.2.) Most development projects that deliver their applications late, deliver them in poor condition, or do not even deliv-

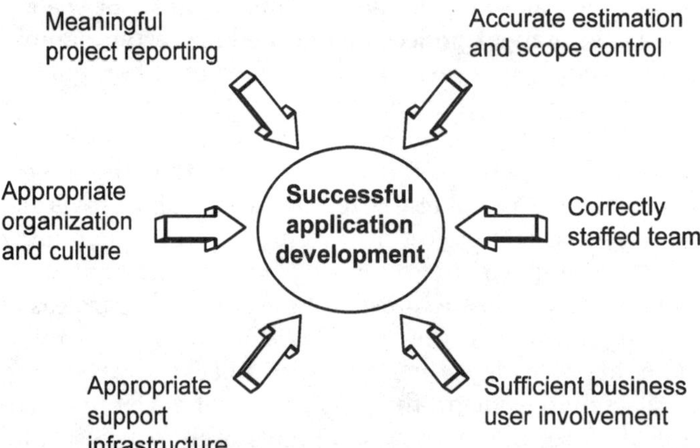

Figure 2.1 Six CSFs for application developing applications in a multiple and evolving technology environment.

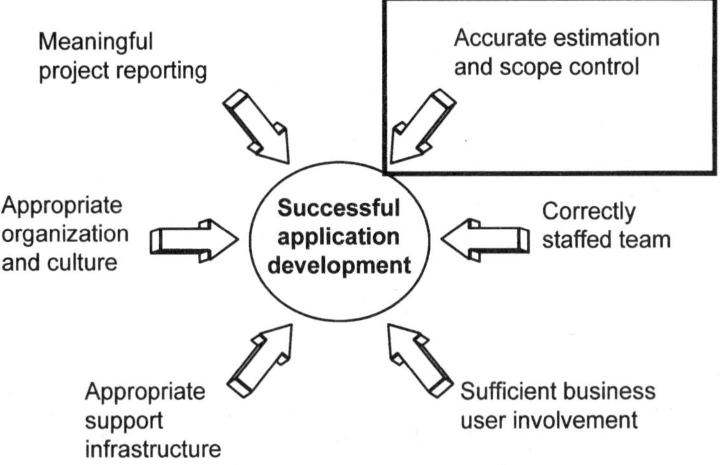

Figure 2.2 Application Management CSF: Accurate estimation and scope control.

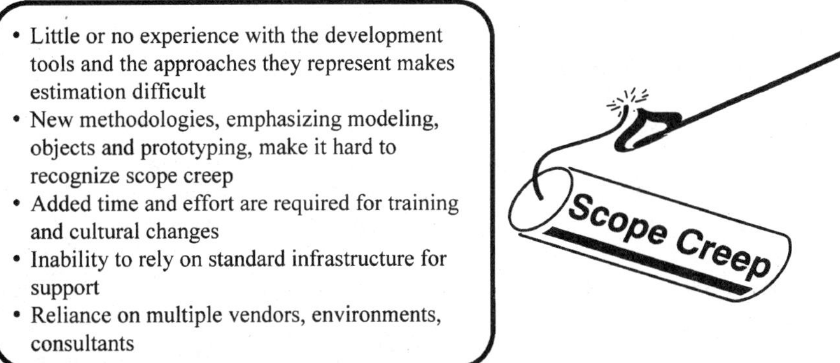

Figure 2.3 Estimation and scoping are a lot more difficult in a multiple and evolving technology environment.

er them at all, can trace their problems to incorrect scoping and estimation.[2] Immediacy of business needs, budgetary constraints, competitive pressures among developers, and lack of commonly accepted and reliable estimation metrics, combine to make this CSF one of the most difficult to achieve—even in traditional development environments. When the technologies are new, and especially when many new technologies are involved, as there are in time compressed environments, our ability to accurately estimate the time and effort required to complete an application development project can quickly degenerate to the point where certain failure is built into the staffing plan before the development project even starts. (See Fig. 2.3) The reasons for this precipitous decline on our ability to estimate include the:

- lack of a suitable experience base for estimating new and unfamiliar tasks,

- lack of familiar information and artifacts upon which reliable estimates can be based,

- lack of experience in recognizing "scope creep" (the propensity of the scope of application development projects to increase as the project proceeds through its life cycle) in terms of the abstract and evolving models are the basis of many new approaches to development,

- unforeseen problems associated with the suite of multiple development and execution technology vendors that are required for many current development efforts,

- additional time and effort required for training and cultural changes, and finally

- lack of a robust and stable infrastructure to support the development project.

To illustrate the problem, let's see what estimation and scope control are like in terms of four of the most commonly used approaches to application development—from the structured design of the 1980s to some very current thinking on OO software engineering. (See Fig. 2.4.)

Although somewhat tired and inefficient by late-1990s standards, the structured design approaches of the 1970s and 1980s provide a rich and understandable array of information for estimating development effort. The application's screens and reports, that are identified and designed near the beginning of most structured design life cycles, during "external design" are easy to understand. And they're also easy to count. With the addition of the application's files and interfaces, mature estimation techniques—based on counts of function points, for example—can be employed. Provided that environmental factors are accounted for, and that the estimation is honest, an accurate forecast in terms of staff-days and time required to complete the project will result.[3] Should the scope of the project expand during the application's development, the results of the expansion are immediately evident in terms of increased numbers of screens, files, reports, and function points.

When an information engineering-based approach is employed along with integrated CASE tools such as HPS or IEF, problems associated with making accurate estimates and controlling scope become

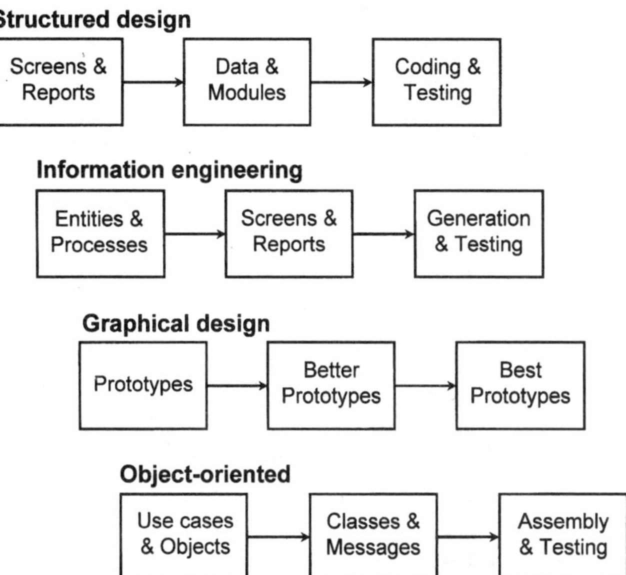

Figure 2.4 Four commonly used approaches to application development yield four totally different sets of forecasting metrics.

more complex. As the IE life cycle begins with abstract data and activity modeling, estimates must be based, not on screens and reports—which don't become available until more than halfway through the development project—but on artifact counts.[4] Although a number of companies have developed successful estimation metrics based on IE entity type and process counts, the combination of learning curve, immature infrastructure, and inadequate user involvement continue to inject uncertainty into the process. Scope control in an IE environment can be equally problematic since increases in scope show up as increases in counts of IE artifacts such as processes and entity types—counts that tend to increase over the development life cycle even when the project's scope remains constant!

Bottom-up estimates of low-level tasks, a tried and true technique for estimating effort in structured development projects, also became problematic for information engineering-based projects. The reason is that bottom-up estimates depend on lots of experience in executing the project's tasks, and as IE projects contained lots of tasks that were radical and new, a reliable experience base simply didn't exist.

The common late-1990s graphical design approach, in which applications are developed as a series of successive "prototypes" using tools such as VisualBasic and PowerBuilder, presents a new and different set of estimation and scope control problems. First, there is no external design, in terms of screens and reports, to serve as a basis for estimation metrics. There are no fixed sets of detailed tasks for making bottom-up estimates. And there aren't lots of early artifact counts, as there are with IE. What graphical developers do have, is a set of early prototypes that continually change, often substantially, as the development project proceeds. The problem of basing project estimates on a set of early and changeable prototypes is exacerbated by the fact that even small changes, when they occur late in the development life cycle, can require large amounts of time and effort to implement.[5] Managing changes in scope can be equally problematic, as the numbers of windows, panes and graphical objects are expected to increase during development as a by-product of the successive prototyping process—even when the scope of the project does not.

From the perspectives of estimation and scope control, OO development potentially offers the best of both worlds. But there are some significant twists. When a use case-driven approach is employed, the OO life cycle can produce an early design that is both understandable and rigorous.[6] Viewing an application in terms of actors (the set of people, systems, and devices that exchange information with the application) and use cases (the "what happens when" scenarios and business events for each actor) provides a solid basis for developing an early understanding of what the application will be like and how it will work. When supplemented by a set of early prototypes, differences, and issues associated with the way users and developers envision the application can be identified, and common ground sought.

As actors and use cases are also countable artifacts, when an OO CASE tool—such as Select Software's Enterprise—is used, counts of actors and use cases can be utilized as a basis for estimating metrics. The catch is that as OO CASE is new to many developers and organizations, and there are lots of hard-to-pin-down environmental factors that can significantly influence the result. As with information engineering, experience with the methodology, tools and language, availability of business users, team business experience and expertise, and geographical dispersion can all exert significant influence. But, as OO development depends mainly on reuse for productivity improvement, two new and significant factors come into play:

- Availability of relevant reusable classes, and
- An infrastructure to support their reuse.

When developing business applications that are large and complex, getting a significant payback from object reuse requires a lot more than the commercially available classes and OO frameworks. Taking advantage of object reuse, to the extent that meaningful productivity gains result, requires development of frameworks and classes that are high-level, reusable, and relevant to the company and its business. But determining which frameworks and classes to build, building them, testing them, so that developers can utilize them with confidence, and developing an infrastructure for maintaining them and helping project personnel to find them, are difficult and time-consuming tasks.[7] The combination of learning curve and cultural transition, development of reusable and relevant classes and frameworks, and development of an appropriate support infrastructure, can take lots of time to implement. It may take 1 to 3 years, for a large organization before many of the substantial productivity gains associated with OO development can be realized.

The predictable result, for OO and as well as for other new development technologies, is that *development productivity can significantly dip before it eventually increases.*[8] The S-shaped productivity curve, common to the adoption of many new development technologies, illustrates this concept. (See Fig. 2.5.)

An equally predictable, and unfortunate, result is that if expectations are not properly managed, and the productivity dip during adoption is not articulated and taken into account, the most promising new technologies can be abandoned long before their impact on productivity is felt.

Developing and using metrics for accurately forecasting the time and effort needed to develop an application is substantially complicated by the multiple development technologies that accompany time

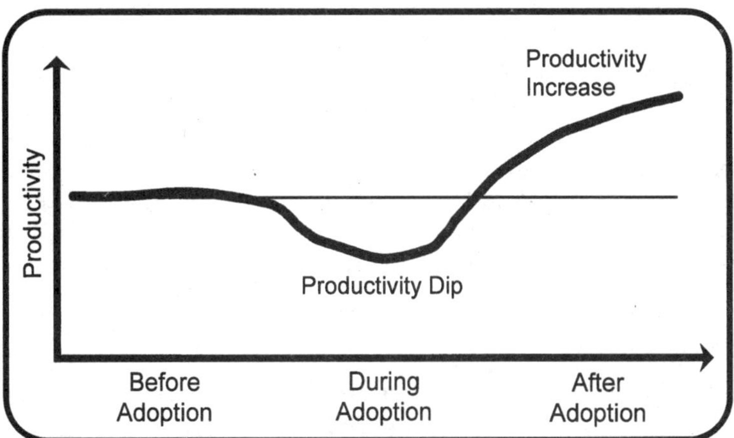

Figure 2.5 S-shaped productivity curve (*Source:* John Stone, *Inside ADW and IEF: The Promise and Reality of CASE,* McGraw-Hill, 1993, Chris Kemerer, MIT CISR Working Papers, 1993).

compressed development environments. There are two main reasons for this. The first is that use of different technologies and technology combinations—Enterprise Upper CASE along with Smalltalk, C++, or PowerBuilder for implementation, for example—can have a major impact on the role of influencing factors as well as on direct time and effort. While all of these technologies represent valid approaches, from an estimation perspective they could hardly be more different. Productivity on Smalltalk implementations, for example, tends to be much more dependent on experience with the technology and familiarity with the Smalltalk class hierarchy than does productivity for C++. Productivity for PowerBuilder implementations tends to depend on the problem domain and its fit for the PowerBuilder development paradigm more than on technology experience.

The second reason is that widespread use of multiple development technology combinations decreases the statistical sample size that can be utilized as a basis for developing predictive metrics for any single technology combination. The result of the smaller sample is, of course, statistical significance at a lower confidence level: a less accurate estimate. While this may not represent a crucial problem for older technologies that enjoy such a wide following that sample size isn't a concern, it can be a serious issue for time compressed technology adoption, where utilization is limited and statistical samples are small. Since it's in the area of new and emerging technologies that practitioners have the least experience, and consequently the greatest need for accurate predictive metrics, the sampling problem represents an estimation "catch 22." Large samples and accurate metrics are abundantly available for older technologies, for which many companies don't need them—as forecasting metrics already in place. Small samples and inaccurate estimates are available for newer technologies, for which companies do not yet have forecasting metrics in place, and therefore need them badly. An additional and most unwelcome problem associated with developing applications in a time compressed environment is that the technologies used are not always fully compatible under all conditions. And when they aren't, combinations of technical issues and the propensity of vendors to blame one another rather than fix the problem, can play havoc with even the best estimates.

Correctly-Staffed Team

It was the end of a sweltering day in July, and having accomplished the last of her objectives, the National Sales Manager for a hot new OO CASE tool vendor was about to leave one of her most successful accounts. But before she could make it to the door, she was stopped by the head analyst on their largest and most important development project. "How can I get certified in your product?" he asked. She knew the answer. And she also knew what the question meant: The head analyst, having become fully competent in her CASE tool and the OO methodology that it supported, was now worth over twice what his company was paying him, and he was positioning himself to leave his employer and turn his newfound skills into newfound wealth. He would be able to purchase the new home that he and his wife needed for their growing family, and his OO development project would become another statistic.

Staffing projects that employ multiple and evolving technologies for application development presents a particularly challenging set of problems. Indeed, despite the importance of this CSF—a fact that's almost universally acknowledged by application developers and management—our inability to staff development projects with teams that have appropriate skills and competencies remains one of the prime reasons why application development projects fail. The combination of stringent business demands, inadequate communications between IT and business management, lack of staffing guidelines, downsizings, head count limits, and budgetary constraints combine to turn development project staffing into a pervasive and recalcitrant problem. (See Fig. 2.6.)

Time compressed technology change makes this problem significantly worse. The principal reasons for this circumstance are that:

- many new technologies and approaches require difficult and fundamental shifts in skills, such as from technical to business,

- the team composition and skill sets required for each approach can be substantially different,

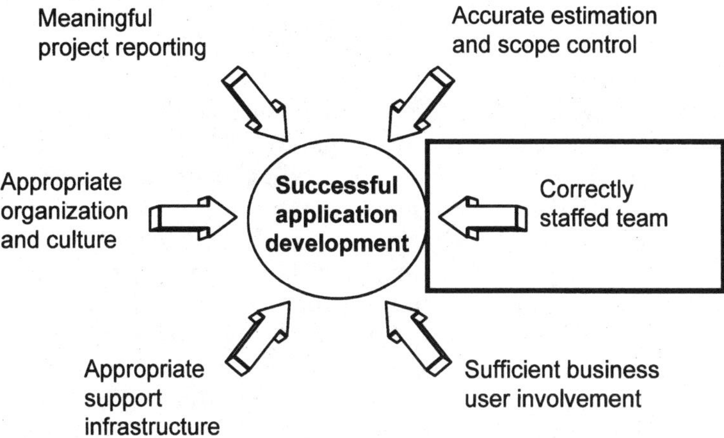

Figure 2.6 Application Management CSF: correctly staffed team.

Structured design

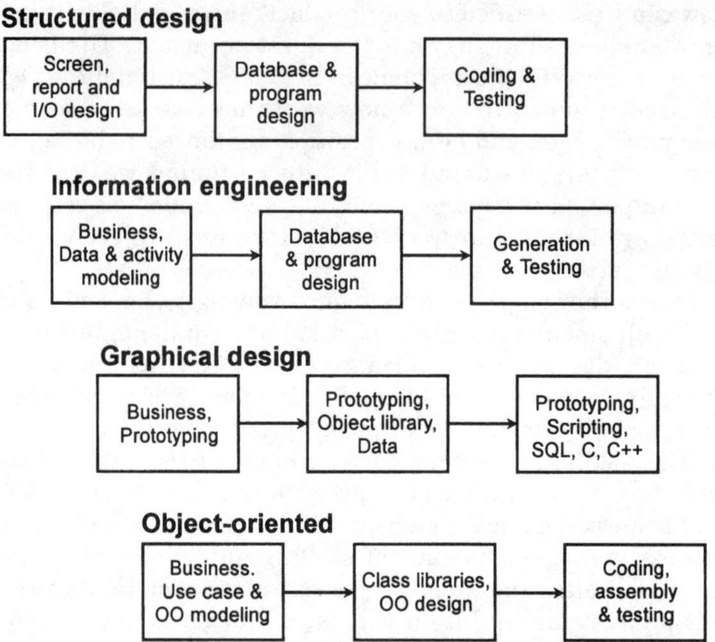

Figure 2.7 Four commonly used approaches to application development and their team composition, skill, and competency requirements.

- the team composition and skill sets required for each technology, within the same approach, can be very different (see Fig. 2.7),

- conflicts arise between the need for staffing continuity, and the need to satisfy specialized staffing requirements of specific activities and tasks, and

- qualified people with relevant new technology experience are scarce.

The evolution of application development over the past 20 years has, in many ways, been an unrelenting progression away from technology and toward business. In the 1970s, when computer hardware was scarce and expensive, programming efficiency was the order of the day. Those who had the technical understanding and prowess to cram applications into ever smaller amounts of memory, who could design programs and databases that got the job done utilizing fewer of that decade's scarce central processing unit (CPU) cycles, who could write programs that other programmers could understand, or who could design character-based screens and reports that were reasonably serviceable, were the IT heroes. Skills in screen, report, program and database design, as well as in programming for the 1970s set of standard mainframe development and execution technologies, were carefully nurtured and developed. As applications were governed not by business needs, but by technology limitations, and business users were resigned to get by with what IT could deliver, business skills—along with the ability to interact successfully with business peers and grasp what they really wanted—were not regarded as central to application development.

In the 1970s world of relatively stable technologies, staffing application development projects with appropriate combinations of skills and competencies was a matter of training, load balancing, and logistics. In many IT organizations, assignment of sufficient numbers of competent COBOL, IMS, and CICS programmers and analysts was all that was needed to fully staff an application development project.

In the 1980s, with less expensive computer hardware, the advent of data-driven design, information engineering and primitive CASE tools, and the emergence of maintenance is a major factor in IT expense, emphasis began to shift away from technology and toward business. Business modeling, in terms of data and activities, became important and sought-after skills. And with business modeling came the need to understand the business, communicate with business peers, and to think and work in terms of concepts such as entity types and IE processes—concepts that were far more abstract than the screens, reports, databases, and programs of the previous decade. But as 1980s code generators required business models to be supplemented by high-level code—IEF procedure action diagrams, for example—and because hardware was still relatively expensive, the transition from technical to business was far from complete. Technical skills were still needed and sought.[9]

The shift during the 1980s to a modeling-based approach was a difficult, and in many ways, unfair, transformation for the IT community. For those who had made successful careers in IT, where highly technical skills could be leveraged and shortcomings in business or interpersonal skills overlooked, the rules of the game had suddenly changed, in midstream. Many had trouble making the switch.

The shift in emphasis from purely technical to a combination of technical and business, along with the need to include business users on development teams, and to work at a higher level of abstraction, seriously impacted the freedom with which IT personnel could be allocated across application development projects. Staffing development projects had shifted from a matter of load balancing and logistics, to procuring sufficient numbers of IT and business people who had the specific skills required for each project.

Application development approaches and technologies had undergone a major shift, and IT organizations that had been carefully optimized to staff 1970s-style development projects were caught short. Many could not make the shift—in terms of budgeting, training, and recruiting—in time to staff large-scale development projects with sufficient numbers of people with the right kinds of skills. Many 1980s CASE projects proceeded with woefully inadequate staffing, and many failed as a result.

The graphical and OO tools and approaches commonly utilized for developing mid-1990s Client/Server applications present an even greater staffing challenge than did the data-driven and IE approaches of the 1980s. For one thing, today's approaches represent a greater departure from traditional application development. They are also trickier, more business oriented, and more abstract. And to make matters even worse, many involve a number of different development, execution, and approach technologies, each with its unique set of staffing requirements.

Consider graphical design. Using graphical development tools such as PowerBuilder and SQL Windows, applications can be developed as a series of prototypes—each successively closer to what their business users really need, each with better features, more robustness. Developers can design and build the prototypes by pointing and clicking on the set of graphical objects provided by the tool, showing the result to their business users, and pointing and clicking once more to correct deficiencies, get more data, or add new features. Where necessary, the functionality that comes with the tool can be supplemented via high-level scripting languages designed for that purpose. Developers do not need to worry about execution technology, data, or even the databases on which the data are stored. There are layers of middleware to ensure that developers remain insulated from these nettlesome bits of reality.

Sound too good to be true? For many small, self-contained, tactical applications, it is true. For application development projects where requirements are well known, needed data are understood and available, performance is not an important consideration, and where single developers with good business and communications skills have good access to their business users—or empowered business users with a flair for technology and good personal computer (PC) skills—do the development, quick and easy Client/Server applications can indeed be the result. But when developing applications that are large and complex, and where one or more of these conditions cannot be met, things can get pretty tricky pretty fast.

For example, the business events that drive the panels, windows, and graphical objects that comprise the application's user interface may not be easy to identify and define. Where many business users are involved, where they are geographically dispersed, or where business process reengineering (BPR) initiatives are changing the work flow and procedures that make up the application's business environment, identifying who will be expected to do what with which the application's graphical objects may not be obvious. Indeed, this information may not become fully apparent until successive prototyping is completed and the flawed application is put into production. To address these challenges, industrial-strength techniques—such as use case modeling, in which classes of users, business events, and the application's objects are modeled and analyzed—are required. And if these kinds of techniques are to be successively applied, development teams, staffed with people who are skilled and experienced in their application, will be needed as well.

Object-oriented concepts, such as abstraction and inheritance, must also be learned and internalized by members of the team. These concepts form an important and integral part of use case analysis, and are fundamental to understanding the libraries of objects that are available to be utilized by graphical tools for complex application design. For large applications, where many hundreds of objects must be utilized, not only for communicating with users, but also for implementing business rules and accessing complex and disparate data, the ability to abstract the objects into classes and to express the classes in terms of meaningful hierarchies becomes a basic and necessary part application development. The result, in terms of appropriate staffing, is that graphical development teams for large-scale applications must include people with OO modeling skills to supplement members with the business, prototyping, and communications skills.

Three additional kinds of skills are often needed. For applications that require functionality that cannot be obtained directly from objects within the library, the tool's objects will have to be supplemented through scripting languages. Although writing scripts can appear at first glance not to represent a significant challenge—a trait that graphical tool salespersons leverage to their advantage—scripting can become surprisingly complex. The enhanced variations of BASIC that come with most graphical development tools, for example, may not be robust enough to achieve needed functionality—such as device control, batch processing or communication with objects outside of the application—or may execute too slowly for the application to achieve acceptable levels of performance. Fortunately, most graphical tools cover this contingency by allowing developers to write scripts in more robust languages, such as C or C++. The impact is that yet another set of skills must be present on application development teams that cannot develop their entire application using the tool's scripting language alone.

Where the data associated with the application are numerous or complex, which is a common occurrence for large-scale applications, data access requirements may not be fully identified until late in the successive prototyping process, when many of the application's panels and windows have been defined and much of the scripting behind the graphical objects has been written. When this happens, large portions of the scripting have to be rewritten to accommodate the new data (or the new structure of the old data). The result is a sharp reduction in development productivity, often by 50 percent or more, and a corresponding extension of the application's delivery date. The cure is modeling, in the form of conventional entity relationship models, or models of "business" or "entity" objects, so that the data required to support the complex application are identified as fully as possible prior to graphical development. Although data modeling has proved to be an effective means of addressing this problem, it adds an additional dimension to the skill set that must be represented on graphical tool development teams.[10]

Performance for large-scale graphically developed applications can also be problematic. Although there are many factors that impact performance, the principal performance drivers often include inefficiency of database designs (for the application's purposes), inefficient SQL generated by the tool, middleware limitations, interpretive scripting languages, and late binding. Where data must be quickly accessed, knowledge of how the data are related to business events—in the use case model, for example—and of how the tool translates scripting language constructs into SQL will be required. Where the application must access data stored in a number of different databases, such as Oracle, Sybase, DB2, and ADABAS, knowledge of each database along with the middleware products that enable its access, also becomes important. As with modeling and scripting, data access and middleware skills must then be represented on the development team.

While the sheer number of different skills that are often needed for successful large-scale graphical application development provides a daunting challenge for today's lean, head count-conscious organizations, two additional factors come into play. These factors are the newness of many of these skills for traditional IT organizations, and the continuity in skills—and the people who have the skills—over different phases of graphical development. (See Fig. 2.8.)

The event modeling, data modeling, and prototyping that comprise many of the early activities of large-scale graphical application development projects, require a combination of business, interpersonal, and communication skills to facilitate working with business peers, as well as the ability to work with abstract modeling and OO concepts. As the application begins to take shape, and object library, class

Graphical design

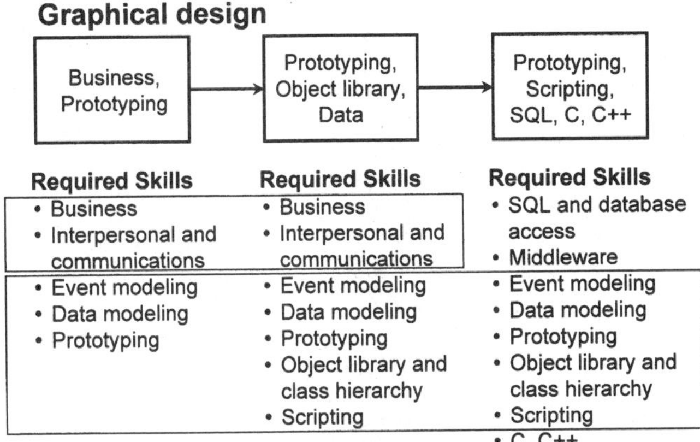

Figure 2.8   Skills and continuity requirements for graphical development.

hierarchy, and scripting skills become important, the need for business and interpersonal skills persists. Indeed, for productive graphical development, not only must business and interpersonal skills persist, but the team members who possess these skills must also stick around for the rest of the project.

Downstream graphical development activities, like their traditional counterparts, require more technical skills. The difference is that many of the technical skills are new. The surprising number of technology competencies that are often needed to successfully bring graphically developed Client/Server applications through implementation, along with their implications in terms of team composition, can be far more difficult to achieve—and to keep up to date with today's time compressed change—than the monolithic implementation skill sets of just a decade ago.

Graphical development also requires similar skills across much of the application development process, although not always for the same purpose. Some skills, such as data modeling, are required during early activities to produce the models, and during latter activities to read the models produced by others. Although models are necessary and effective analytical and documentation tools, and they can certainly be used to transmit information from one activity to another, when it comes to moving information efficiently and quickly down the application development cycle, they a poor substitute for continuity of people. There would be far fewer failures if application development managers paid more attention to this simple fact.

At first glance, OO development utilizing C++ or Smalltalk presents staffing needs that are similar to those encountered in graphi-

Object-oriented

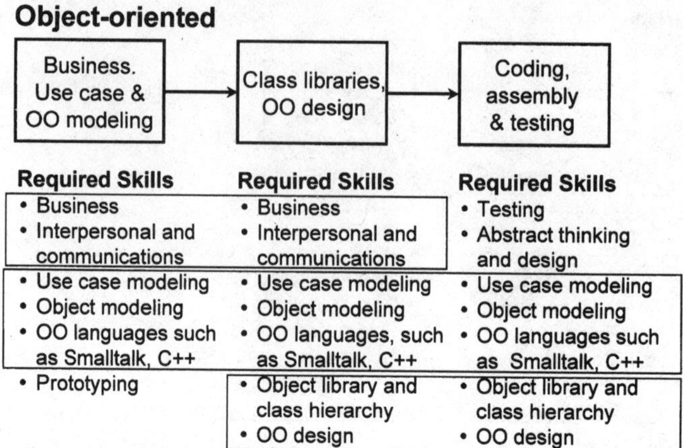

Figure 2.9   Skills and continuity requirements for OO development.

cal development. Consider requirements analysis. (See Fig. 2.9.) As with other modern approaches to application development, business requirements for large and complex applications must still be fully analyzed, modeled, and understood, before the applications can be successfully designed and built. Indeed, the consequence of forgoing this kind of formal analysis and modeling, when implementing in C++ or Smalltalk can be even worse than they were for graphical design. As requirements are "discovered" late in the OO development cycle, the frameworks and class hierarchies that fully supported the application the developers thought they were building, can turn out to be far less appropriate for what their business users really want. When this happens, reuse is substantially reduced and the development team spends substantial amounts of costly time and effort modifying their frameworks and classes to support the real business requirements. The inevitable result is an implementation that takes a whole lot longer, and costs a whole lot more, than it should have. This scenario assumes that management is more tolerant than our Wall Street trader, and allows the development project to get that far. Many managers do not.

To get the job done in an OO environment—so that the requirements model not only reflects the business users' true needs, but also provides appropriate frameworks and classes for OO design and construction—abstract thinking, along with skills in techniques such as use case analysis, object modeling and state transition analysis are needed. And if the use case model is to aid the business users and developers in achieving a common vision of what the application will look like, prototyping skills can become as important for OO development as they are for graphical design.

But compared to graphical design, in which sophisticated prototypes can be built simply by pointing and clicking on the right objects, building prototypes in C++ or Smalltalk is language intensive, requiring knowledge not only of graphical objects, but class hierarchies and language syntax as well. The result is that C++ and Smalltalk prototypes can be more cumbersome to build, and they take more time and effort to modify in response to input from business users. The staffing impact is that prototyping in C++ or Smalltalk requires language, graphical object, listening, presentation, and communication skills, in addition to a good working knowledge of class hierarchies and objects.

This point is underscored by the dependence of OO development on multiple technologies, often in the form of graphical objects procured from a variety of third-party vendors. The problem here is that purchased objects can come with their own problems, schedules, and agendas, and if the implications are not fully understood by the team, and taken into account, significant downstream development problems can result. This is what happened to an East Coast service company that utilized a number of very impressive C++ graphical objects in the development of an important new application. Their selection process was very thorough, ensuring that not only each graphical object provided the functionality required to support their users' requirements, but also that each represented the best in its class, and that the vendors were cooperative and financially sound. What their selection process didn't take into account was that two of the vendors weren't planning to support the 64-bit hardware, that they needed to achieve required performance levels, until a year after their application was to be delivered. The result was a set of unhappy users, along with lots of scrambling on the part of the development team as they found and implemented acceptable substitutes.

Downstream implementation, OO design, construction, and testing, can also be more demanding in terms of the application development team and the skill sets that must be present. Abstraction and class hierarchies, that at once are more important, more complete, and more complex than in graphical development, must be assimilated by team members before they can be productive. For example, it's hard to productively design and code functionality in Smalltalk, where every variable is part of a complex class hierarchy, if the Smalltalk class hierarchy is not only understood but also assimilated to the point where the programmers have it in their heads, so that they don't have to stop and think about each new component and how it fits into the Smalltalk model.

But class hierarchy knowledge along with language and coding skills are not sufficient. Team members responsible for design and construction must also understand, and be able to interpret and add

to the use case and object models that represent the business requirements. And as with graphical development, the requirements models
may not provide every subtlety that those who design and code OO
applications and who assemble applications from reusable classes
need to understand. The reality is that for complex applications, the
models produced during requirements analysis must be supplemented by team continuity. Some of the members of the team that worked
with the business users to develop the requirements models must be
represented on—or at minimum, be readily available to—the teams
doing OO design and construction.

There are a number of conclusions that we can draw from these
examples on how new and multiple development technologies impact
the skills and composition of development teams. The first is that, new
development technologies are taking care of more and more of the
basics, freeing development teams from mundane tasks, such as writing
code for user interfaces and data access. And business knowledge—
along with interpersonal, communications, and prototyping skills—
takes on greater importance, especially during early phases of development. As many of the newer technologies are based on object- or
data-based models of business requirements, modeling skills, along with
ability to work with abstract concepts also become more important.

During implementation, two team- and skills-related trends are
apparent. The first trend is a shift of deep technical expertise away
from application development teams, as teams using OO and graphical
development tools are doing less coding and more assembly work.
There is a corresponding shift of deep technical expertise toward development support in the form of development tools and OO classes and
frameworks that support multiple development efforts. (See Fig. 2.10.)

A final, but by no means less significant, skills shift is that for
implementation (design and construction) phases, skills in a greater
number of technologies are needed. The proliferation of execution
technologies, along with new reusable components—in the form of
graphical objects and OO classes, and middleware products—are, at

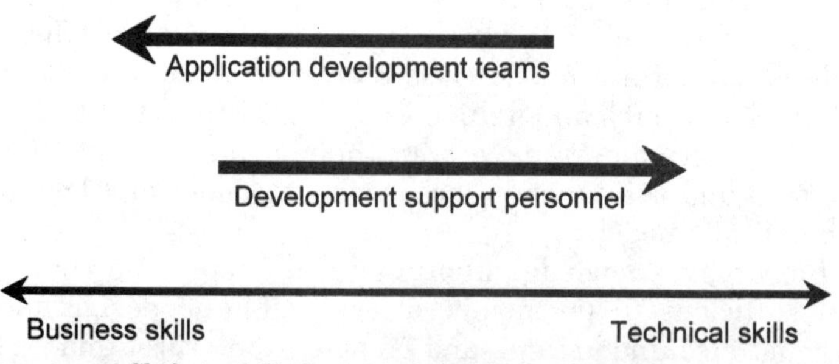

Figure 2.10 Shifts in skills for development and support personnel.

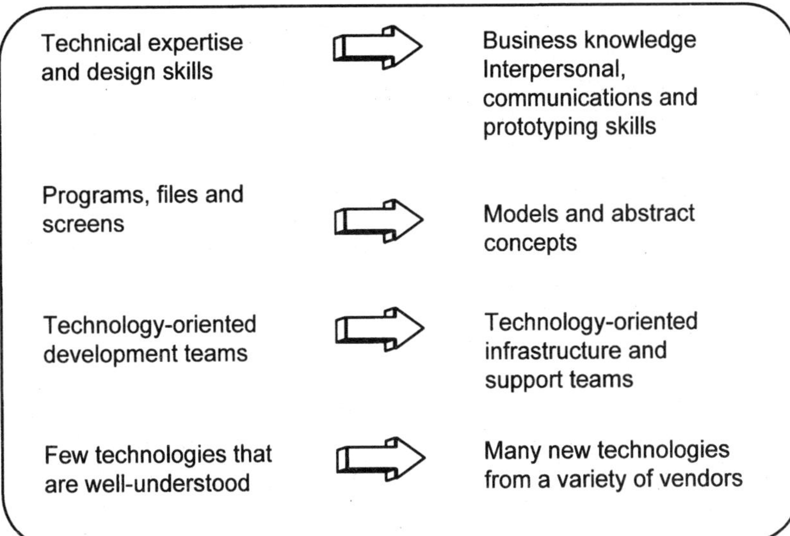

Figure 2.11 Major shifts in team composition and skills resulting from new and multiple development technologies.

least for the moment, ensuring that familiarity with more and more technologies is required.

There are a number of additional new technology-related team and skill observations that I believe are appropriate to make. The first is that although development is becoming a lot more graphical—and will, in all likelihood, continue to do so—the alacrity with which modern tools can construct graphical interfaces belies the technical complexity behind their graphical facades, and with it, the skill sets required to utilize them effectively, especially for large and complex applications. This problem is often exacerbated by the inappropriate set of expectations fostered by many development technology vendors and naive or unscrupulous consultants.

The second observation is that new development technologies tend to be incomplete, sometimes even lacking basics, such as debugging software, that can operate effectively through multiple layers of middleware and execution technologies. The rapidity with which new technologies are becoming available often means that there is too little time to develop what Dave Siegel of Sony Music Entertainment of calls "magicians"—people with the skills to come in, quickly assess a technology-related problem, fix things up, and get a development team back on track.[11]

The third, and final, observation is the inability of the compensation infrastructure in many companies to keep pace with what people, who become highly skilled in current technologies, can be worth. (See Fig. 2.11.) It's not at all uncommon for companies—especially large organizations—to lose many of their most effective people partway through development projects, and for the projects to suffer, sometimes irreparably, as a result. Until managers give this problem the attention it deserves, and differences between the current technology job market and compensation models are dealt with, and alternative means for achieving staff loyalty are developed, this is likely to be a persistent and troublesome offshoot of time compressed change and the abundance of hot new technologies that it brings.

Sofficient Business User Involvement

Considering the fundamental importance of computer applications to conducting late-1990s business, it's saddening and somewhat surprising that business users' involvement in the development of their applications remains as low as it does. (See Fig. 2.12.) Indeed, while lack of sufficient business user involvement may not solely account for the high rate of failed application development projects, which is by many accounts, over 50 percent, it almost certainly plays an important role in the proliferation of applications that don't fully support the business.[12] Although it's tempting to think that late-1990s development technologies, with their business orientation and graphical interfaces, might mitigate this problem, what actually happens is that time compressed change, and the introduction of multiple and

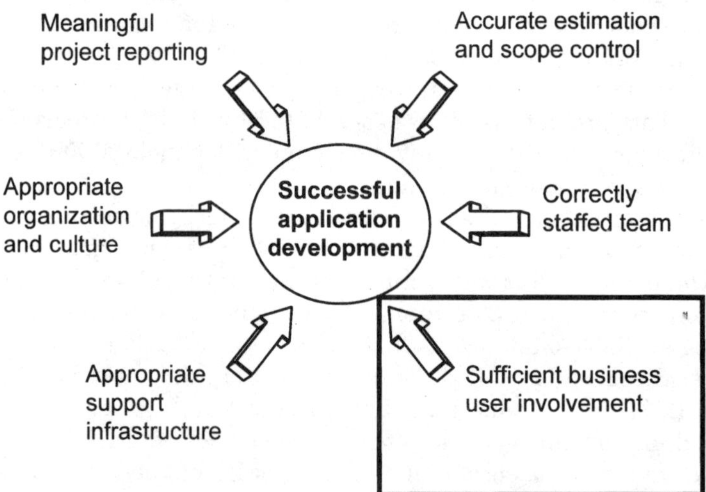

Figure 2.12 Application Management CSF: sufficient business user involvement.

evolving development and approach technologies that it brings, can make this already pervasive problem worse. To illustrate this phenomenon, let's take a closer look at what happens to the amount and nature of business user involvement in terms of our four commonly used technologies and approaches to application development.

By today's standards, traditional structured design required only a modest amount of business user involvement, which was typically limited to explaining what they needed, as best they could, and approving screens and reports. As long as the application's screens and reports looked OK, and the developers seemed to understand what was needed, the project proceeded with no further user involvement, until the application was delivered, and the business users began their acceptance tests. The results spoke for themselves, with over 70 percent of applications requiring extensive rework before they were usable, if indeed they were usable at all. Many were not.[13] The 1990s business user involvement problem, and the structured design legacy that we must still address, is that the low user involvement of the 1960s, 1970s, and much of 1980s set the standard in terms of expectations for amount and nature of business user involvement. Many of today's most critical application development projects are still hobbled by this constraint.

Information engineering represented the first technology shift in which business users were required to actively participate in the development of their applications—in this case, by developing detailed and rigorous models of their business requirements. Two things happened as a result. The first was that many business units weren't prepared to supply the quantities of qualified business users demanded by their IE projects. With over three decades of minimal involvement, they were caught off guard by this new requirement. The second thing that happened was that the seemingly interminable modeling sessions—along with the barely comprehensible data, activity, and interaction models that the sessions produced— alienated many business users from the process. Although the nature of their involvement would change, as information engineering gave way to newer and better development approaches, the bitter lesson stuck. Many of today's business users remain disenfranchised from their application development process, and many current application development projects move forward without the achievement of this CSF.[14]

The problem of insufficient user involvement has been mitigated— at least for small-scale applications—by two mid-1990s information technology trends. The first is the progression of computer hardware out of the insular IT "glass house" and into the business user community, a progression that was enabled by inexpensive and environmentally tolerant networks and servers, and by the acceptance and proliferation of powerful PCs as standard business tools on everyone's desk. The second is the emergence of graphical application development tools that enable business users to develop their own Client/Server applications by themselves—through contracting with independent software vendors, by hiring consultants, or for the growing number of business users who are computer literate, it's not particularly difficult, or even uncommon, for business users to develop their own tactical applications using tools and databases such as VisualBasic, PowerBuilder, Excel, and Access. To the business community, this trend represents an attractive option for quickly procuring needed IT support. To the IT community, as we shall see, it represents yet another source of development, execution, and approach technologies; and with them, a number of problematic implications. (See Fig. 2.13.)

For large and complex applications, where successful graphical development requires detailed and rigorous data models, development tools such as PowerBuilder and VisualBasic can be used to help attain the required user involvement. By incorporating

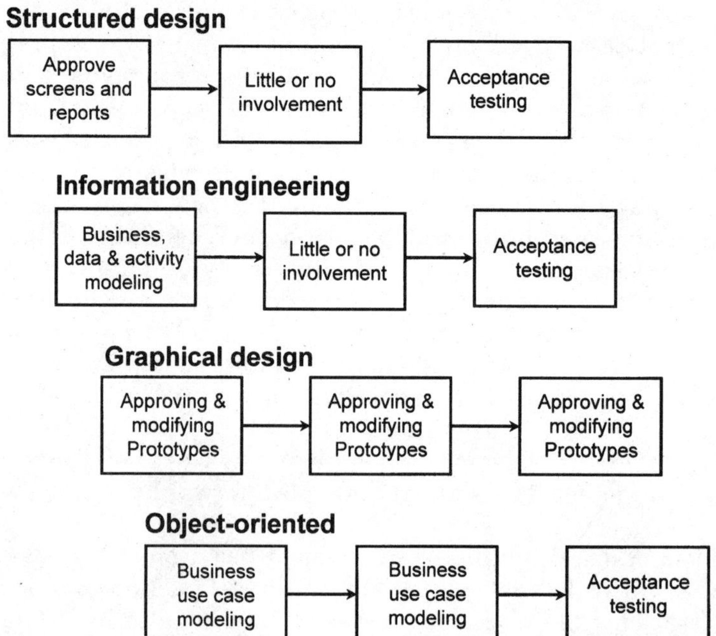

Figure 2.13 Business user involvement required by four commonly used approaches to application development.

rapid prototyping into the data modeling, discovery and validation processes, sufficient business user participation can be more easily achieved.[15]

Although large-scale OO development requires construction and validation of object models that are far more conceptual and complex, and correspondingly more difficult for business users to deal with, the problem has been mitigated by the emergence of OO use case analysis. Utilizing OO CASE tools such as Rational Rose or Select Enterprise, business requirements can be expressed and analyzed in terms of nonthreatening stick figures called "actors" and what happens when scenarios called "use cases."[16] When combined with rapid prototyping, using tools such as PowerBuilder and Visual Basic, requirements models that are detailed and rigorous enough to support OO analysis, yet business-oriented and straightforward enough to be meaningful to business users, can result. Use case requirements modeling is an example of a means for not only assuring a common envisioning of the application among developers, users, and management, but also for overcoming the business disenfranchisement that resulted from previous modeling involvement.

What does this mean? In terms of achieving the user involvement CSF in a time compressed technology environment, two things become apparent.

The first is that the amount of user involvement required by recent advances in development and approach technologies is increasing, and that the resulting time compressed demands on business users are difficult for many organizations to cope with. While recent advances in development have been achieved, approach and execution technologies have moved application development out of the "glass house," making it more directly accessible to the business community, the combination of business user disenfranchisement and low business involvement, left over from past development practices, continues to thwart achievement of the CSF for current development efforts.

The second is that the time compressed proliferation of development approaches are creating a set of very confusing signals, that the business community is often at a loss to interpret. It is not uncommon for large organization business users to find themselves simultaneously involved in a number of different application development projects, each making a different, and in some cases conflicting, set of demands on the dwindling amounts of time that they can afford to spend on application development. The problem is exacerbated by the fact that many of the newest and most promising development technologies and approaches—OO, for example—are increasingly dependent on business user involvement. Fortunately, some of the same approaches are also being implemented along with techniques, such as rapid prototyping and use case analysis, that help facilitate the achievement of this most important CSF.

Appropriate Support Infrastructure

Perhaps it's our unbridled enthusiasm for the latest development technologies, our fascination with new approaches, our drive to quickly apply them so that the businesses we support can realize their immediate benefits, or our misguided attempts to fulfill business demands that cannot be met with our current arsenal of approaches. Maybe it's nothing less cynical than a collective desire to be the first on the block with new technology experience so that we can command higher compensation in the volatile IT job market. Whatever the reason, we seem to have an unerring propensity to implement new development technologies and approaches without the benefits of the support infrastructure needed to make them work. At best, we implement the new technology and its support infrastructure concurrently, while the (hopefully not too visible) initial development project languishes in the mayhem and confusion that results.

The simple, if unpopular, truth is that new development and approach technologies fail if the infrastructure they require is not in place to support the people who must use them. (See Fig. 2.14.) And, considering the time compressed rate at which we are being bombarded with new technologies and approaches for application develop-

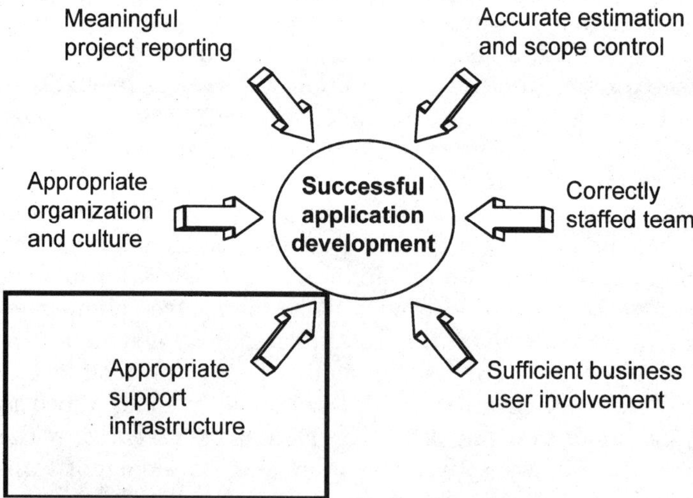

Figure 2.14 Application Management CSF: appropriate support infrastructure.

ment, the correspondingly increasing numbers of technologies and approaches already in use at many companies, and the relatively static nature of most IT organizations, there is typically too little time and too few resources available to put the required infrastructure in place. Perhaps the most frightening aspect of this problem is that, in many organizations, it isn't even acknowledged.

Although the specifics depend on the development technology being implemented and the complexity of technology infrastructure into which it must integrate, the following figure represents the minimum set of core application development infrastructure components that must be in place to support most new development technology initiatives. (See Fig. 2.15.)

As new development technologies are introduced, the need for compatible approach technologies, in the form of an application development methodologies to guide developers in their use, should be obvious. Methodologies provide work breakdown structures (WBSs)—in the form of phases, activities, and tasks—for developers to follow. Methodologies show developers who should participate, where in the WBS they will be needed, and what each participant should do. They provide sample work products for the development team to create, and guidance on who should get them, and why. Some methodologies also supply quality assurance guidelines, check lists, danger flags, and help with estimation and project planning.

Yet in spite of the obvious benefits that methodologies bring, and the need for explicit guidance when tools and techniques are new and not well understood, many new technologies are introduced, and utilized on a number of important projects without the assistance of a compatible methodology. There are a number of reasons why this happens. For one thing, methodologies must be fitted into a company's culture. Such an activity can take copious amounts of time to imple-

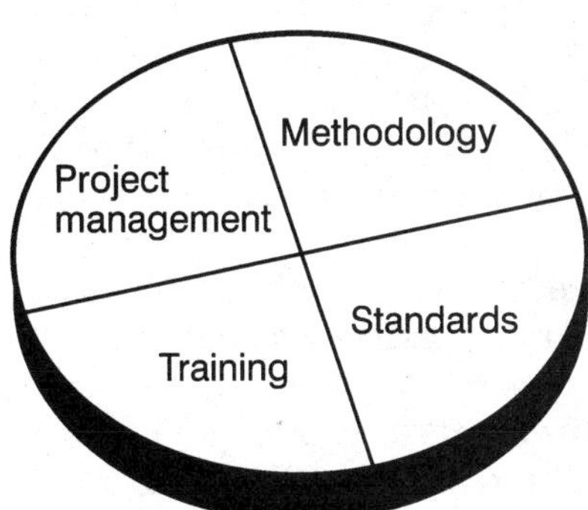

Figure 2.15 Minimum set of core application development infrastructure components.

ment, amounts of time that aren't available in many of today's time compressed IT environments. Methodologies are also enigmatic, sometimes existing only in a process management tool, a web site, a consultant's approach, or in the form of a book. Without the visibility or cachet of a new technology or tool, the cost of such methodologies, which is often considerable, can be hard to justify. Indeed, the allure of a development tool can be so compelling that I've seen seasoned developers—who should, and do, know better—overlook the methodology requirement for a development tool with an exquisite user interface.

Methodologies are also sometimes viewed as obstacles by unethical vendors and development technology proponents, to whom methodologies represent expensive bits of reality that shouldn't be allowed to get in the way of a sale. Finally, methodologies represent one of the key areas in which multiple development technologies come into direct conflict, with new technologies as well as with each other. When new development technologies call for different things to be done, by different people, for different reasons and in a different order, such as object modeling instead of data modeling, or starting with use case requirements modeling instead of prototypes, it's in the methodology that many of these key changes show up. And it's also in the methodology that many of the cultural issues and conflicts over different technologies and approaches must be addressed. Given this daunting set of circumstances, it's not at all surprising that many IT organizations choose to address these problems, not by fixing them, but by "shooting the messenger"—deferring the methodology through which they are seen.

Closely related to methodology is project management, which builds on the foundation provided by the methodology's WBS and deliverables. Indeed, many methodologies come with interfaces for exporting their WBSs and deliverables into popular project management tools, such as Microsoft Project and ABT Project Workbench. Once the export is complete, the application development team can utilize the tool not only for day-to-day management of the project, but also for identification of staffing needs, tracking effort and expenditures, critical path analysis, identification of problems, and reporting progress. It's all very neat. Or is it?

In today's time compressed technology environment, in which different application development paradigms exist—consisting of IE, visual development, and OO development, for example—rolling up progress, staffing and support requirements becomes problematic. How, for example, can an IT organization roll up progress from a portfolio of several development projects, when different projects are reporting progress in terms of the phases and activities of vastly different WBSs? And how does management interpret the resultant roll-up in a meaningful way, so that it can identify problems, ensure that needed resources are available, monitor progress?

From the perspective of a single application development project, where the problems of reporting progress across multiple technologies doesn't exist, project management problems associated with many new development technologies can still exact their toll. The evolutionary nature of many of their deliverables conflicts with more traditional "one-and-done" styles of management that view development projects in terms of a series of completed deliverables. While some managers are beginning to understand and deal with evolutionary deliverables, most project management tools do not. Armed with management tools that have little or no means for tracking and reporting progress within activities or tasks, such managers must utilize facilities outside of their company's standard management tool to provide this kind of support for their projects—a practice that's discouraged in many organizations.

I recently attended a Smalltalk demonstration provided for the managers of a large Southeast company. After expounding on the virtues of its Smalltalk implementation, the vendor proceeded to demonstrate, for their VP and her direct reports, just how easy it would be for their developers to use. The demonstration was impressive. The salesperson—who by his own admission, had little technical expertise—was able to quickly and easily link a number of different objects together to form a working application. Although the salesperson dutifully suggested that their developers "go through a few days of Smalltalk training," the implication was obvious. This stuff was easy. A minimal amount of training would do. And if her budget was too tight....Well, you can fill in the rest.

The graphical nature of most modern development paradigms certainly does make it easy for developers to become proficient at mousing around the tools that support them. The problem is that, from a training perspective, their graphical interfaces are too good, masking the complexity that lies beneath, and the training that's required for developers to master it. The problem is compounded by the fact that training for new development technologies is usually not readily available, and when it is available, it's likely to reflect the specifics of the development, execution, and approach technology environments of the organization at which the training materials were developed rather than those of the organization receiving the training. And the training curriculum is likely to be focused solely on the needs of application developers, the people most directly affected by the technology.

Orientation components for business users and management, two groups who are becoming increasingly involved with application development, are typically given short shrift, if indeed they are present at all. In time compressed environments, where lots of different development technologies are involved, training rarely takes this into account, leaving confused developers to make analogies and sort out differences on their own. The result is the combination of confusion, misunderstanding, and inappropriate expectations that accompanies our time compressed application development environments.

The fourth, and final, core component is standards to guide developers in the production of quality work products. When new technologies are involved, standards become particularly important for two main reasons. The first reason is that may of the work products are likely to be new, with members of the development team having little or no experience in producing or utilizing them. And the few individuals who do have experience producing the new technology's deliverables are each likely to have done so in a different environment representing a different, and possibly conflicting, set of ideas about what they should look like. Even when consistent, the standards, along with the concepts they promote, may not be appropriate to support the company or its goals. The second reason for the importance of standards is that, when the technologies are really new—as they often are in our time compressed environments—standards may not yet exist. No one may have thought it through.

The solution is to implement a set of standards appropriate for the organization doing the development. As standards, procurement, development, dissemination, and training can take substantial amounts of time to implement—time that many IT organizations don't have as they strive to cope with their time compressed environments—these activities are typically carried out in parallel with the initial development projects. The all-too-common practice of developing standards in parallel with developing initial applications results in substantial amounts of:

- thrashing, as standards are quickly developed and then redeveloped in response to the conflicting perceptions and needs of ongoing application development projects,

- rework, on the part of application developers, to bring work products into conformance with standards that weren't available during their initial development, and

- confusion, on the part of developers and support personnel, who know what to do, but have trouble reaching consensus on the conventions used to do it.

Where multiple technologies are involved, standards can easily come into conflict, usually with confusing results. Differences in user interfaces, modeling notation, and development tool capabilities, can legitimately require different standards for equivalent work products such as object models or user interface prototypes. If the standards cannot adequately address these differences, developers have trouble utilizing their analysis and development tools to produce work products that conform to the standards, and the standards can quickly lose their value. To development teams that are under pressure to produce working applications on schedule, the predictable result is that the standards will be ignored.

An Appropriate Organization and Culture

Compared to the time compressed pace at which development, approach, and execution technologies are changing, organization and culture are docile, slow-moving creatures. The problem is that technology change and a company's organization and culture are tightly coupled. They interact. And it's in the jagged interaction of these very differently paced corporate components that many of the organizational and cultural upheavals that companies experience with multiple and emerging development technologies get their start. (See Fig. 2.16.)

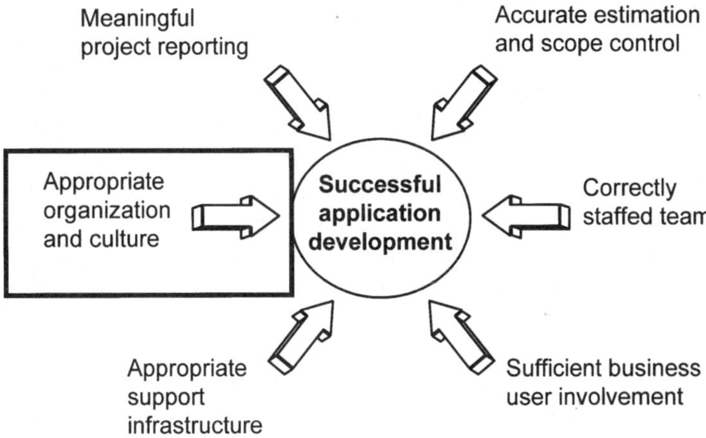

Figure 2.16 Application Management CSF: appropriate organization and culture.

Consider OO development and reuse. A company can implement object technology for application development by switching from the C programming language to C++ or Smalltalk, purchasing an OO methodology such as OMT or Objectory, and making sure that everyone is properly trained in their use. But increased productivity and decreased maintenance—the two principal benefits of object technology—depend on reuse. If substantial reuse isn't achieved, the company will have switched from conventional to OO development without realizing the benefits.

The problem is that reuse requires reusable classes—the OO software components that developers assemble to build applications—and reusable classes are hard to develop. Indeed, it can many times the effort to develop components that are reusable than it does to develop conventional nonreusable components. Developing reusable classes (OO components) also requires a separate process with demands that differ in a number of significant ways from those required to build applications: At a minimum, reusable component development requires:

- a different, that is, less business oriented and more technical, set of analysis, design, and programming skills,

- a different set of objectives: maximum reuse, instead of fast development, and

- much tighter Quality Assurance (Q/A) and testing, so that the resultant reusable components will be worthy of the increased confidence that developers will have to place in them.

In short, they require a separate organization, with a unique set of objectives, skills, and motivation. Even the basic mission of the organization must be different.

The result is that to derive real benefit from object technology, the IT function must be configured totally differently from its traditional counterpart; it must have a separate organization dedicated to developing, maintaining, and administering the reusable components used by application development projects. When compared to traditional application development organizations, the organization represented in the following figure, from Ivar Jacobson's book on OO software engineering, illustrates the magnitude of the difference.[17] (See Fig. 2.17.)

Implementing this kind of organizational change requires lots of time and effort. New organizations, for component management as well as for component construction and maintenance, have to be created and staffed. Organizations that do application development must

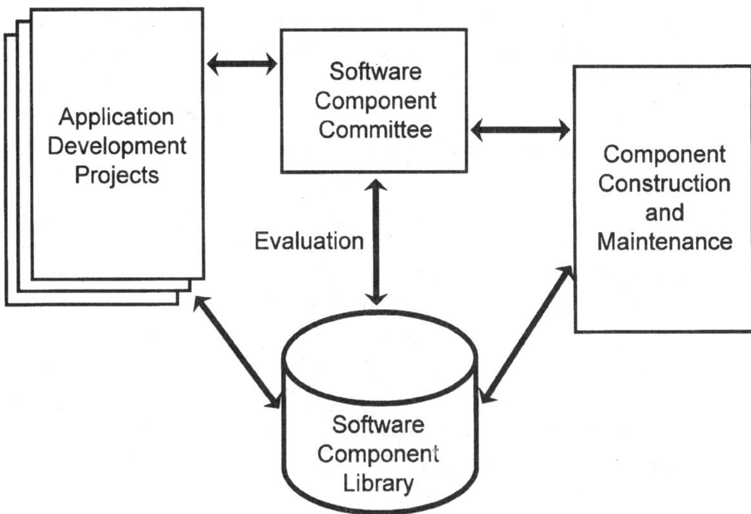

Figure 2.17 An organization supporting OO software reuse (*Source:* Ivar Jacobson, *Object-Oriented Software Engineering,* Addison-Wesley, 1993).

be reengineered away from developing entire applications into organizations that develop OO applications largely from reusable components. And in most companies, where applications must be developed using a mixture of traditional and object technologies, application development support organizations—such as Data Administration, Database Administration, Testing, and Quality Assurance—will have to be enhanced so that they can simultaneously support both modes of development.

The cultural changes required to implement new and multiple application development technologies can be equally jarring. Object-oriented software engineering, for example, calls for a fundamental and difficult shift, away from developing applications as quickly as possible, to taking the time to understand, model, and implement the business requirements so that the developed applications can be delivered correct.

There are other problems. Achieving high levels of reuse can require equally fundamental changes in organizational culture. To illustrate this problem, consider the cultural imperative in many application development organizations not to adopt things that were "not invented here." Getting developers, in such organizations, to reuse frameworks and classes that were developed and maintained by others can represent an especially challenging task, as such attitudes are often the result of attempts to reuse subroutines and procedures in a traditional environment with most unsatisfactory results. Achieving reuse requires not only a rich library of components that have been designed for reusability, but also application developers who can locate the reusable components they need, and who have incentives to utilize them once they are identified. These kinds of changes require basic revisions in how developers are measured and rewarded; revisions that, in many IT organizations, are no less significant than redefining the meaning of failure and success.

In large organizations, it's unrealistic to move the entire IT function over to a new technology and methodology for application development. The transformation is likely to be gradual, and even after many years, may be incomplete. Other new application development technology initiatives, possibly involving different and conflicting technologies, may be under way, as are applications being developed using traditional technologies. And the additional risks of developing certain critical applications in a new technology may be too great.

The result, for many organizations, is a requirement that major changes in application development be implemented in such a way that they can coexist with a combination of traditional development and with other new approaches to application development. While the achievement of coexistence for organization and methodology doesn't pose a particularly difficult challenge, such a challenge *is* posed by achieving coexistence for the set of disparate cultures required to support a time compressed array of different application development approaches. When the extent of the requirement for cultural change and coexistence are taken into account, the unfortunate reality that new application development technologies are typically implemented without the support of compatible cultures becomes easier to understand.

Meaningful Reporting

Honesty, openness, candor, and understanding are not attributes that many business managers would use when describing how progress is reported on their application development projects. Indeed, most business executives that I interact with find application development to be a source of immense frustration. Despite the importance of application development to their businesses, they don't feel that they have control over it. Many aren't even confident that they know what's really going on. And as if these common complaints aren't already bad enough, the late-1990s time compressed injection of new and multiple development technologies into this already flawed communications process is making things a lot worse. (See Fig. 2.18.)

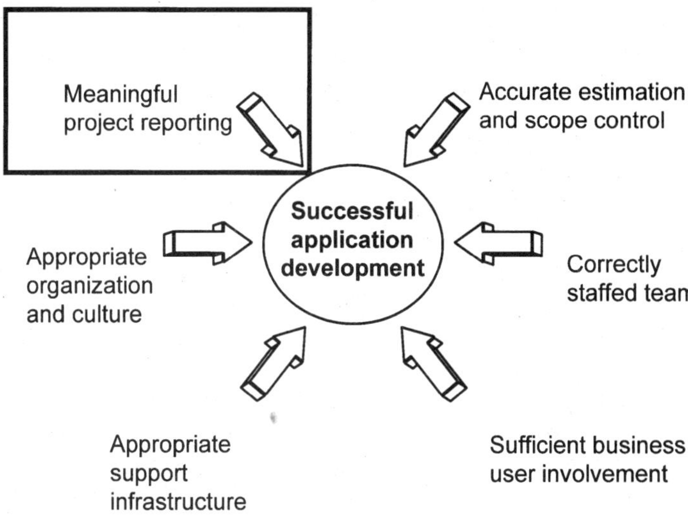

Figure 2.18   Application Management CSF: Meaningful project reporting.

As an example, consider the Department of Transportation of one of our most heavily traveled states. Their application development projects were overseen by an Executive Committee consisting of civil engineers who took considerable pride in knowing—if necessary, down to every nut and bolt—how each of their construction projects was doing. Yet the same engineers were not at all sure how the first of their multimillion dollar suite of application development projects was doing. What they were sure of was that the project was at least a year behind schedule, that delivery of the business application it was supposed to produce was in doubt, and that they were going to do something about it. They had to get the situation under control.

What the Executive Committee did was appoint one of its members—a civil engineer, and commissioner over one of their major functions—to temporarily leave his post and move in with the application developers on a full-time basis. The idea was that even if he couldn't totally fix things up, he would see what was happening on a day-to-day basis, and report his findings back to the Committee in a manner that they could understand. A year after he moved in with the project, the committee found itself just as much in the dark. Although a year had gone by, and the Commissioner "felt as if the project was making progress," he couldn't quantify their progress or tell with any certainty when the developers would deliver the application. The Executive Committee was concerned, and began discussing how to pull the plug on the project and the new technology that it was based on.

The project was, in fact, on schedule and doing fine. The problem wasn't with the project. Nor was the problem the new application development technology that the project was based on. The problem was a lack of reporting that was appropriate to the project, to the application development technology, and to the Executive Committee whose job it was to oversee the project. As soon as the reporting was corrected, the Executive Committee calmed down and the project was allowed to proceed to a successful conclusion.

New application development approach technologies can and do send a confusing set of signals to IT and corporate management, especially where multiple development projects utilizing a number of different technologies are involved. The problem stems principally from the new and confusing set of signals that accompany new development technologies and approaches.

Consider the fact that many new application development technologies are based on evolutionary deliverables, often in the form of business models that evolve throughout the application development life cycle. It is not uncommon, for example, for OO use case models to go through several iterations as the development team learns more about the business and their problem domain, and for new actors, use cases, classes, and interactions to be added as a result. Revisiting the same territory, so it can be understood and modeled with increasing detail and accuracy, is one of the signs that experienced OO developers look for. They know that such revisiting means the development team is probing and that good models are being developed. But the same sign can appear quite different to the company's IT and business management. To a management that's not prepared for the evolutionary nature of many OO deliverables, and that cannot discern the added detail associated with each successive iteration, the project can easily appear to be spiraling round and round through the same set of tasks with no progress or end in sight. When combined with unreliable metrics, surprises, environmental factor dependencies, and vendor pointing problems, even the most well-run project can appear to be in serious trouble. (See Fig. 2.19.)

To be effective in an multiple and evolving technology environment, progress—what is happening and what should be happening to an application development project—must be reported in ways that are meaningful and relevant in terms of the organization culture and needs of those who interpret and act on the information. Without an understandable framework, in terms of what should happen, when it should happen, why it should happen, and the likely consequences if it doesn't happen, management cannot be expected to provide useful and appropriate support for new technology projects. Indeed, when—

Figure 2.19 The same set of signals can appear very different to developers and to management.

in addition to confusion and poor performance—the combination of a new and different set of signals and tasks, the increased risk associated with developing in new technologies, and the attractiveness of new development and execution technologies as scapegoats for the missed deadlines are added as effects of the technology adoption productivity dip, it should come as no surprise if management has a propensity to "cut its losses" and throw them out.

References

1. The following books provide a good perspective on problems associated with estimation and management of application development projects. Roger Pressman, *Software Engineering: A Practitioner's Approach*, McGraw-Hill, 1992. Also see Robert Charette, *Software Engineering, Risk Analysis and Management*, McGraw-Hill, 1989; Vaughan Merlyn and John Parkinson, *Development Effectiveness*, Wiley, 1994; and the updated edition of Frederick Brooks, *The Mythical Man-Month*, Addison-Wesley, 1995.
2. Robert Charette, *Software Engineering, Risk Analysis and Management*, McGraw-Hill, 1989; and Vaughan Merlyn and John Parkinson, *Development Effectiveness*, Wiley, 1994. Also see Lois Zells, "Litigated Disaster: Anatomy of a Major Project Failure," *Application Development Trends*, November 1994.
3. For more information on function points, contact the International Function Point Users Group, 5008 Pine Creek Park, Westerville, OH. Also see Chris Kemerer and

Benjamin Porter, "Improving The Reliability Of Function Point Measurement: An Empirical Study," *IEEE Transactions on Software Engineering,* 18(10):1011–1024, 1992; and Chris Kemerer, "Reliability of Function Points Measurement: A Field Experiment," *Communications of the ACM,* 36(2):85–97, 1993; and Capers Jones, *Programming Productivity,* McGraw-Hill, 1986.

4. John Stone, *Inside ADW and IEF: The Promise and Reality of CASE,* McGraw-Hill, 1993.

5. John Stone, "CASE Plays A Role In Visual Development," *Application Development Trends,* January 1994.

6. Ivar Jacobson, *Object-Oriented Software Engineering: A Use Case Driven Approach,* Addison-Wesley, 1993.

7. My experience indicates is that developing reusable objects requires not only substantially more time and effort, but a different set of objectives and quality assurance as well. Ivar Jacobson, in his book *Object-Oriented Software Engineering: A Use Case Driven Approach,* Addison-Wesley, 1993, reports that constructing reusable objects can be up to 10 times more expensive than equivalent nonreusable objects. Also see Robert Fichman and Chris Kemerer, "Object-Oriented and Conventional Analysis and Design Methodologies: Comparison and Critique," *IEEE Computer,* 25(10):20–39, 1992.

8. Chris Kemerer "How the Learning Curve Affects CASE Tool Adoption," *IEEE Software,* May 1992. Also see John Stone, *Inside ADW and IEF: The Promise and Reality of CASE,* McGraw-Hill, 1993

9. John Stone, *Inside ADW and IEF: The Promise and Reality of CASE,* McGraw-Hill, 1993.

10. John Stone, "CASE Plays A Role In Visual Development," *Application Development Trends,* January, 1994; and Ivar Jacobson, *Object-Oriented Software Engineering: A Use Case Driven Approach,* Addison-Wesley, 1993 for a discussion of entity objects.

11. David Siegel, of Sony Music Entertainment, observed the lack of highly skilled technical people who could support several teams developing in a given technology when his organization switched from COBOL and CICS to PowerBuilder for a major implementation. He solved the problem by hiring the PowerBuilder magicians he needed from an external consulting firm specializing in PowerBuilder implementations.

12. Robert Charette, *Software Engineering, Risk Analysis and Management,* McGraw-Hill, 1989; and Vaughan Merlyn and John Parkinson, *Development Effectiveness,* Wiley, 1994.

13. Robert Charette, *Software Engineering Risk Analysis and Management,* McGraw-Hill, 1989.

14. In some organizations, the disenfranchisement was so complete that organizational barriers were erected—in the form of IT-to-business liaison groups—to guard against the problems that they associate with direct business user participation in application development. My experience is that once user disenfranchisement is institutionalized, in the form of an organization whose existence depends on keeping application developers and users apart, the sufficient user involvement CSF can no longer be achieved and application development suffers irreparably as a result.

15. This technique is by no means limited to data modeling for visual development. I have seen similar techniques applied to information engineering-and OO-based application development, with similarly good results.

16. John Stone, "Objectory product review," *Application Development Trends,* June 1994.

17. Ivar Jacobson, *Object-Oriented Software Engineering: A Use Case Driven Approach,* Addison-Wesley, 1993.

How the Time Compressed Change Affects Our Companies, Cultures, and Professional Lives

Changes in application development have become a positive and enabling 1990s business force. New application-related opportunities are being recognized and seized. Applications to support business initiatives are implemented in record time, and their IT developers become heroes in the process. Empowered business users are developing and running applications tailored to meet their own unique needs.

Sound good? It is good—generally. But there are also problems. The same advances in application development that enable our companies to quickly turn new business opportunities into better positioning, increased market share and profits are also increasing problems and risk. Many development advances require difficult changes in infrastructure, culture, and governance, and those who develop and use applications that are based on them often find that they must operate under new and unforeseen constraints. As a result, the basic orientation of application developers and users is changing, as are their roles and many of their tasks. Some bask in the light of newfound skills and wealth. Others lose their jobs.

To illustrate how organizations and people are being impacted, we'll examine the 10 principal ways in which time compressed changes in development, approach, and execution technologies impact companies and the corporate lives of their IT professionals, business users, and management. (See Fig. 3.1) We'll examine how time compressed changes impact development productivity, along with the resultant increases and decreases in IT and business responsiveness. We'll also

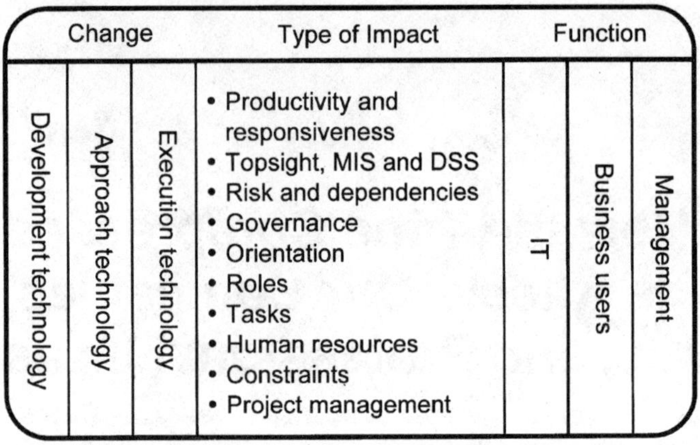

Change			Type of Impact	Function		
Development technology	Approach technology	Execution technology	• Productivity and responsiveness • Topsight, MIS and DSS • Risk and dependencies • Governance • Orientation • Roles • Tasks • Human resources • Constraints • Project management	IT	Business users	Management

Figure 3.1   The 10 principal ways time compressed IT change impacts companies.

look at what happens to dependencies and risk, and how the same changes impact development of management information systems (MIS) and decision support systems (DSS) along with their implications in terms of ability to help management achieve "topsight."[1] In addition to the organizational changes that were introduced in the last chapter, we'll look into how people are affected—in terms of governance, orientation, roles, and tasks. Finally, we'll examine what happens to project management from the perspectives of development teams and project managers.

How Time Compressed Change Impacts Productivity and Responsiveness

There's little doubt about the impact that new technologies are exerting on application development productivity and responsiveness. A developer utilizing Smalltalk, for example, can build applications at many times the speed of his or her peers developing the same applications in a traditional language such as COBOL or C. And, in addition to being developed in a fraction of the time, the Smalltalk application is likely to be easier to use and far less expensive to maintain. (See Fig. 3.2)

But before Smalltalk developers can outperform their traditional counterparts in creating fast, accurate, and usable business applications, substantial amounts of time—many months, often years—are required to adopt Smalltalk as a productive application development technology. Time is required to learn the Smalltalk syntax, paradigm, and class hierarchy structure, and to develop a library of reusable

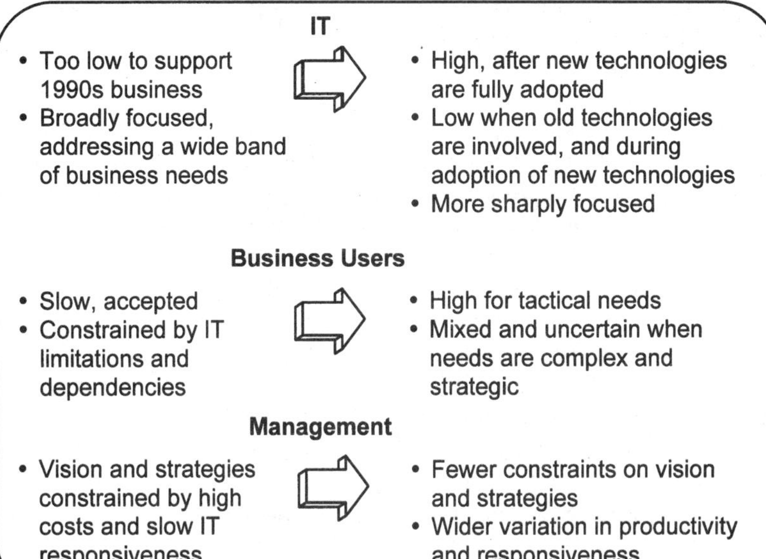

Figure 3.2 How time compressed changes in application development impact productivity and responsiveness.

classes and frameworks that are relevant to the business.[2] In addition, for technologies such as Smalltalk to be productive in a business environment, the problem domain itself must be insulated in many ways from other applications developed in other technologies. For an isolated business requirement, such as a trader workstation, achieving an insulated and bounded problem domain isn't difficult. For business requirements for which many diverse applications must interact, such as a trade processing system, achievement of an isolated problem domain can be problematic.[3] The same kinds of constraints hold, although sometimes to a slightly lesser extent, for other new development technologies, such as distributed objects and C++.

The recurring theme, and principal underlying constraint, is that as we progress from low-performance application development based on technologies that have broad applicability, to high-performance development based on new technologies and approaches:

- the learning curve, and time required for adoption, can be substantial,

- integration with legacy systems, and with current systems being developed using different technologies, can be problematic, and

- the spectrum of problems that can be productively addressed, narrows and becomes more sharply focused.

For many business users, time compressed changes in application development have been a liberating force. Unconstrained by highly technical developer interfaces and expertise required to program applications in traditional languages, business users in increasing numbers, are developing their own tactical applications.[4] Indeed, surprising sophistication and functionality can be quickly achieved using simple development tools such as Excel, VisualBasic, or Access. As we saw in Chap. 2, the result has been a sharp increase in productivity and responsiveness for tactical applications. Today's business users, who are computer literate or have access to people who are computer literate, are developing applications on an as-needed basis to retrieve information, capture and store information, analyze data, develop custom reports, and create presentations. Some of these applications are developed to address one-time business needs, and then discarded. But many are not.

Productivity and responsiveness for user-developed applications that are large and complex become much more mixed and uncertain. One problem is that, due to their complexity and integration requirements, many such applications are built largely by outside vendors. To be sure, many of the outside vendors are better equipped to handle new development technologies than their internal IT counterparts.

It's easy for an outside vendor, that is skilled in one or more new development technologies and approaches, to quickly develop applications in response to increasingly time-constrained user demands. It is also easy, as we shall see, for the same vendor to introduce technologies that are right for solving its client's business problems, but that are wrong when viewed from the perspective of the company or its management. Even when the technologies are right from both corporate and customer perspectives, additional technologies are likely to have been introduced, accelerating the amount of time compression that the company must deal with.

For management, the problem thus becomes one of balancing business requirements for increases in development productivity and responsiveness, with equally stringent requirements that time compression—resulting from development technology evolution and proliferation—be held to manageable levels. Management must also ensure that individual gains in productivity and responsiveness don't impair the ability of the company's MIS and DSS to provide a meaningful perspective of the company and its business.

How Time Compressed Change Impacts Topsight, Management Information, and Decision Support

Developing meaningful MIS and DSS applications for today's companies can be a challenging endeavor. (See Fig. 3.3.) In addition to traditional governance- and data-related problems, such as:

- ownership, confidentiality requirements and privacy issues,

- incompatibilities among business rules (e.g., management, regulatory, and shareholder reporting),

- inconsistent identifiers for customers, suppliers, locations or parts, and

- stewardship disputes over who accepts what kinds of responsibility for which data, a new set of development technology- and execution technology-related problems and issues must be addressed.

Consider what happened at an insurance company, with a top management initiative to develop a companywide view of its customers, so that it could analyze buying patterns across its organizations and products, take advantage of cross-selling opportunities, and recognize

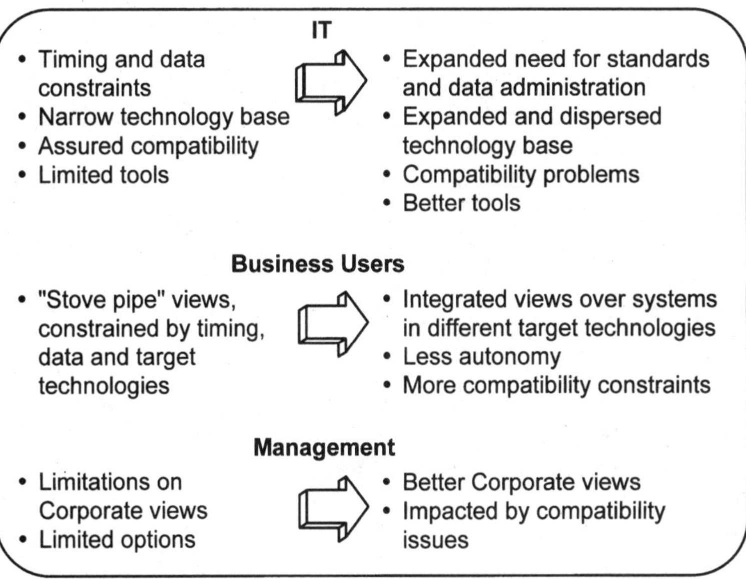

Figure 3.3 How time compressed change impacts topsight, management information, and decision support.

good customers—purchasers of multiple products from multiple business units—when the company comes into contact with them. The company had a strong and proactive Data Administration in place for a number of years, and many basic data-related issues were under control. Customers, for example, has common identifiers that were issued on a companywide basis. But the company's application development was decentralized. with individual business units responsible for developing their own applications and were free to choose the development and execution technologies that were best for their needs. The result was that four of its most important business units stored their analytic customer information in four different databases, and utilized four different technologies to access their data. While each unit was individually successful in fulfilling the needs of its business users, accessing the same data for corporate MIS and DSS proved to be expensive and difficult. Although the company's MIS and DSS developers had little trouble with the Access-based Personal Life data or with Group Life's Oracle database, accessing mainframe data in DB2 and ADABAS was problematic. Two separate and expensive middleware products had to be installed before the Property & Casualty and Annuities data could be accessed. Installation was time-consuming and difficult, as Annuity and Property & Casualty's mainframe-oriented IT organizations has trouble understanding and providing much of the PC, network, and protocol–related information needed for installing the middleware product. Once installed, corporate MIS developers were frustrated by the narrow set of SQL database access commands that the much-touted middleware would support.

The result was that the MIS developers' applications executed too slowly, the minimal performance levels required to make their MIS and DSS applications usable could not be attained, and there was little that they could do to speed them up. (See Fig. 3.4.)

Group Life's developers, concerned about corruption of their encapsulated Oracle data (that was supposed to be accessed only through C++), provided access to their customer data on a read-only basis. Although at first this didn't seem to be a significant problem, it meant that the same customer data had to be stored on two different databases, that were maintained by two different groups. It wasn't long before significant differences between what was supposed to be the same customer data became apparent, as corporate and business unit managers began to clash over different conclusions based on the different numbers in their reports. In addition to substantial and highly visible embarrassment, lots of time and effort were required to isolate, reconcile, and correct the errant data, and to put controls in place to ensure that the problem wouldn't recur.

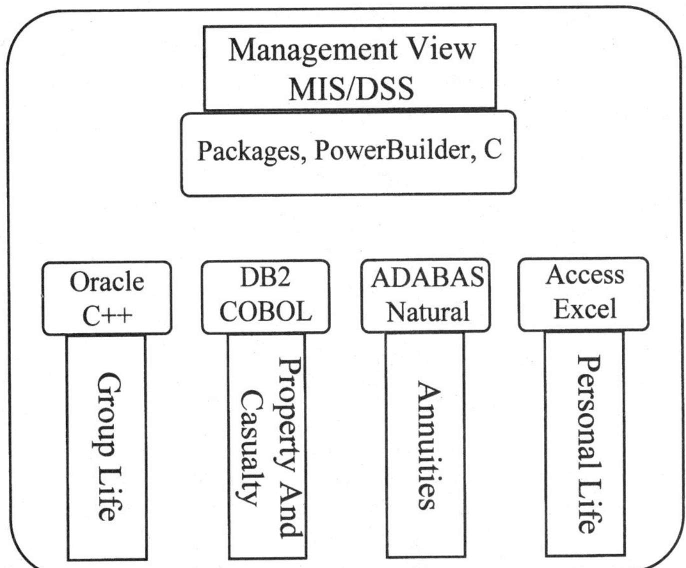

Figure 3.4 How differences in execution technology and development technology architectures impact management views of company information.

As an organization's development and execution technology base expands, and the new technologies become dispersed throughout many business units, developers of management applications—such as MIS and DSS—that require information from a number of different applications and databases, are forced to face new and difficult challenges in terms of basic compatibility. Many such challenges result not only from technology architectures, but also from fundamental differences in development and approach technologies. Even languages as seemingly close as C and C++ can represent fundamental differences in approach—differences that can wreak surprising amounts of havoc on attempts to leverage information contained in the applications they were used to develop. The result is that, although development tools are getting better and can be utilized over wider ranges of technology architectures, many developers and their business users are finding that they have less, not more, autonomy than before in developing the applications they need.

Although MIS and DSS tools are also becoming more usable to managers at an accelerating rate, time compressed change has not been an unfailing friend to management. The accelerating rate at which application development technologies are evolving and proliferating places real constraints on management's ability to utilize their

MIS and DSS tools to get at their companies' information so that they can develop the topsight they need to run today's businesses. This is especially true when the data, on which the information is based, are associated with different development and execution technologies.

How Time Compressed Change Impacts Dependencies and Risk

For a number of years, substantial reductions in numbers of suppliers has been a steady trend in almost every sector of our manufacturing economy, as companies strive to increase quality, reduce costs, compete in our global economy, and become world class.[5] An exception that stands in sharp contrast to this trend is the manufacturing of software, that is, application development. The time compressed increases in the number of suppliers—the development, approach, and execution technology vendors utilized by today's application developers—results from the:

- extent to which application development is not only technology-dependent, but to a large extent, *driven* by innovations in development and execution technologies, the

- proliferation and diversity of application development technology vendors, and the

- accelerating rate at which development and execution technologies evolve and proliferate.

It's not uncommon, for example, for an application development team to utilize products from different vendors for methodology, analysis tools, development languages, graphical user interface (GUI) widgets, query tools, reporting tools, transaction processing monitors, databases, database design tools, database connectivity, testing, and configuration management. The resulting risk to application developers is that effective utilization of products from large numbers of vendors requires not only that their products cover the requirements of the development project, but also that:

- they remain in business, continuing to evolve and support their products, that

- their products are compatible with each other, and that

- their products continue to evolve in consistent ways, so that compatibility doesn't decrease with every new release of every product.

Adding to these problems is the widespread practice among development technology vendors of bringing new releases of their products to market before the full set of features needed by developers is available—and in some cases, before they have been fully tested. The reason for this practice is that, with time spans between development technology releases down to only 6 to 9 months, vendors in this competitive arena are finding themselves thrust into a "catch 22" dilemma. If they take the time to ensure that their new releases are fully tested and usable products, they run the risk of losing market share to other vendors who get to the market with the new set of widely touted features first. If they don't take the time needed to ensure that their new releases are tested, usable products, they run the risk of alienating the application developers who are their customers and tarnishing the reputation of their products. Adding to this problem are management and scoping risks associated with new tools, technologies, and approaches that are not well understood. Lack of basic project management aids, such as standards for assessing quality, metrics for estimating effort, formats for reporting progress, and warning signals for controlling scope, add to these already substantial risks. (See Fig. 3.5.)

For business users, lost opportunity risks, due to their IT organization's inability to deliver quality applications when and where they are needed, are being traded off for a host of new risks associated

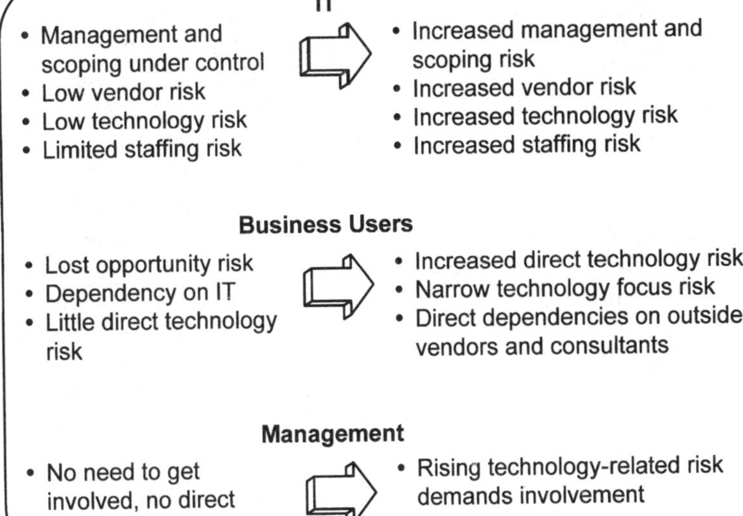

Figure 3.5 How time compressed change impacts dependencies and risk.

with developing the applications themselves. In addition to taking on the vendor and technology risks associated with all current application development projects, business users must now contend with two additional risks.

The first risk stems from their narrow focus, as nontechnical business people confront specific business problems. The risk is that in developing applications that address their specific business needs, it is easy to unwittingly create significant technology-related problems that may not be immediately apparent. Common examples that typify this class of risk include:

- creation and storage of key business data—on things like customers, exposures, products, suppliers, locations, inventory items—in ways that aren't compatible with other applications,

- introduction of languages and development environments that produce run-time images that can't execute on standard desktop workstations or that don't fully interoperate with other desktop- or server-based applications, and

- applications that capture information at nonstandard times, in response to their sets of business events, resulting in data that are correct, but that reflect a different set of circumstances from their counterparts in other parts of the organization.

The second risk is the product of their direct dependencies on application vendors and consultants. It's often difficult for business users, unaccustomed to large-scale application development, to sort the wheat from the chaff—to discern system integrators and consultants who are good from those who are not. It's also far easier for unscrupulous vendors of business applications to sell inferior products to business users than to combinations of business users and IT professionals.

As an example of how this can happen, and of just how insidious it can be, consider what happened when a vendor of a finance and accounting system sold their product to a large Midwest services company. Their system was a mature product. It had a large installed base, included many desirable user features, and supported over 20 databases, including DB2, the database that the company had selected to support, with the aim of helping ensure the integrity of its new IEF-based applications. But the way the vendor supported the large number of databases was by seeking the lowest common denominator, which in their case was Index Sequential Access Method (ISAM)—a robust and innovative data management technology of the early 1970s! While treating 1990s DB2 tables as though they were a collection of 1970s ISAM files permitted their finance and accounting system to execute in a DB2 environment, it didn't permit the system to take advantage of DB2's 1990s features, such as referential integrity, that were essential to ensuring the consistency of the company's highly-integrated application environment.

When confronted with the problem and its implications, what the vendor heard was a clarion call for damage control. It wasn't about to lose a multimillion-dollar sale on a mere technicality. To address the problem, the vendor's management, in a presentation to their customer's top business managers, stood up and lied! Their sale was saved, the system was implemented, and as a result, the company spent many times the budgeted cost of the system developing the workarounds that were needed to keep the system from corrupting their highly integrated data.

The dependencies of today's businesses on information technology, the complexity of today's integrated application environments, and the numbers and complexities of the technologies upon which they depend demand knowledge and direct involvement of business users, IT, and company management.

How Time Compressed Change Impacts
Governance, Roles, and Responsibilities

A colleague recently asked if I was referring to the "application development backlog" at a lecture I gave on the gap between business's information needs and the availability of applications to fulfill them. If it had been 1985 instead of 1995, his assumption would have been correct. In the mid-1980s, business users did indeed have to wait—often many months, sometimes years—for their IT departments to get around to developing their applications. But this was 1995, and business users, in increasing numbers, were busy closing the gap between their needs and the applications required to fulfill them, by developing applications themselves, and by contracting with outside vendors to develop applications for them.

Although governance, roles, and responsibilities are quickly changing in almost every aspect of corporate life, when it comes to application development, roles and responsibilities are changing to the extent that roles are often reversed—with business users developing applications and IT being left to deal with the results. The combination of Client/Server technology's low entry cost, familiarity, and acceptance of PCs as part of our everyday business environment and the proliferation of graphical user-oriented development tools have enabled business users, in increasing numbers, to get into the business of developing their own applications.[6] (See Fig. 3.6) To business

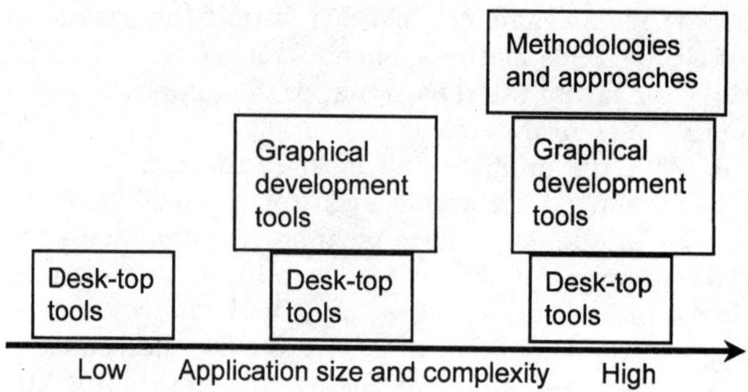

Figure 3.6   Drivers of user involvement in application development.

users who develop their own applications, time compressed change
has been a friend, a source of liberation and empowerment.

To IT developers, many of the same time compressed changes have
been the source of a unwelcome governance shift—from sole owners of
application development to shared ownership and responsibility.
Indeed, many of today's business applications are the product of mul-
tidisciplinary development teams composed of IT and business participants. For low-end tactical applications, this phenomenon is driven
largely by desktop tools that business users have on their workstations, and that are powerful enough to invite application development. For applications of moderate size and complexity, it is also the
result of graphical, easy-to-use, user-oriented development tools, such
as PowerBuilder and VisualBasic. For high-end mission-critical applications, it is just as often the result of IE, prototyping, and OO–based
development approaches that not only emphasize, but also demand,
high levels of business user participation in the development process.

If IT has been relegated to the role of observer for tactical application development, and to that of shared developer for applications
that are larger and more complex, IT's roles as sole development
technology source, and owner of production facilities, have been
equally diminished. (See Fig. 3.7.) While IT continues in its role as
owner of the mainframe, with full governance over its administration
and use, more and more development is taking place on
Client/Server platforms located in user-run business units, for implementation on user-administered local area networks (LANs). In
terms of network infrastructure, IT's governance is being increasingly relegated to administrator of the organization's internet. These
trends are a direct result of time compressed changes that have
made development and production technologies not only simpler and
easier to use, but also significantly less expensive. And as development technology vendors follow the trend and directly approach the

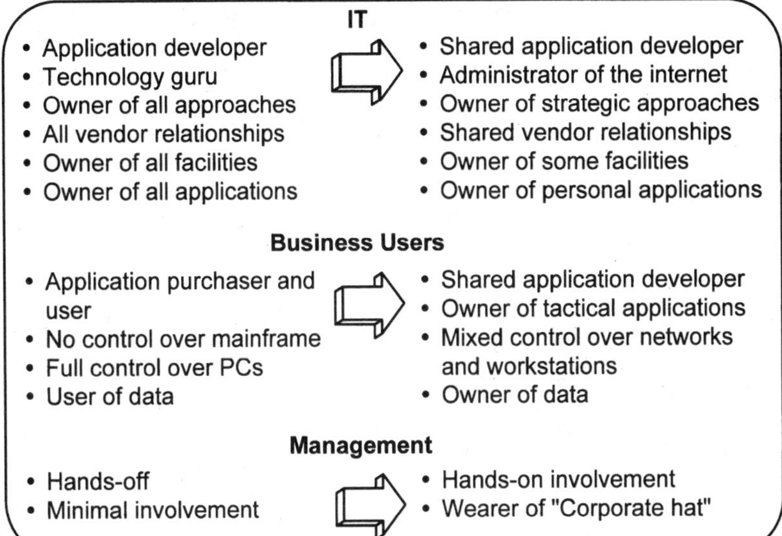

Figure 3.7 How time compressed change impacts governance, roles, and responsibilities.

business community, development and production technologies are becoming more accessible as well.

For business users, the same time compressed forces are resulting in a governance shift from no governance over mainframes and full governance over PCs, to shared governance over LANs and workstations.[7] As PCs become nodes on networks and gateways into network-based applications, their users lose control over the software that runs on them, the applications they support, their icons, and their desktops. Even personal applications—such as word processors, presentation software, and spreadsheets—are becoming less "personal" as they fall more and more under the governance of IT. The results of the exposures and risks that accompany unauthorized access, infections by software viruses, and being out of compliance with software licensing requirements have made the administration of personal software one area that bucks the general IT-to-business application governance trend.

A final, and not always welcome, business user governance shift caused by time compressed change is the shift from data user to data owner. The accelerating proliferation of development and execution technologies, and the resultant proliferation of the ways in which data are stored and accessed, have complicated the task of data administration and increased the need for a single point of responsibility for each part of a company's information. If data are to be stored in multiple execution technologies—relational, object, and OLAP databases, for example—and accessed by applications developed through different and conflicting approaches—such as C and C++—someone must own up to being responsible for their correctness and to being the definitive source for their values and formats. If data governance issues are not specifically addressed and straightened out, applications that are developed on and run in a time compressed multiple technology environment will, as in our previous example, soon degenerate, and their users will be left to make do with unreliable and inconsistent results.

The roles associated with resolving the conflicts that arise as governance, role, and responsibility issues are sorted out inevitably fall to management. In time compressed multitechnology development and execution technology environments, it is management that must wear the "corporate hat" and sort out the resultant issues for the overall good of the organization. This role calls not only for direct involvement, but also for the judicious weighing of conflicting requirements such as productivity and empowerment versus the ability to leverage key corporate information in terms of its strategy and corporate vision.

How Time Compressed Change Impacts Orientation

One of the most fundamental effects that time compressed change has on IT, and all who come into contact with IT, is to transform its orientation from the tried and true to the new and not yet proven. (See Fig. 3.8.) The combination of time compressed technology change, increases in business's information needs, and the viability of alternatives to the internal IT organization for procuring needed applications has fueled the transformation. Taking 2 or more years to develop a strategic application, for example, that utilizing newer technologies could be developed in 6 months, can put a company or strategic business unit at a serious competitive disadvantage. Today's application development organizations—whether part of corporate IT, the research and development (R&D) arm of a software company, or an independent application development vendor—no longer have the option of developing new applications based on traditional approaches, technologies that are fully understood, tested, stable, and secure. To be competitive in the fast-moving late 1990s they must reorient themselves, not only to work with new and not fully proven approaches and technologies, but also to successfully harness these new technologies and approaches to develop better applications more quickly and at an increasingly lower cost. Considering material already covered, the extent of the reorienta-

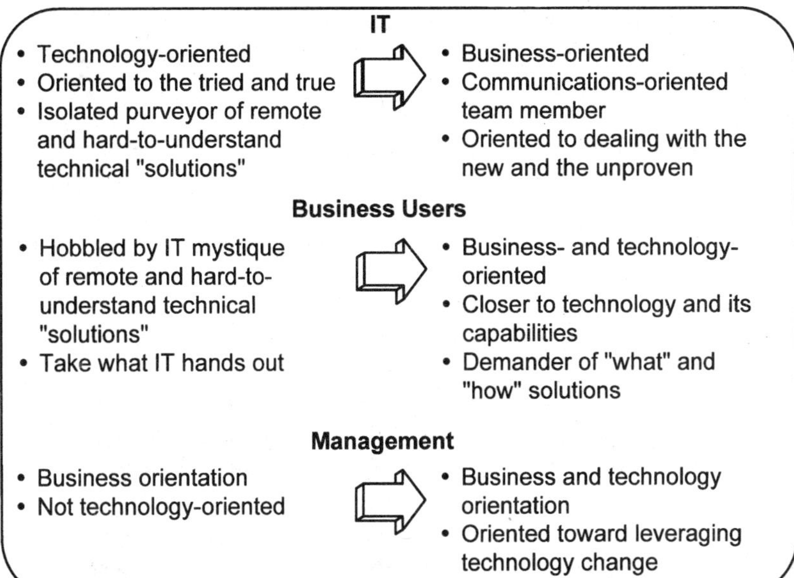

Figure 3.8 How time compressed change impacts orientation.

tion becomes clear. It must, at minimum, include a reorientation of application developers:

- away from technical and toward business,

- away from isolated development and toward codevelopment through participation on interdisciplinary teams, and

- away from the known and toward the not yet fully proven.

Business users, as prime beneficiaries of time compressed technology change, are undergoing a corresponding reorientation away from development, approach, and execution technologies as remote and hard-to-understand necessities, toward development technologies as usable—and in many cases, comfortable, even familiar—business tools. One result of this transformation is unrealistic expectations. The combination of enthusiastic development technology vendors, graphical interfaces that are beguilingly simple, acute business needs, and unscrupulous consultants is usually sufficient to quash the skepticism that business users would otherwise have, and to help ensure the continuation of this already ubiquitous problem. A second result is more ambitious specifications and demands. It is not uncommon for business users, bolstered by quotations from a number of outside vendors, to demand that their IT functions provide comparable service in terms of time, cost, and functionality.

Demand for functionality is likely to include not only *what* users require to support their business needs, but *how* they want the required functionality delivered as well. The UNIX-oriented IT developers at a Canadian software company were recently confronted by this reality when their proposal, that the interface for a new product be developed in Motif—a UNIX-based GUI—was soundly rejected. The company's Marketing Department—their business user—was only tangentially interested in the advantages of Motif and in the goodness with which it emulated a Windows GUI. What they were after was interoperability with other Windows applications, and the cachet that Windows had in their market.

Time compressed change is exerting a similar impact on management in the form of a transformation from being strictly business oriented toward a broader business- and IT-based orientation that includes application development. For management, execution technologies—and in an increasing number of instances, many development technologies as well—are joining the ranks of familiar and usable business tools. The key difference is that for management, time compressed change can be leveraged: to achieve competitive advantage, to increase productivity, to lower costs, to increase communication, and to help in the achievement of its strategies and vision. Indeed, many managers who have successfully made the transformation to embracing time compressed change are joining the ranks of the most innovative development technology users.

One CEO—a businessperson through and through, but one who had also developed considerable insight into information technology and application development—saw surprising and innovative possibilities when exposed to Linda, a coordination language designed to tie workstations together so that they could be used for parallel processing. Although he was shown a coordination language, what the manufacturing-oriented CEO saw was a better means than the currently available set of EDI products for achieving supply chain integration. Time compressed development technology change, and the business opportunities that it enables, represent too great an opportunity to be ignored by business management.

How Time Compressed Change Impacts Tasks

"When are we going to start coding? Four months have gone by and we still don't have anything to show for it—our competitors in Retail Banking have written half their code, and we haven't even begun! This project, along with my career in this bank, are going down the tubes fast!" shouted a very concerned Senior Vice President at a major East Coast bank. He was furious. And in a sense, he was right. His application development effort had the distinct appearance of a project that was out of control and going nowhere—in terms of traditional tasks. In terms of OO development tasks—the tasks required to complete his project—it was doing just fine.

Coding, the once ubiquitous staple of application development—the task, that for many people, defined application development, the task by which developers have been proven, and the task by which their progress has been measured for over 40 years—is being quickly rendered obsolete. Time compressed changes are swiftly replacing coding with a variety of tasks—from developing business and design models, to stringing pre-coded OO components together, to pointing and clicking on the graphical icons. And what little coding that is left is becoming far more likely to be automatically generated by CASE tools than written by hand.

As time compressed changes are evolving application development from a hand-wrought craft into an automated process with engineering roots, the tasks performed by developers—and indeed, by almost everyone associated with application development—are evolving as well. (See Fig. 3.9.) Program design and coding are being replaced by business and application modeling, which—with the aid of OO frameworks, classes, and CASE tools—are generating the application. Debugging and testing, still significant development tasks, are

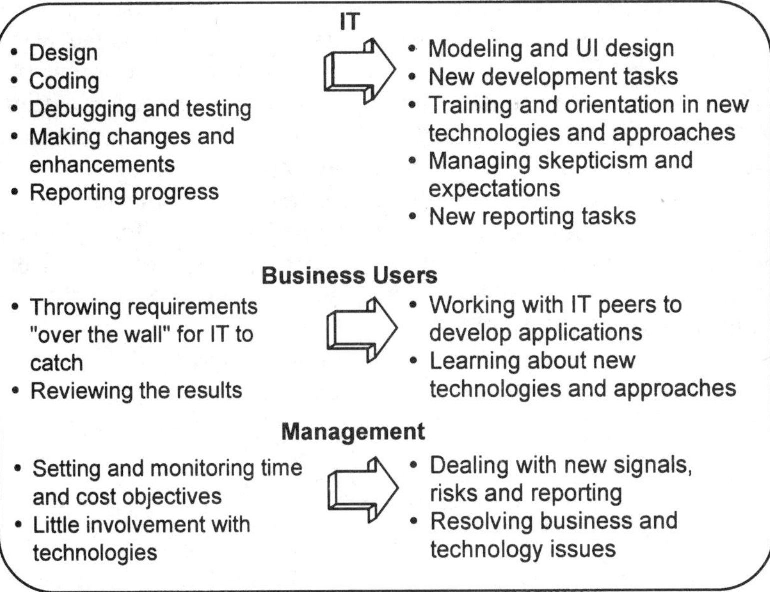

Figure 3.9 How time compressed change impacts tasks.

becoming more closely associated with design and requirements models than with programs.

Adding to the already significant tasks associated with working together, as peers, utilizing new technologies to model business requirements, and developing applications that successfully address them, IT developers and business users are finding themselves increasingly burdened by a set of new, and not universally welcome, sets of tasks. Developers and business users, for example, are spending increasing amounts of time, not on tasks associated with developing applications, but on tasks associated with keeping up with new technologies and with managing the substantial changes that often accompany their introduction. In addition to training in how new technologies work and in how to apply them to develop applications, nettlesome tasks facing today's developers include:

- managing, and striking an appropriate middle ground between, the inflated expectations and deep skepticism on the parts of business users and company management, as they become aware of hot new development technologies;

- evaluating, procuring, and in some cases developing and customizing, infrastructure needed to support new technologies; and

- developing and justifying new procedures and formats for explaining differences in approach and reporting.

For management, new—and not always welcome—tasks include dealing with the mixed and confusing sets of signals produced when applications are developed using a variety of technologies and approaches. It is not uncommon for managers of large organizations to find themselves saddled with the unwanted task of comparing and making sense out of an array of disparate application development projects—some developing data models, others analyzing use cases, and still others developing series of rapid prototypes. Adding to this burden are increased demands on management's time resulting from the accelerating stream of business, organizational, and technical critical path issues produced by many current technology projects.

The halcyon era, when management could deal with development technologies by setting and monitoring time and cost objectives, has become yet another casualty of time compressed change.

How Time Compressed Change Impacts
Human Resources

Time compressed change is a strong destabilizing force, impacting companies' human resource infrastructure in a number of significant, if not immediately obvious, ways. (See Fig. 3.10.) In addition to the continuous additional burden it places on training, communications, and change management, time compressed change creates marked scarcities of IT personnel who are proficient in new and emerging technologies.

When a new technology is hot, market demand can outstrip IT personnel with the key skills needed to make it work, to the extent that the disparity seriously compromises the technology's success. At its worst, it can bring progress on new development to a grinding halt. There are three reasons why this happens. The first is obvious, the others are not.

The obvious reason is that IT professionals, anxious to capitalize on newfound skills, are difficult for companies to retain. I've seen entire technical staffs of hot-technology projects leave partway through—as soon as they have delivered enough to ensure their credibility in the new technology job market—to double their compensation for the same amount of effort. The predictable result is a stalled project— until a new crop of resources can be hired, trained, brought up to speed on progress to date, and for a short time, put to productive work. Although the project may eventually be completed, the sought-after productivity gains, if realized at all, typically fall far below the technology's potential. Companies simply can't get high productivity from projects that are cycled through many different teams.

Even when resources with new technology skills are convinced to stick with their projects through completion, this problem can still exact a significant toll on the organization's ability to achieve the return on investment (ROI) required to make the technology pay off. The problem is that sticking it out through a single development project isn't sufficient. Moving up through the new technology adoption curve, so that positive productivity gains commensurate with the technology's potential are achieved, requires developers who are experienced, who have utilized the technology to develop two—even three—applications, and if the gains are to be widespread, who are able to propagate the technology into other development efforts.[8] If getting developers who are proficient in a hot new technology to stick it out through a single development effort is hard, getting them to stay through three or four projects, while compensation disparities become even greater, can be close to impossible.

The second, just as significant, but far less obvious, reason is that the new technology skills that are most needed tend to be the ones most quickly dissipated and dispersed. The dispersion results from the accelerating number of required development skills that accompanies time compressed change. For example, staffing two concurrent development projects—one utilizing PowerBuilder and LBMS, the other using VisualAge, and Objectory—requires four times the number of skills that would be needed if the same two projects were executed in VisualBasic, or COBOL and CICS. If the PowerBuilder project supplements its PowerScripts with C or C++, and the VisualAge project utilizes object-oriented COBOL to supplement Smalltalk, the multiple can quickly grow to six, or even seven times the number of skills.

The problem is that as the number of technologies and approaches concurrently in use grows, the skills of those who participate in development must be dispersed among a greater number of technologies:

- more people get involved,

- time lost to training goes up,

- hiring becomes more difficult, and

- management's ability to balance uneven demand by reallocating personnel to other projects is reduced.

A related, and equally significant, problem is that time demands on individuals who do acquire multiple skills, or who possess key skills in several sought-after areas, can easily reach the point at which their time is dispersed among so many projects that they lose much of their effectiveness. (See Fig. 3.10.)

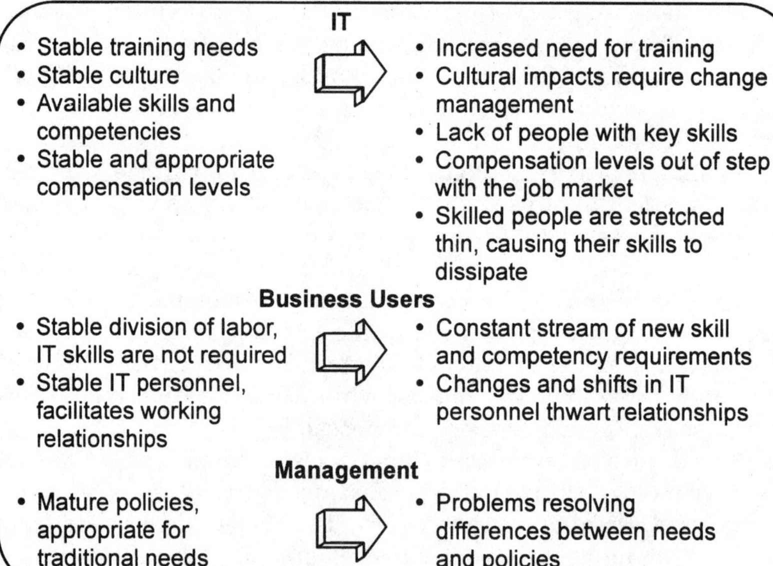

Figure 3.10   How time compressed change impacts human resources.

For the increasing number of business users who find themselves in some way associated with application development, a direct opportunity and an indirect problem become apparent. The direct opportunity is to work with IT, as development peers, to produce better and more relevant applications for their business units. But effective participation in the application development process requires an understanding of the development approach, and in a growing number of cases, some technical skills as well. Consider use cases, a popular OO technique for defining requirements. While business users don't need technical skills to participate in use case-based requirements analysis,

- understanding how use cases are constructed helps them to express their ideas and requirements in a more appropriate way—and more importantly—to determine for themselves the extent to which their needs are reflected in the use case models that result,

- understanding OO fundamentals, such as abstraction, helps them spot opportunities for abstracting parts of use cases for reuse that may not be obvious to developers who are not as close to the business, and

- knowledge of the company's frameworks and class libraries of OO components and user interface widgets will help them leverage their development participation and codesign applications that are more usable and easier to develop.

The indirect problem is that the high turnover rate of IT personnel who acquire skills in hot technologies makes it more difficult for business users to establish the kinds of long-term personal relationships that make really productive work with their IT counterparts possible. Scarce time must be taken from productive development and reallocated to teaching each new crop of "business analysts" the fundamentals of their businesses, as common language is sought, differences are identified and ironed out, subtleties are revisited, and requirements models double and triple checked. It all takes a toll, not only on business users who participate in development, but also on sought-after goals such as development productivity and the quality of the applications that result.

How Time Compressed Change Impacts Constraints

Among the main attractions of application development to IT professionals are the opportunities it offers to press the latest technologies into useful service, to be creative, and to invent clever solutions to solve business problems. These prerogatives, to the chagrin of developers of applications, are fast falling victim to time compressed change.

Time compressed proliferation of development, approach, and execution technologies aggravates technology interactions, increasing constraints on application development. (See Fig. 3.11.) Selection and implementation of technology architectures in any of these areas represent de facto commitments to technology strategies—strategies that can persist over time, constraining future options for the other two.[9]

In the 1980s, when development, approach, and technology architectures were relatively stable, and IBM's dominance imposed de facto standards, such constraints were acceptable. Everything fit. In the late 1990s, with technology proliferating and evolving at an accelerating pace, and the lack of a clearly dominant commercial force capable of stabilizing most aspects of application development, things can get pretty dicey pretty quick. Development utilizing a particular C++ compiler and library of C++ reusable classes, for example, can place constraints not only on execution technology hardware architecture (Pentium versus Power PC, 32 bit versus 64 bit), but also on approach technologies (OO versus Graphical Design, versus data-driven) The problem for application developers is that while no one can predict, with a high degree of certainty, how each of these architectures will evolve, everyone must make technology architecture decisions, and everyone else must deal with the resultant legacy of the constraints.

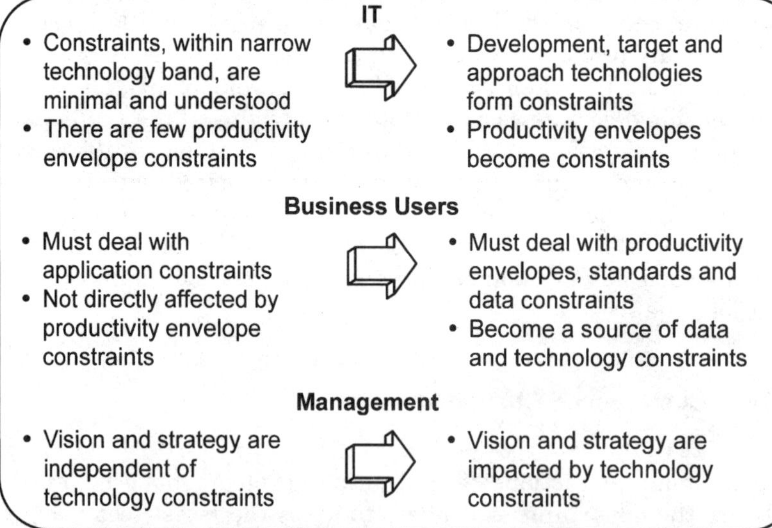

Figure 3.11   How time compressed change impacts constraints.

Another significant, but often unforeseen, constraint results from development tool productivity envelopes: the narrow bands of implementation flexibility, within which application development tools are most productive. In general, as development tools become more advanced, and more productive, they do so, at least in part, at the expense of flexibility. Productivity in OO development—using Smalltalk or C++, for example—is achieved primarily through reuse of classes, with the highest productivity gains resulting from reuse of the highest-level classes. Developers who can reuse classes such as "Customer" or "Sales Order" get a lot more for their efforts than do developers whose reuse is limited to low-level classes such as dialogue boxes, radio buttons, or floating-point numbers. Although some flexibility can be maintained by adding new methods to reusable classes, the highest levels of productivity are achieved by concentrating development efforts on assembling applications from reusable high-level components—such as OO frameworks—rather than on a combination of assembly and component development. Similar situations exist for most current approaches to application development. High productivity from information engineering-based IEF depends on extensive reuse of high-level procedure templates. Productivity from graphical development tools, such as PowerBuilder, depends on extensive reuse of standard objects and limited use of custom objects and scripts.

The problem is that in each of these cases, the added productivity comes at the expense of flexibility. The required functionality, although achievable through surprisingly modest amounts of time and effort, is achieved in standard ways, through reuse of standard prefabricated components. Developers produce, and business users get, what the business needs, but not necessarily precisely the way the developers or business users wanted it.

The key to achieving high levels of productivity from modern development and approach technologies, such as OO development, graphical development and IE-based CASE, is to operate within the tool's productivity envelope—to constrain designs such that required functionality is achieved through high levels of reuse. The benefit is fast, low-cost application development through significant reuse. The cost is productivity envelope-based constraints.

Data that must be accessible by different sets of business users, through applications implemented using a diversity of development, approach, and execution technologies, can become an additional source of constraints. In the multiple and diverse technology environments typical of most large organizations, applications that access strategic data—on customers, schedules, products, or suppliers, for example—must ensure that constraints, in the form of common data standards, are observed. The inevitable consequence of not doing so is creation of islands of data that are supposed to be the same, but as we saw in Chap. 2, can easily diverge, presenting inconsistent and unreliable views of the business. The consequence of following strict data standards is the imposition of additional constraints on developers, sometimes in a form that's neither intuitive nor fully compatible with all of their development, approach, or execution technology needs. The problem is that each application developed by a business unit in a new development, approach, or execution technology adds to the set of already substantial data constraints.

Addressing data constraints, as we shall see, requires a data administration function that is broad enough to address data issues—such as governance, standards, integrity, and security—using paradigms that are compatible with the increasing diversity of technologies that results from time compressed change.

Management's vision and strategy are also impacted by multiple and evolving development, approach, and execution technology constraints. The combination of:

- increased reliance on IT for enablement and implementation of business initiatives,

- time compressed increases in data and technology constraints, and

- governance and issues that arise when different business units utilizing different approaches to application development come into conflict

requires that management become involved. For example, a strategy to leverage database marketing techniques to increase sales and to generate cross-selling opportunities among a company's business units, cannot be successfully executed if the company cannot recognize the same customer across the diverse applications that serve the needs of each business unit.

The tricky problem for management is ensuring that a workable balance is maintained between managing the time compressed acceleration in diversity of data technology, and fostering the autonomy required to attain high levels of performance from today's flattened and empowered organizations.

How Time Compressed Change Impacts Project Management

The impact of time compressed technology multiplication and evolution on development project management can be every bit as devas-

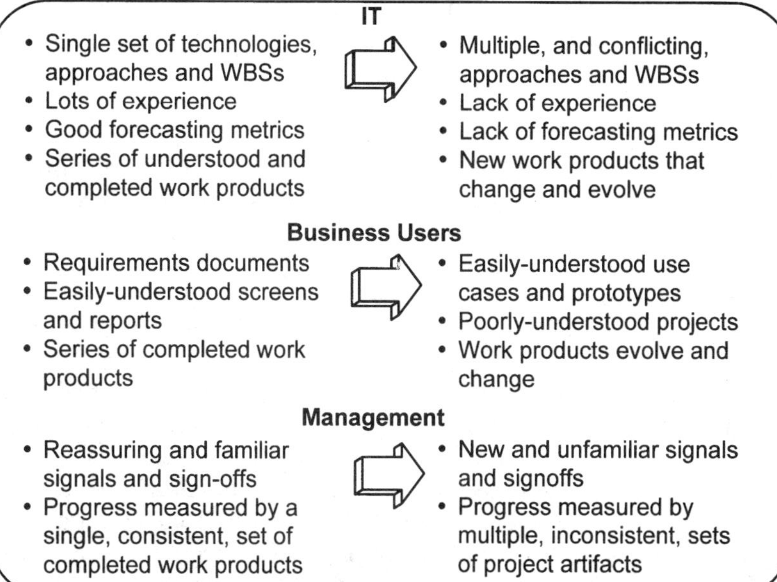

Figure 3.12   How time compressed change impacts project management.

tating for those who must make sense out of an organization's application development as it is for managers of individual projects. (See Fig. 3.12.) Indeed, it can be more so, for they must contend not only with the vagaries of developing applications in new and evolving technology environments, but also with copious amounts of inconsistent and conflicting information from a number of development teams, each utilizing what are arguably the best technologies and approaches. In today's increasingly flattened and empowered organizations, application development can take on as many appearances as there are business units engaged in it.

While it is not uncommon for large organizations to find themselves engaged in developing their business applications utilizing a diversity of IE, graphical, and OO approaches, the impact on project, business unit, and company management can be problematic. The array of project signals and artifacts presented to management can easily include:

- life cycle phases that don't match, and in some cases seem to be leading their developers in totally different directions,

- work products and deliverables that are fundamentally different and hard to compare,

- different needs, in terms of business user involvement and support infrastructure, and

- a different set of development tools and vendors.

Without the benefit of a consistent yardstick for comparing and measuring different development projects in a meaningful way, application development management is increasingly finding itself at a loss to effectively plan and manage.

In terms of project management, developers and their business users often fare no better. Indeed, the combination of new and poorly understood WBSs, work products, and deliverables and support requirements can turn project management into a real challenge. When the lack of basic management tools—such as meaningful milestones and estimation metrics and new, unforeseen, and in many cases, inexperienced—vendors are taken into account, it can become difficult to envision how today's application development projects can be managed with any consistency at all. In fact, without a means for addressing management in a time compressed environment, they cannot. The alarmingly high percentage of failed development projects speaks for itself.[10]

References

1. David Gelernter coined the phrase "topsight" in his book *Mirror Worlds,* Oxford University Press, 1992, and defined it as "what comes from a far-overhead vantage point, from a bird's-eye view that reveals the whole—the big picture; how the parts fit together." I believe that this is what should be achieved—but doesn't always happen— by corporate management as a result of their Management Information Systems (MIS) and Decision Support Systems (DSS) support.
2. All Smalltalk classes are, of course, reusable in a technical sense. What I am referring to here, are business classes, or components, that are meaningful to the business and its problem domain, that are large enough to substantially impact the productivity with which business applications can be developed, and most importantly, are robust enough to be reliably reused by many developers for many applications.
3. One-way integration—Smalltalk applications utilizing other business applications in other technologies—can be achieved, through "wrappers," for example. Achievement of two-way integration—in which the applications can call or message each other—is much more difficult.
4. Developer interfaces, such as C or COBOL workstations, that require their users to develop low-level code using text editors and debuggers represent highly technical interfaces to most business users.
5. John Emshwiller, "Suppliers Struggle To Improve Quality As Big Firms Slash Their Vendor Rolls," *Wall Street Journal,* September 2, 1991. Also see Steven Ray, "Building World Class Suppliers," in *Total Quality: An Executives Guide For The 1990s,* Dow Jones-Irwin, Ernst & Young Quality Improvement Consulting Group 1990; and Tom Gunn, *21st Century Manufacturing,* Harper Business, 1992.
6. For an interesting discussion on the clash between IT and business user governance over information technology acquisition, see "CIOs Business Units Wrestle Over Control Of Technology Spending," Bob Violino, *InformationWeek,* April 10, 1995.

7. My shift in terminology from "PC" to "workstation" is intentional, and is meant to emphasize the fact that there is little that is personal about desktop computers that run significant LAN-based applications.
8. Chris Kemerer, "How the Learning Curve Affects CASE Tool Adoption," *IEEE Software,* May 1992.
9. For a fascinating, in-depth, and relevant discussion of how commitments can persist over time, placing unforeseen—and unwanted—constraints on strategies and options, see Pankaj Ghemawat, *Commitment: The Dynamic Of Strategy,* The Free Press, 1991.
10. Chris Kemerer and Glenn L. Sosa, "System Development Risks In Strategic Information Systems," *Information and Software Technology,* 33(3):212–223, 1991.

Potential and Achievable Benefits—What We Should, and Should Not, Expect

The business users at a large Midwest car company were astounded. Despite an aggressive schedule, the software vendor that they had selected—a small Smalltalk development company—was about to deliver their application on the day it was due. And they weren't ready to receive it. Based on past experience, the bewildered business users weren't expecting the application for another 3 to 6 months, and they didn't know quite how to respond to their vendor's "early delivery." The new work flow and procedures, that were required to take advantage of the application's capabilities, hadn't been fully implemented, training on the new system hadn't begun, and the 1000 workstations that were needed to run it hadn't even been ordered. What they did know was that Smalltalk was a resounding success, and that it would be their technology of choice for all subsequent application development.

As the automotive company's business users were struggling to cope with their "early delivery," the CIO of a large East Coast bank was getting ready to throw the same technology out. The bank's two initial Smalltalk development projects had also been completed on schedule, each producing a viable business application. But the CIO, who was anticipating immediate and dramatic productivity improvements, wasn't impressed. Indeed he had already previewed a new graphical development environment—something he felt was potentially a lot more productive than anything he had seen before—and begun negotiating with its vendor for a license to use it.

Although the car company and the bank achieved similar results with comparable development technologies, they came to strikingly different conclusions— conclusions that were based not on results, but on how results were perceived. And their different perceptions were the product of their equally different expectations.

In the time compressed world of late-1990s application development, in which new technologies and approaches are thrust upon companies with increasing rapidity, maintaining a realistic perspective in terms of what to—and what not to—expect can be a real challenge. And not maintaining a realistic perspective can be downright dangerous. But before we tackle this important and pervasive problem, we must first be sure we understand it. To develop our common understanding, let's take a close look at expectations for application development technologies and approaches—those that are achievable as well as those that are not—on the part of IT, and particularly on the part of business and management.

Achievable IT Expectations

The realities that development technologies are moving forward at an accelerating pace, and that many new development technology products really do represent significant advances, provide the means for some of IT's most enthusiastic expectations to be met. (See Fig. 4.1.)

Indeed, many new development technologies, if properly utilized and given half a chance, can be harnessed to deliver applications in surprisingly short amounts of time and with correspondingly small amounts of effort. IT professionals, utilizing standard late-1990s

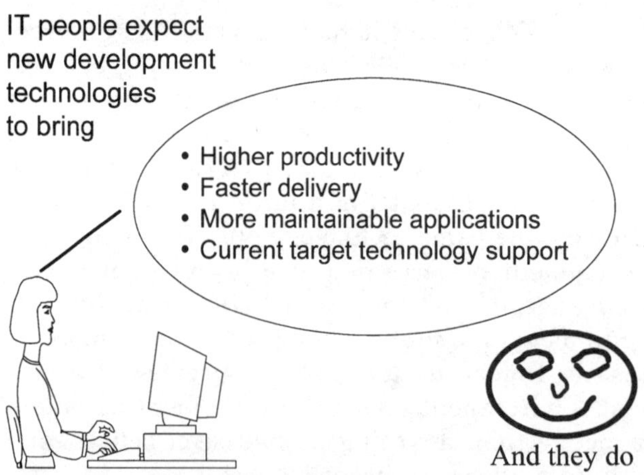

Figure 4.1 Achievable ITs expectations for new technologies.

tools, such as PowerBuilder or VisualAge, are routinely delivering applications in fractions of the time that would have been required using technologies—such as hand-coded COBOL, C, 4GLs, or IE-based CASE—that were popular less than a decade earlier. Maintenance of applications, so that they can follow today's fast-changing business requirements, can also be markedly reduced. And when implementation is preceded by robust requirements and analysis—utilizing technologies such as OMT, Rational Rose, and Select Enterprise—corrective maintenance can be reduced as well.

But the pervasive problems resulting from inappropriate expectations, such as the misperceptions that caused our car manufacturer and bank to reach such wildly different conclusions based on their similar experiences, are not the product of expectations that can be achieved. They are the product of:

- expectations for new development technologies that aren't achievable, and

- significant and unforeseen new development technology consequences for which expectations don't even exist.

Unachievable IT Expectations

The area in which perhaps the largest and most persistent gaps between IT's expectations and what can actually be achieved occur is in the amount of time it takes for new development approaches and technologies to yield positive results. (See Fig. 4.2.) The amount of

Figure 4.2 IT's expectations for new development technologies that can't be achieved.

time that can go by before even short-term benefits can be realized is, in fact, almost universally underestimated. In terms of major companies with large IT organizations, traversing the productivity dip in the technology adoption S-curve (presented in Chap. 2) so that significant and tangible benefits can be realized, 2 to 3 years is not an unusual amount of time. For smaller companies, with simpler IT organizations and infrastructures, somewhat smaller amounts of time can suffice. Although there are many reasons why this happens, factors that account for the unexpectedly large amounts of time that are often required before short-term benefits can be achieved, almost always include:

- training IT developers on the technology and associated approach,

- utilization of the new technology and approach on two to three real projects (tiny proof-of-concept pilot projects don't count) so that they can gain practical, hands-on, experience,

- development of new support infrastructure components (such as class library management for OO) development, and

- enhancement of existing support infrastructure components (DA, DBA, Q/A, project reporting, for example) so that the specialized needs of the new technology can be successfully addressed.

Equally problematic, but sometimes less obvious, are unrealistic expectations for the long-term utility of a technology or approach. Staying with a perfectly useful and appropriate technology or approach, beyond the time during which it represents a viable market segment for new technology developers, can place an IT organization at risk of becoming isolated from the development technology mainstream—and from many of the advances that come along with it. Collateral technologies—from industry-specific class libraries and frameworks and middleware, to testing tools, help systems, and software configuration management (SCM) software—developed by independent software vendors to serve the lucrative mainstream application development market will diminish in number, as the development market moves on to the next technologies and approaches. Given sufficient time, such technologies will become stagnant, with fewer and fewer new releases, support will diminish, and in the end they'll no longer be generally available. Companies that stay with development technologies beyond their time also find that the best managers, analysts, and programmers—the human resources upon which successful development ultimately depends—will also have moved on to more current technologies, leaving behind a population that's less competent and more expensive than its predecessors.

Although a strategy to stick with tried and true technologies can offer temporary refuge from the turbulent onslaught of time compressed technology advancement, such benefits are likely to be short-lived. In the end, when viewed over periods of time longer than 2 to 3 years, the benefits of development technology advances generally far outweigh the costs and problems of adopting them.

Two additional, and ubiquitous, problem areas for IT expectations include expectations that new technologies will be applicable to a wide range of business problems and that the company's business users and management will share IT's enthusiasm for the technologies and their benefits. The reality is that new technologies, especially when first introduced, are likely to be most useful for addressing narrow ranges of business requirements—such as isolated (workstation-based) applications for Smalltalk, low-volume connectivity for Open DataBase Connectivity (ODBC), or low-performance LAN-based systems for Common Object Request Broker Architecture (CORBA) Object Request Brokers (ORBs). As development technologies mature, utilization becomes more wide-spread, and collateral technologies become available, the range of business problems that the technology can be successfully used to address undergoes a corresponding expansion.

Many of the most insidious expectation-related problems that come along with time compressed technology change result from things that aren't fully expected, but happen anyway. (See Fig. 4.3.)

Consider cultural impact. Moving from a single paradigm for application development, or a few well-defined paradigms, each satisfying equally well-defined needs, to multiple and constantly expanding

Figure 4.3 What IT should, but doesn't, expect new development technologies to bring.

development paradigms that conflict and overlap, can throw even the most well-run IT organizations into cultural upheaval and chaos. The problem is not so much that they conflict and overlap, but that the time compressed rush of new paradigms and technologies is so fast and so relentless that organizations don't have sufficient time to sort things out. Fueled by vendor claims, slick demonstrations, trade journal reviews, and a host of real and imagined reasons for successes and failures, rumors fly, and reality often gets lost in the dust. With little else to go on but hearsay, hype, intuition, and their own initial experiences, and with rapid career advancement in the offing for those who are proven right, IT organizations can easily degenerate into a series of armed camps, each utilizing "the best" technology or approach—the one that the entire company should quickly adopt. As companies try to resolve the substantial cultural shifts discussed in Chap. 3 against this backdrop, it's not difficult to understand why so many fail.

With the proliferation of new technologies and retrenchment of developers into armed camps, come new, and often conflicting, demands on the infrastructure that supports application development. (See Fig. 4.4.) As the following figure indicates, much of the infrastructure needed to support application development can be surprisingly technology-specific. As a consequence, infrastructure components that provide exemplary support for one technology are often of little use for projects executed in another. For example, consider mainframe COBOL, integrated CASE, PowerBuilder, and Smalltalk. Although at least three of these common late-1990s development technologies can be found in simultaneous use at many large IT orga-

- A methodology that is consistent with the development technology and approach
- Training in methodology and tools, with just-in-time refresher and mentoring
- An independent organization for constructing and managing reusable components
- An independent quality assurance organization that understands the technology
- Project management with check points for re-estimation utilizing technology- and approach- based metrics
- Progress reporting that translates what is happening into a common format that management can understand

Figure 4.4 Technology-dependent development infrastructure support requirements.

nizations, there's little overlap in terms of infrastructure support. Even when these vastly different development technologies are utilized on different projects—certainly, this idealization is not always the case—conflicting infrastructure requirements can at a minimum cause unexpected increases in support infrastructure costs. In many cases, I've seen these kinds of conflicting demands bring progress to a grinding halt as budgetary and governance battles over development support supersede development of applications that are needed to sustain the business.

Limitations on the latitude designers have in developing applications that meet their users' requirements precisely as they want them to, or on the range of execution technologies that the development approach can support, can quickly lead to similar kinds of problems. Unexpected inconsistencies in user interfaces, resulting from conflicting development technology requirements, can make applications more difficult to deploy and tarnish the reputations of those who built them.[1] Unforeseen execution technology requirements can also cause expectation problems. Their adverse impact on deployment costs that, for large systems, can amount to many times the original cost of development, often results in late delivery and significant cost overruns.

Achievable Management Expectations

Although many of the expectation-related problems wrought by time compressed development technology change directly affect IT, their impact is often most acutely felt by management. Indeed, management's development technology naiveté—their lack of technology sophistication, paucity of direct development technology experience, and consequent insulation from the direct affects of time compressed technology change—can make them especially vulnerable to making decisions based on expectations that aren't correct.

Yet in spite of these limitations, many managers have developed a good feel for how development technologies can be harnessed to further their objectives, to help achieve their visions for the business units they run. I often encounter business managers who understand what development technologies can do, and who have no trouble articulating the outcomes they're looking for, but who are frustrated because they feel they aren't getting the outcomes. Paradoxically, I also run into a considerable number of business managers who have been jaded by information technology failures to the extent that their expectations are far too low for what today's development technologies can achieve. What I don't come across often very are business managers with realistic expectations for what today's multiple and evolving development technologies can and can't do.

To gain some insight into this unfortunate set of circumstances, let's examine management's' expectations for time compressed development technologies. We'll begin with management expectations that can be achieved.

Of the expectations that management harbors for evolving and proliferating development technologies, among the most achievable, but at times least obvious, are expectations for higher productivity, quicker delivery, and reduced development cost. Although there are lots of vendor examples and abundant anecdotal evidence that support the existence of these gains, I know of no controlled scientific studies, the kind utilized to validate new medical drugs, for example, that quantify and validate them.[2] The few studies that are available tend to be privately executed internal pilot project projects, with little or no attempt to control important variables such as scalability, experience with the new technology, or adequacy of the support infrastructure.[3] Nevertheless, it's the firm belief of many who work with new and proliferating development technologies that gains in productivity and delivery time, when the technologies are properly deployed, are achievable. (See Fig. 4.5.)

The problem, and the principal reason why these potential gains aren't always reflected in managements' expectations, is that real-world considerations such as:

- measurements made too early on the technology adoption curve,

- attractiveness of new technologies as scapegoats for projects that failed due to management, resource and scoping problems,

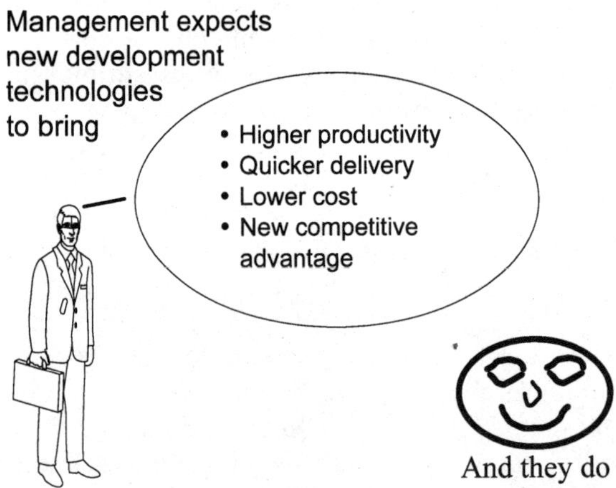

Figure 4.5 Achievable management expectations for new technologies.

- inadequacy of most IT organizations to deal with multiple and evolving development approaches,

- denigration of specific development technologies by groups interested in promoting others, and

- the offsetting of productivity gains by increased development costs resulting from the accelerating utilization of applications in today's business

tend to cloud their appearance to the extent that they are not always obvious, or even visible, to management.

What is visible to management, are the potential competitive advantages and increased empowerment that result when application development is successfully leveraged to further the business. Competitive advantages afforded to companies that are first to market with strategic applications are well known. As more and more strategic business initiatives depend on—indeed, are often built upon—unique applications that enable them to be implemented before competitive companies can respond with initiatives of their own, the key words here are "first to market." And fast delivery of new and strategic applications, the enabling force behind "first to market" is, to an increasing extent, the result of the technologies and approaches utilized in their development. The converse is also true. Companies that are unable to successfully leverage time compressed changes for quick and low-cost application development are likely to become the strategic laggards in our increasingly fast-moving and competitive global market.

Unachievable Management Expectations

Management expectations for productivity, development time, and cost benefits from time compressed development technology change, although eminently achievable, are not immediately achievable. Nor are they achievable long term. The differences between IT's expectations of time compressed technology change, for short-term benefits and long-term utility, and what can really be achieved, are frequently reflected to management in terms of ROI on their (often substantial) technology investments. In the late-1990s, these differences between management expectations and what can be achieved can play a crucial role in determining application development success. When they're adequately addressed, the benefits of new and multiple technologies can be leveraged to improve application development and garner competitive advantage for the business. When they are not, the resultant misperceptions can swiftly lead to the downfall of need-

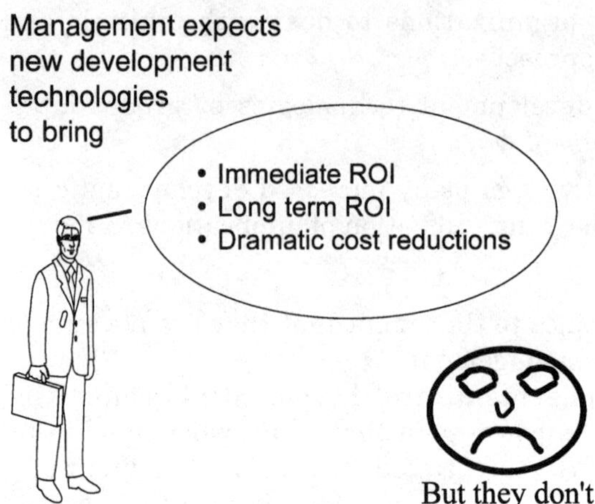

Figure 4.6 Management's expectations for new development technologies that can't be achieved.

ed development technologies, and with them, the potential for productive, fast, and cost-effective application development. (See Fig. 4.6.)

When the S-shaped productivity adoption curve presented in Chap. 2 is viewed in terms of ROI, what management actually sees is presented in Fig. 4.7. From this perspective, with "profitability" substituted for "productivity," the adoption curve bears a striking resemblance to the proforma income statement for a new business initiative with the "investment" occurring during an initial period of negative cash flow followed by a period of positive cash flow as the initiative matures and begins to pay its investors (management) back.

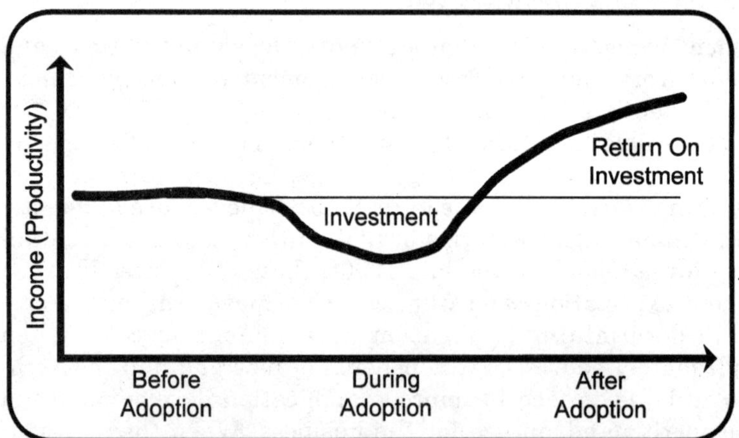

Figure 4.7 S-shaped productivity adoption curve reflected to management in terms of ROI.

The key difference is that in the case of the business initiative the proforma income statement is presented to management as part of the initiative's business plan, so that management knows exactly what to expect in terms of:

- how deep the investment will be,

- when it will bottom out,

- when it will break even, and

- when it will begin to generate a return.[4]

And as the business initiative is launched, its progress is continuously monitored against these criteria. But when IT launches a new development technology initiative, it is rarely presented to management in these terms, in terms of the investment that it really represents. The typical result is that management's expectations for the initiative are set, not by the realities of technology adoption, but by a melange of hype from IT proponents, technology vendors, industry pundits and consulting firms, backed up by "gee whiz" articles in technical journals, business publications and airline magazines.[5] (See Fig. 4.8.)

The result is a divergence between managements' expectations and what management observes during adoption. In the absence of realistic expectations for what a development technology adoption curve will do, what the management of many organizations concludes is that instead of going up (as expected), their return on investment is actually going down. Given this set of circumstances, the businesslike

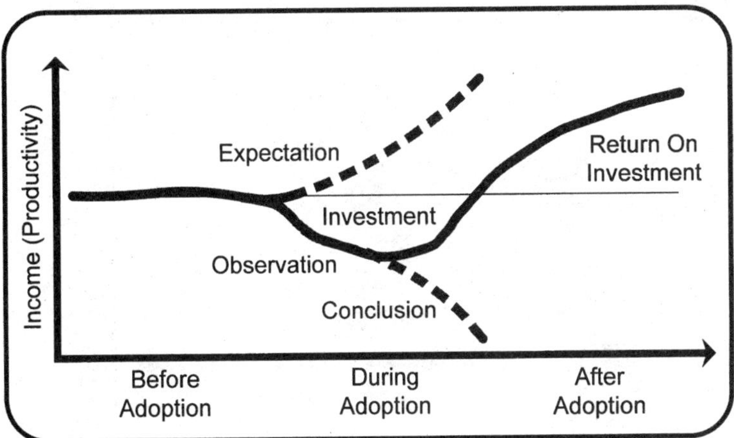

Figure 4.8 Divergence between management's expectations, observations, and conclusions.

management decision is clear. Management cuts its losses and bails out, without waiting for the adoption process to complete.

But, as we discovered earlier in this chapter, baling out half way through adoption and switching off to the latest development technology, as the CIO of our East Coast bank did, before it can pay its investors back causes thrashing, minimizing achievable development technology ROI. The predictable result is the self-fulfilling chain of new development technology catastrophes experienced by many companies, and additional unwarranted lowering of new technology expectations. (See Fig. 4.9.)

Unfortunately, as we also discovered early in this chapter, the converse is just as true. Sticking with development technologies too long, because new technology expectations have been set too low, often as a result of thrashing through too many technologies too quickly, results in companies staying with older technologies too long. Although such companies may do marginally better than those that thrash, they too reap small returns on their development technology investments. (See Fig. 4.10.) The typical result is a bizarre paradox in which managements' expectations for application development are at once too high and too low.

The challenge for management—the people who ultimately decide where on the technology adoption curve to operate, so that their company can realize a decent return on its development technology investment—is to ensure that decision makers have realistic expectations so that they can make the right technology decisions in spite of loud and eloquent pleas from technology proponents and equally eloquent pleas from those who have been burned by change and want to

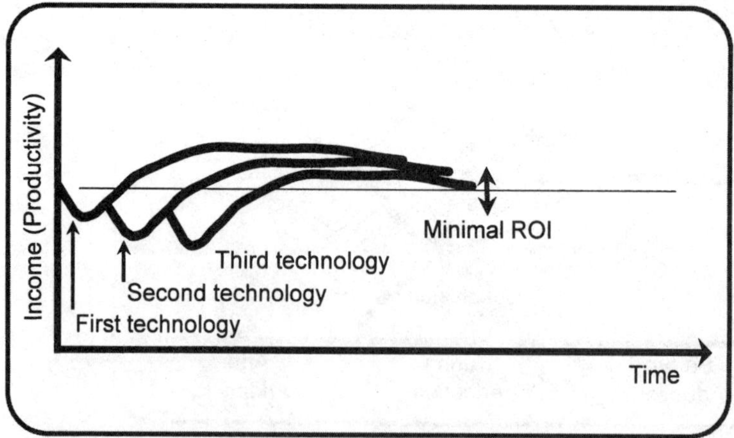

Figure 4.9 Minimal ROI due to thrashing through too many development technologies too quickly.

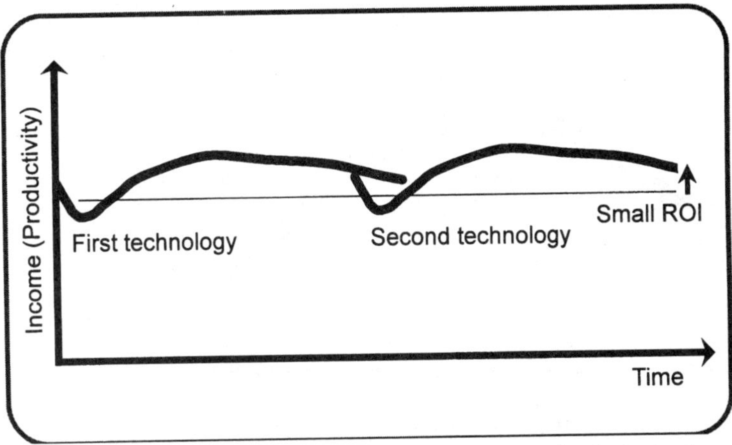

Figure 4.10 Small ROI due to sticking with development technologies too long.

stand pat. Given a set of correct decisions, it's not difficult to reap substantial development technology ROI from time compressed change, even though adoption often requires a substantial investment. (See Fig. 4.11.)

In terms of expectations, it is therefore important for management to understand that development technologies and approaches have useful lives during which substantial ROI can be achieved. Move off the technology too soon and you run the risk of thrashing and minimizing your ROI. Stay with the technology too long, and for a different but equally valid set of reasons, your potential for substantial ROI goes down too. (See Fig. 4.12.) In Chapter 11, we'll revisit this

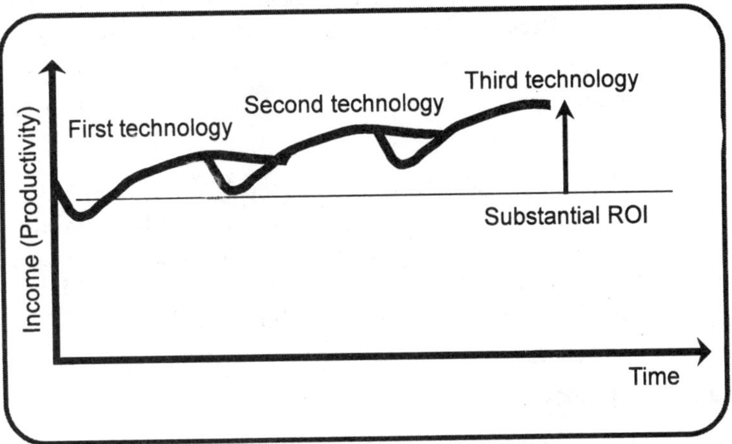

Figure 4.11 Development technology adoption optimized to achieve substantial ROI.

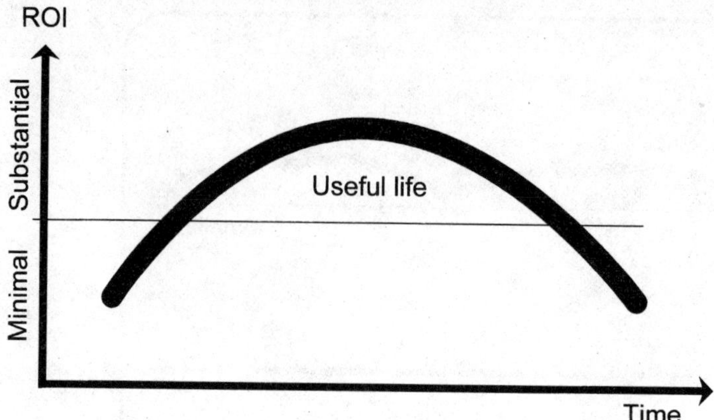

Figure 4.12 Realistic expectations for a development technology's useful life.

concept with the objective of maximizing return on information technology investments.

Management expectations of dramatic cost reductions from development technologies and approaches can also be problematic. The underlying issue is not the degree to which development is becoming more productive, but that by the time management sees the results—in terms of development budgets and output—much of the gains have been offset. The culprit, in most organizations, is a combination of:

- inability to realize potential gains due to thrashing through too many development technologies too soon or sticking with technologies too long,

- inefficiencies generated through conflicts between the sets of different—and often conflicting—technologies that comprise today's development environments, and

- increased organizational reliance on, and demand for, application development.[6]

Given this set of circumstances, the potential for dramatic reductions in application development costs cannot be realized. What management can realize, and has every right to expect, if time compressed technology change is correctly managed, is quicker, cheaper, higher-quality applications that can be leveraged for business benefit.

Unexpected Management Impacts

Management of most organizations doesn't like surprises. Yet there are a number significant, and often unexpected, ways in which the

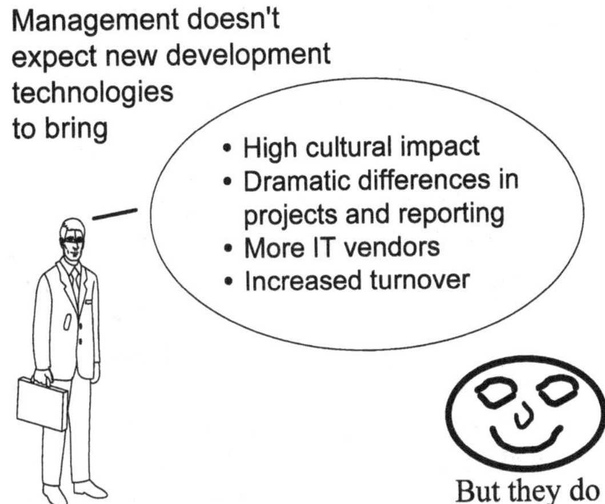

Figure 4.13 What management should, but doesn't, expect from new development technologies to bring.

accelerated proliferation of new and multiple technologies impacts management. (See Fig. 4.13.) And as with other management expectations, if they are not understood and managed, so that management knows what to expect and why to expect it, the surprises that result can seriously thwart the technology adoption process.

Consider cultural impact. If management isn't prepared for the substantial IT and business cultural impacts that, as we discussed in Chap. 3, can result from new and evolving development technologies, adoption of the technologies that cause the cultural impact adoption will be put at serious risk. The problem is not the magnitude of the cultural impact, or management's ability to address it—technology-based cultural change is well understood, and there are abundant resources available to help organizations cope with it.[7] It's that the breadth and magnitude of the cultural impact is often unexpected. And when cultural change is unexpected, and consequently neither planned for nor managed, the results are often disruptive and chaotic. Faced with significant numbers of IT and business employees who are not able to cope with the cultural changes wrought by a technology that "someone in IT is using for application development," management's reflexive response will be to ditch the technology and save the organization. A company can survive without the latest and greatest technology for application development. It cannot survive with its employees in chaos.

Fortunately, addressing this problem in most organizations is not difficult. What it takes are:

- understanding the cultural impact that a development technology or approach is likely to bring,

- taking the trouble to ensure that management is aware of it, and

- enlisting the help of internal and external resources to manage it.[8]

My experience is that proactively addressing the problem in this manner not only prepares management to cope with technology-based cultural change, but also often brings management's involvement and active support. Cultural change is a serious management issue that almost always raises the stature, in management's eyes, of the IT personnel who bring it to their attention.

Some cultural changes will directly impact management. And of those that do, one of the most difficult to cope with involves management and reporting of new technology development projects. To illustrate just how different management reporting can be, along with the origin and severity of the cultural changes that can result, consider an OO development project at a large East Coast financial services company. As the project was one of the company's first forays into the world of OO, its progress was under careful scrutiny by the company's IT and business management, a group of concerned executives that were experienced in, and oriented to, traditional development.

It wasn't long before the group became concerned with what they saw. What they expected was an OO rendition of the series of head-to-tail life cycle phases that they were used to, so that progress—and in terms of their "one and done" culture, the health of the project—could be measured in terms of completed deliverables. What their progress reports showed was that the project team was working on every phase at once, and completing nothing in terms of final deliverables. From their reports, the managers could see that for the project to successfully complete, each of the OO phases would have to be completed at the same time, on the date the application was due, "which was," as one of the more benign executives put it, "a highly unlikely series of events."

But as Fig. 4.14 indicates, that's precisely what happened. With the exception of Requirements Analysis, which ended a month earlier, each of the project's life cycle phases ended in October, the month in which the application was due. The working application was delivered, the project manager and her boss both got promoted, and the group of befuddled executives was disbanded, with its members still not quite sure about what they had just seen.

What happened was, in fact, appropriate for well-run OO and graphical development projects. What was reported to the IT and business executives was obviously not. But with concurrent life cycle

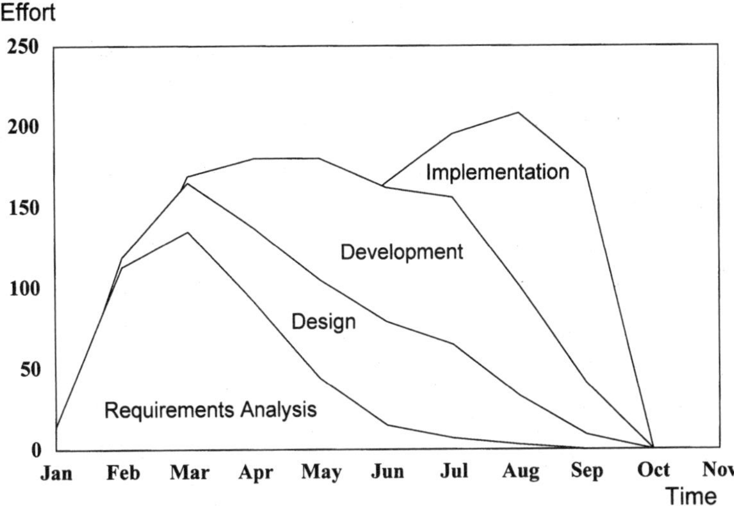

Figure 4.14 Concurrent life cycle phases from an OO development project.

phases—Requirements Analysis, Design, Development, and Implementation were all active from June through September—and Requirements Analysis lasting to within a month of delivery, what would have been appropriate for reporting to management? What should management expect?

For OO and graphical development projects, the answers to these questions can be seen by taking a closer look at the figure depicting the life cycle of the project. (See Fig. 4.15.) Examination of the Requirements Analysis phase reveals that, with the exception of the initial 2 months during which the project was getting started, the level of effort expended by the project team (shown as staff-days per month, along the vertical axis) went down in each successive month. The team expended 135 staff-days of effort in March, but only 91 in April, 44 in may and just 15 in June, a trend that continued through the end of the project. What was happening, was that the requirements models they were producing were *converging* on the business requirements. For a similar set of reasons, the effort expended during the project's Design, Development, and Implementation phases displayed a similar convergence as each phase got closer to completion.

Had the management team been looking for convergence, as a measure of the health of their OO project, and had they been shown convergence in their management reports, much of the misinformation and confusion would have been eliminated. The point is that new development technologies and approaches can require significant dif-

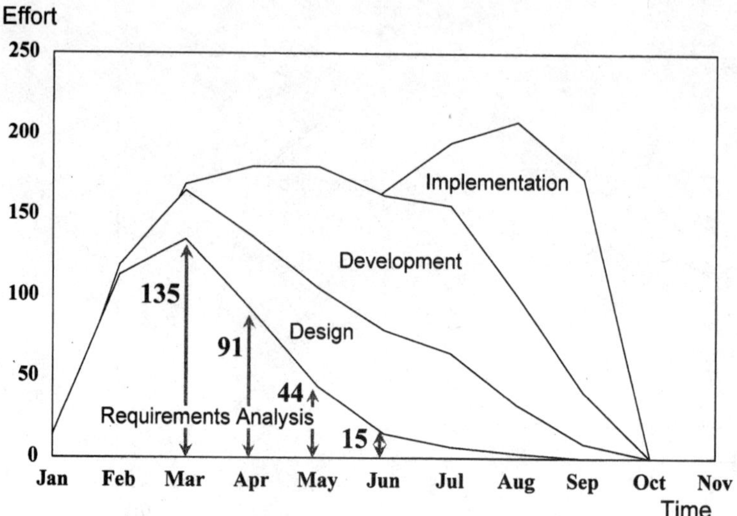

Figure 4.15   Convergence of life cycle phases from an OO development project.

ferences in management expectations, and equally dramatic differences in development project reporting as well.

There are two additional time compressed development technology consequences that are highly visible, and that therefore require that management expectations for them be properly set. They are the number of different vendors on IT's books, and the high turnover rate among IT staff. Both are, in many ways, the unavoidable by-products of an industry that is changing and fragmenting as quickly as IT. Both are tough problems that represent significant challenges to management. And both are a lot more difficult to manage when management isn't prepared for them in terms of what to expect.

I've seen many application development efforts falter due to the development team's inability to purchase the technologies they need, to procure required expertise, or even to hold onto the expertise they have begun to develop. In one OO development project at a West Coast manufacturing company, the team of Smalltalk programmers turned over three times (300 percent) in an 18-month period, seriously thwarting development and putting the entire project—for a mission-critical system that the company had to have—at risk. The frightening thing is that this happened right under the nose of an astute project manager, who was keenly aware of what was going on and was working diligently with the company's management to prevent it.

The underlying issue here is management expectations. Had management been aware of what was going to happen, along with the reasons why it was going to happen and the potential consequences of not managing it—had they known what to expect and why to expect it—they could have been better prepared to handle it. This is a classical management problem that has a number of viable solutions, depending on the organization, its structure and its culture.[9] But they all require time and planning to implement, which was just what our manufacturing company's management didn't have. Had they known what to expect, the crisis might have been avoided, and to the extent that it could have been avoided, its impact on the project could certainly have been blunted.

These kinds of problems do not fall solely on the shoulders of management. Business users, especially those who work in information-centric companies and business units, tend to share many of the expectation-related problems being experienced by management. They, like many of their management counterparts, tend to harbor bimodal expectations for application development technologies that are too negative and too optimistic.

Achievable Business Benefits

Although I regularly come into contact with business users whose operations are critically dependent on delivery of new and updated applications, I can think of few who have been able to develop a realistic perspective on application development, especially in terms of what's achievable and what's not. This observation should not be surprising. It's a predictable result of the:

- redirection of industry pundits and development technology vendors to target business users—the corporate population with the most acute needs and the largest amounts of money,

- liberation and empowerment experienced by the growing segment of business users who have become sufficiently comfortable with the workstations that grace their desks to develop their own simple, but effective, applications, and the

- disappointments experienced by business users when, for a host of reasons that they cannot fully understand or control, their application development projects fail to deliver what they expected—or in an alarming number of instances, fail to deliver anything at all.

Given this seemingly schizophrenic set of inputs, what should business users reasonably be able to expect from the increasing numbers of evolving technologies and approaches that time compressed change

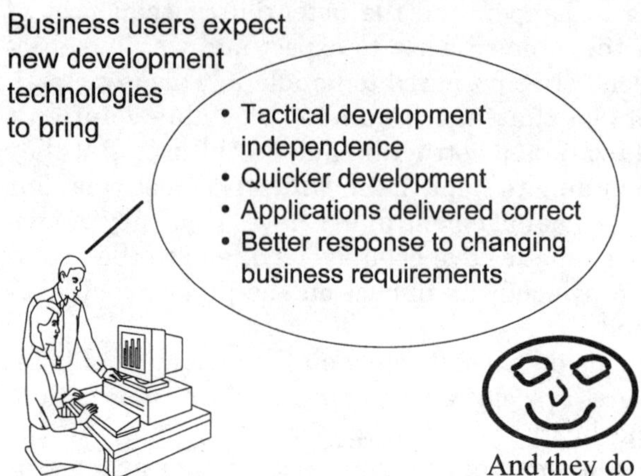

Figure 4.16 Achievable business user expectations for new development technologies.

brings to bear on their application development? Let's start with business user expectations that can be achieved. (See Fig. 4.16.)

Provided that time compressed technology change is properly managed, achievable business user expectations for application development can include applications that are delivered more quickly, that are less expensive to develop and to run, and that are more flexible so that they can be more easily changed to meet changing late-1990s business requirements. Although these expectations are achievable for many business users, they are not universally achievable for all types of applications developed for all kinds of users under all kinds of governance.

Consider autonomous development. To increasing numbers of business users, an overriding expectation, based on experience with development technology already on their desktops, is ability to control their own development. Indeed, many of today's business users do develop successful applications, either directly or by contracting with a software vendor.

For business users who have developed successful local applications to satisfy pressing needs, and who in doing so have exceeded the modest expectations they had before they tried it, a collateral expectation that they can continue to do so doesn't involve an unwarranted leap of faith. Nor does a seemingly similar expectation that, having mastered the development of simple tactical applications, they can meet with equal success in tackling strategic applications that are larger, less isolated, and more complex. The first set of expectations is both reasonable and achievable in many organizations, given today's rich user-oriented development environments. What isn't reasonable, as we saw in Chap. 3, are expectations that the technologies and approaches that so successfully facilitated tactical development can be successfully scaled up to develop applications that are large and strategic. (See Fig. 4.17.)

The problem is that although the viability of autonomous development decreases precipitously as applications become large and complex, expectations often do not. The insidious nature of the inverse relationship between hubristic expectations and reality for business user-developed applications, as applications go from small and tactical to large and strategic, is illustrated below. (See Fig. 4.17.)

Unachievable Business Benefits

Aside from expectations for development independence, which are achievable only for applications that are isolated and limited in scope, the next most unachievable expectation is intuitive development. The problem is not that modern approaches to application development aren't intuitive. They are. Object-oriented and graphical development, for example, are among the most intuitive approaches to developing applications. The problem is the number of approaches to application development and the diversity of development technologies in concurrent use. In large organizations, especially those in which application development is decentralized, it is not uncommon for business users to be exposed to a number of divergent technologies, approaches, and

Figure 4.17 Expectations and reality for autonomous application development.

processes for developing applications. To business users who are confronted with a seemingly continuous stream of new and different technologies and approaches, sometimes for applications that are in other respects similar, expectations that they will gain familiarity with, and insight into, the development of their applications, so that they can interact in a familiar and consistent manner with their IT peers, are not likely to be met.

Nor are business user expectations for consistency in interfaces and application behavior. The culprit is often the number of different technologies utilized in their development and the differences in user interfaces that result. The problem is exacerbated when business requirements are met through a combination of applications that are acquired from a number of different organizations, each embracing a different set of technologies and standards. (See Fig. 4.18.)

Fortunately, this problem can be successfully addressed through the innovative use of development technologies. By utilizing a graphical development tool to develop and control a common presentation layer, a large energy company was able to achieve a consistent user interface for its Clean Air System in spite of the fact that major parts of the system were procured from a number of different vendors who developed their applications using an equal number of different development technologies and approaches.[10]

Unexpected Business User Impacts

Most business users who have been touched by application development have come to expect increased contact with their IT peers and

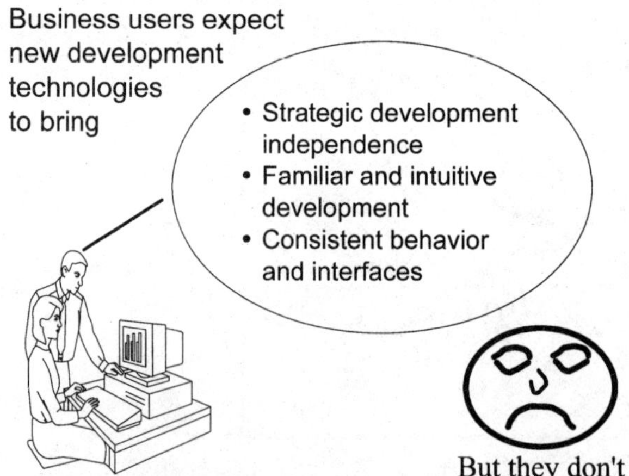

Figure 4.18 Business users' expectations for new development technologies that can't be achieved.

greater involvement in the application development process. What they don't always expect is the extent to which the nature of their involvement changes along with the development technologies and approaches. To illustrate how this kind of involvement impacts business users, consider how it can change based on our four commonly used approaches to application development. (See Fig. 4.19.)

As application development progressed during the past two decades, from 1970s-style structured design, through information engineering, to visual development and OO, involvement of business users in the development of their applications experienced a significant increase. But years of application development, using structured analysis techniques, had taught many companies that direct involvement of their business users wasn't needed. As a result, the late-1980s information engineering requirement that business users be highly involved in the modeling of their requirements, took the business community by surprise. Business users didn't expect it, weren't prepared for it, and as a result, had a tough time making what looked to many like a sudden and unaccountable shift—a shift that was aggravated by the abstract and technical mature of the models.[11]

Although prototype-based graphical development and use case requirements modeling are a lot less alienating, and therefore more welcome, to business users, when viewed from the perspective of the business community, what is seen is a whipsawlike shift back and

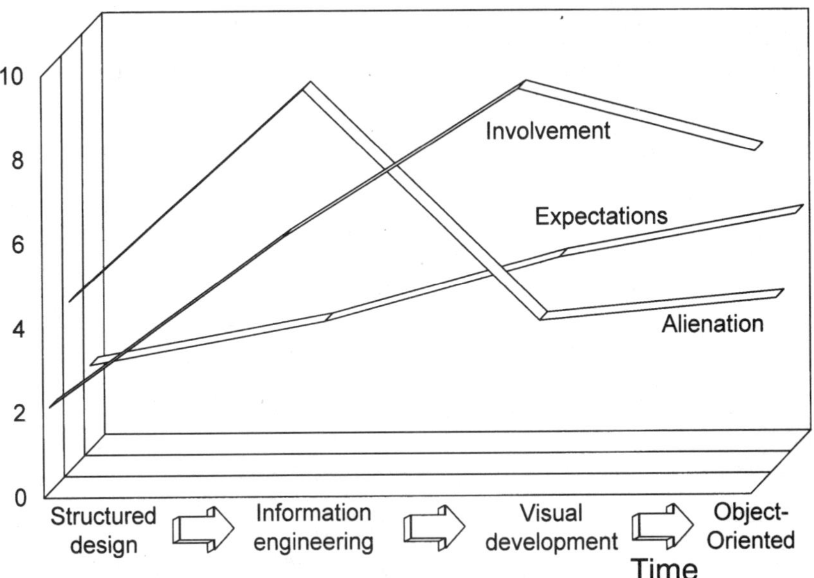

Figure 4.19 How development approaches impact business users.

forth among these radically different approaches to application development. In large organizations, in which these approaches are often utilized concurrently by different IT organizations on different projects, the problem is even worse.

Equally unexpected, and sometimes a lot more welcome, are the insights into a company's business that surface as a by-product of IE and OO requirements modeling processes—insights that can make meaningful contributions to business reengineering efforts.[12] But in the real world, they can make meaningful contributions only to the extent that they are expected, so that the right business users participate and the results can be factored into business reengineering initiatives that would otherwise have little to do with application development. (See Fig. 4.20.)

References

1. In addition to business applications, development tools often fall victim to this problem. ObjectView, a PowerBuilder-like product marketed by KnowledgeWare in the mid-1990s, came with no less than three completely different interfaces—depending on the functionality its users were trying to utilize.
2. Robert Fichman and Chris Kemerer, "Adoption of Software Engineering Process Innovations," *Sloan Management Review* 34(2):7–2, 1993.
3. For additional insight into the importance of variables, such as experience with analysis and implementation technologies, see Michael Tuk, John Stone, and Stephen Fogarty, "Use Case-Based OOSE Forecasting Model," OOPSLA 94 Metrics Workshop White Paper.
4. In business initiatives (such as launching a new fashion or product line, opening a new store, adopting a different style, or adding a new feature) the business units responsible for their success don't, of course, know how well things will go. The investment might bottom out sooner or later than what they predicted. Some initiatives are wildly successful, while others don't bottom out at all. The point is that, in well-run

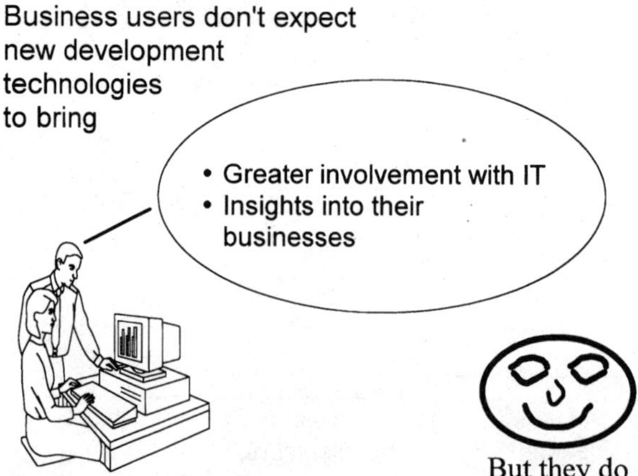

Figure 4.20 What business users should, but don't, expect from new development technologies to bring.

business organizations, the risks are explicitly articulated for everyone to see, the investments are better quantified, and the results are more closely tracked.

5. There are, of course, many responsible companies among technology consulting firms and publications. But in my experience, many companies are not responsible. Articles in technical journals owned by consulting firms that specialize in particular development technologies, for example, are not always as objective as they might be had they appeared in publications that were independent.

6. Dr. Howard Rubin, Howard Rubin Associates.

7. There is a rich body of knowledge on managing technology-based cultural change. For a good perspective on information technology and organization-based change management, see Walter J. Utz, Jr., *Software Technology Transitions,* Prentice Hall, 1992; John F. Rockart and Debra Hofman, "Improving Systems Delivery: Evolving New Strategies," *Sloan Management Review* 33(4):21–31, 1992; and Colin A. Carnall, *Managing Change In Organizations,* Prentice-Hall International (UK).

8. When seeking this kind of help, a company's Human Resources organization is often a good place to start. For an insightful perspective on managing technology-based cultural change, see Beverly Goldberg, "Manage Change—Not The Chaos Caused By Change," *Management Review,* November 1992.

9. I have seen a number of successful and innovative solutions to this problem. One manager of a large Midwest company solved it through a "contract" with his employees under which they agreed to stay until the end of his project and he agreed to either match their market value or help place them as highly paid consultants when they were finished. Another company addressed it by spinning off their application development organization as a separate company that was partially owned by the IT people who staffed it. Both initiatives were successful. And both required significant amounts of time and planning.

10. John Stone, "CASE Plays A Role In Visual Development," *Application Development Trends,* January 1994.

11. Information engineering business models were difficult for many business users to grasp. The information engineering data model, for example, which is a good analysis tool views business requirements from the perspective of a relational database. While this view may be appropriate for IT developers, it alienates many business users, who cannot understand or deal with it. For a more in-depth view of this problem, see John Stone, *Inside ADW and IEF: The Promise and Reality of CASE,* McGraw-Hill, 1993.

12. Ivar Jacobson, Maria Ericsson, and Angela Jacobson, *The Object Advantage: Business Process Reengineering With Object Technology,* Addison-Wesley, 1994.

Development Tools, Methodologies, Infrastructure, and Support—Why They Fail in Our Multiple and Changing Technology Environments

Russ carefully stashed the book on object-oriented system performance that he had just finished under his desk, where it joined more than a dozen others. Although his cubicle had been assembled with what Human Resources determined to be more than ample shelf space, there was no other place for him to stow his new book. Indeed, over half of his cubicle's 12 feet of linear space was taken up by the two system development methodologies that graced the bookshelves of each Project Manager's office.

As he gazed up at the methodologies that were supposed to guide his development teams through successfully executed projects, Russ was struck by how useless they really were. The first methodology—the older of the two—had been purchased, at considerable expense, from the Big 6 firm that was his CIO's consultant. Although it was comprehensive and well executed, Russ and every other project manager knew that if they followed the methodology, completing all of its work products, their projects would be delivered hopelessly late and over budget by at least 50 percent. Moreover, it was IE-based, and therefore of little use for Russ's current OO project.

His company's newer methodology, delivered not only in the form of bound volumes, but in a hypermedia-based process management tool as well, so that it also took up copious amounts of disk space, was no more useful than the first. Although the new methodology was OO, it had been developed by his company's corporate IT organization to cover the multitude of different OO approaches that were in use by the business units that funded it. As it met this requirement by concentrating on generalities rather than on the specifics of each approach, it provided little discernible added value to development teams who needed detailed day-to-day guidance on things like properly sizing use cases, getting the most out of their OO frameworks, figuring out how to identify and abstract common behavior, and striking the right balance between inheritance and performance.

To development teams and Project Leaders like Russ, who are rewarded for on-time delivery of the applications they develop, methodologies that aren't relevant and that don't provide high added value to development teams doing the work on a day-to-day bases, are "less than useless." The inevitable result is that such methodologies wind up on Project Managers' book shelves, where they're most visible and do the least harm.

Data Incompatibilities

A significant and unfortunate reality of late-1990s application development is that, like the methodologies on Russ's book shelves, the tools utilized by most IT organizations don't hold up well against the pressures of time compressed technology change. Instead of addressing the needs of each development and execution technology in the multiple technology environments that today's developers face and leveraging new technologies as they become available, our methodologies, tools, and infrastructure tend to do well only for specific approaches and narrow ranges of technology. This tendency is exacerbated by our development infrastructures and cultures that, like the methodologies and tools that they support, address the needs of our multiple and expanding technology environments from singular perspectives, and rigid dogma. Indeed, our tendency to compartmentalize development technologies and approaches is so pervasive and so great that tools and techniques from one culture and approach often never make it to the next, even when they are sorely needed and could be put to excellent use.

To gain some insight into this problem, along with the consequences and opportunities that it represents, let's examine it in terms of our three popular approaches to application development: IE,

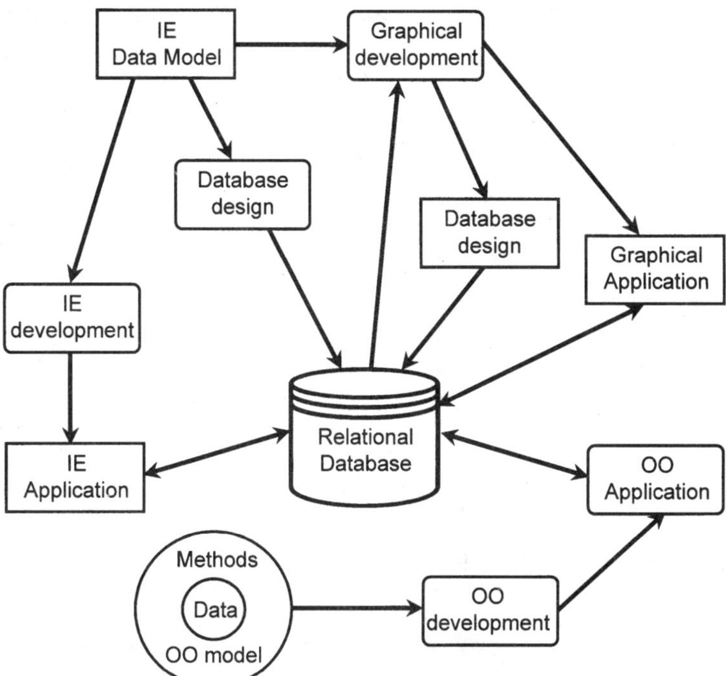

Figure 5.1   How three common application development approaches view data.

graphical development, and OO development. We'll do so by exploring their strengths, differences, and especially their methodology, tool, and infrastructure incompatibilities, from the perspectives of data, requirements, participation, and support. (See Fig. 5.1)

Let's start with data. Although an organization's data can collectively represent one if its most important assets—an asset that's taken very seriously by each of our approaches, they do so in ways that can lead to serious problems and incompatibilities.[1]

Information engineering ensures integrity and compatibility through detailed data models. Information Engineering does so by modeling each element of information in a logical data model (a fully normalized entity relationship diagram that's independent of the databases that might implement it), and by ensuring that the data model is capable of fully supporting the business's requirements. If the data model fully supports each of the business's requirements, if it's faithfully implemented in the form of one or more databases, and if each application accesses the data it needs in a manner consistent with the model, everything's OK. As most IE tools provide their users with ample facilities to ensure that each of these conditions is met, high levels of data consistency and integrity can be ensured, within the IE environment.

But a company's IE environment rarely encompasses the entire enterprise. External forces—such as business units that have chosen other development paradigms, outsourcing, non-IE packages, user-developed systems, and DSS applications, to name a few—act to prevent that from happening. The result for all but the smallest and most autocratic organizations, as Figure 5.1 suggests, is that a number of different development paradigms must exist side by side, and they must share many of the same data.

Outside of the IE environment, IE data models lose their ability to ensure that data integrity is achieved. Many graphical development tools—PowerBuilder, for example—can easily read the schema (the database's design) directly from the database, constructing their own data models in the process. When the schema is first read in, all is well and good. But as soon as iterative prototyping calls for it, as a by-product of the graphical development process, these tools can just as easily modify their data models, along with the database, to accommodate their users' requirements. Integration of such modifications with the IE data models, and with the IE-based applications that depend on the data models, is a manual process—a process that data administration functions in today's downsized and empowered organizations have neither the resources nor authority to fully address. (See Fig. 5.2.)

When the OO paradigm is added to the fray, things get even worse. Like IE, OO development takes a pedantic view of how data are accessed, and depends on the enforcement of that view for achieving many of its benefits. The object technology paradigm assumes that all data that are accessed by OO programs are encapsulated within objects, so that the only way to access them is by sending a message to the object that encapsulates them. It's all very elegant. As long as the OO development analysis and design were correctly executed, data integrity is enforced, and the problems associates with data corruption are held at bay.

The problem, of course, is that in large organizations, in which many of the data reside in databases that are accessed and updated by non-OO applications, this elegant scheme doesn't work. When implemented in organizations with independent and diverse IT environments, the OO paradigm, like IE, can lose much of the control that it depends on for achieving its benefits.

This leads to an application development paradox. Information Engineering- and OO-based development depend on, and achieve, much of their benefits through, autonomous control of the data they access. Yet when they exist side by side in the same organization, or

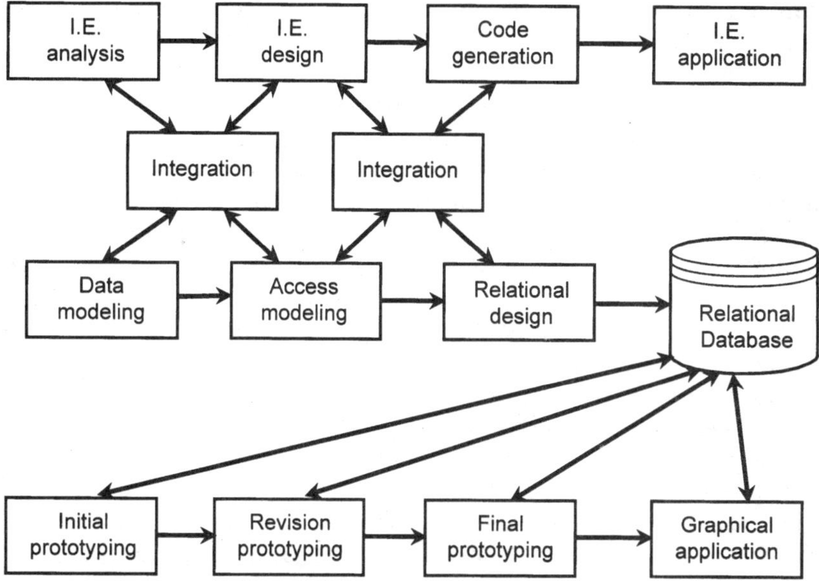

Figure 5.2 Integration problems for IE and graphical development.

when their data are also accessed by graphical applications created by "empowered" employees—both common occurrences in large and diverse companies—autonomous control over data they access is precisely what they don't have.

This conundrum would be easy to solve if the tools and methodologies utilized for IE, OO, and graphical development were broad enough to address it, if they took an expansive view of the data that they model, encapsulate, and access, so that needs of other development paradigms could be taken into account. But they aren't. IEF's data models provide a great foundation for IEF-based implementation, and a solid basis for graphical development as well.[2] But when they support graphical development—using tools such as PowerBuilder, that are outside of the IEF paradigm—the support becomes unidirectional (IEF-out). Mechanisms for helping developers identify differences between the way IEF-based and PowerBuilder-based development projects view data, cannot be found in either tool. Nor can mechanisms for helping them to resolve such differences once they're identified. Without the inclusion of such mechanisms, as integral parts of development tools, there is no way of ensuring that the reverse integration—from code models, through design models, to analysis models—will be achieved. And without reverse integration, the analysis models, upon which much of the benefit of these approaches depends, degenerate over time and eventually lose their value completely.[3]

For applications developed using OO tools, such as Smalltalk or C++, the problem takes on an additional dimension. Object-oriented applications are, of course, susceptible to the same uncoordinated forces as IE and graphical development. Technologies representing different and conflicting development paradigms pull databases in different directions at the same time, but don't provide the ability to communicate what they are doing so that they can let each other in on when it's happening. Nor do they provide mechanisms to resolve the resulting differences.[4] And, also like IE, methodologies and tools utilized to develop applications in Smalltalk and C++ typically don't provide reverse integration—or even reverse traceability—so that what happens to the database can be reflected back through the database interface software to the Smalltalk image or C++ objects, and on to the object models used for analysis.

The additional dimension stems from the fact that much of object technology's benefit depends on inheritance, and on encapsulation of data within objects. These properties help shield OO developers from data-related concerns—such as how the data within objects are utilized, how the data are accessed, or even which object does the accessing.[5] The result is that OO developers can concentrate on solving business problems instead of worrying about data, which makes them more productive.

But when the data are stored on relational databases, as they almost always are in organizations with lots of non-OO systems and complex data interactions, the same properties that free developers from having to concern themselves with data can also become the sources of significant problems. The reason is that although objects can be stored on relational databases, the mapping of persistent object instances to relational tables is neither simple nor obvious—a situation that, borrowing an analogy from electrical engineering, is sometimes referred to as an "impedance mismatch."[6] The result is that while OO applications' data can be stored on and retrieved from relational databases, the ways in which they are accessed can wind up being far from optimal—sometimes involving lots of relational joins and table searches. When this happens, the applications that are produced can require many minutes to perform operations that should take no more than a few seconds. As the database changes to support the needs of new non-OO applications, and as new-OO applications (that access the relational database via methods somewhere in their class hierarchy structures) are added, things can degenerate even further. As a result, applications slow down, so much that over time, they can lose much of their business benefit.

This scenario doesn't have to take place. The problem can be solved through data and access modeling, along with traceability from OO analysis down through design and code models, and into the relational accesses that the OO classes must make. But it typically isn't solved—at least not until the OO applications are implemented and fail because they don't perform. The underlying problem, and a principal reason why the problem isn't properly addressed, is that relational databases, along with their modeling, accessing and performance, are not part of the formal OO paradigm. Nor are they part of the knowledge and culture of most OO practitioners, to whom relational technology represents a temporary solution to achieving object persistence—an inadequate solution that will soon be replaced by object databases and that therefore doesn't merit serious attention. Relational databases are therefore not addressed in a meaningful way by the methodologies and tools utilized by OO practitioners in their development processes.

The shame of the situation is that integration of the OO and relational design processes is neither difficult nor complex. With the exception of the two integration processes, each part of the development scenario presented below must be executed anyway for successful development. The two differences are inclusion and timing. To effectively address this problem, they must be included within the OO development process, and they must be included before, not after, the applications are implemented. (See Fig. 5.3.)

With relational database design integrated into the OO development process, the relational data design process could become the foundation for integration of OO development with IE and graphical development as well. Although such integration might be regarded as a corruption of the formal OO paradigm, and some OO benefits might

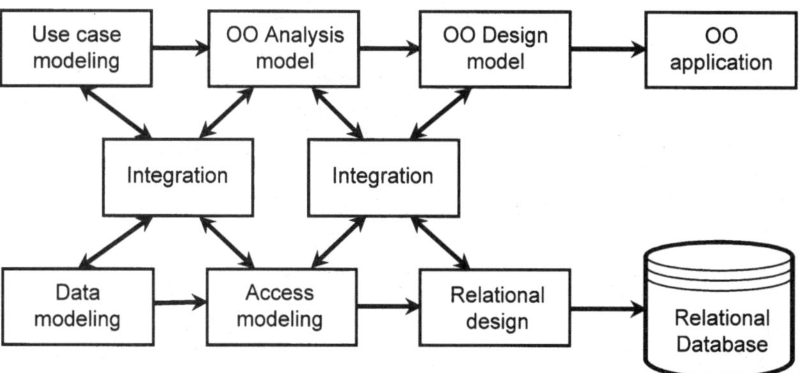

Figure 5.3 Integration of OO and relational technologies into the development process.

be compromised as a result, it would effectively address a real and pervasive problem found in many organizations. In such companies, the net positive result in terms of business benefit would be substantial. As Figs. 5.4 and 5.5 suggest, and as we'll see in Part 2 of this book, effective data integration of OO development with IE development and of OO development with graphical development is a problem that can be solved.

On the data side, the tools, methods, and techniques required to address the problem have been around since the late 1980s, and there is an available body of IT practitioners who understand them and are skilled in their use. So their skills and knowledge could be put to good use in facilitating OO design and implementation. But it doesn't happen. The three cultures, along with the individuals who populate them, are too far apart, and there are no tools or methodologies that I know of that successfully integrate them.

Incomplete Requirements

If different development paradigms have trouble dealing effectively with data and relational databases, they have a great deal more difficulty with requirements. The reason is that although they address data differently, when the differences are stripped away the information underneath is essentially the same. A customer's address,

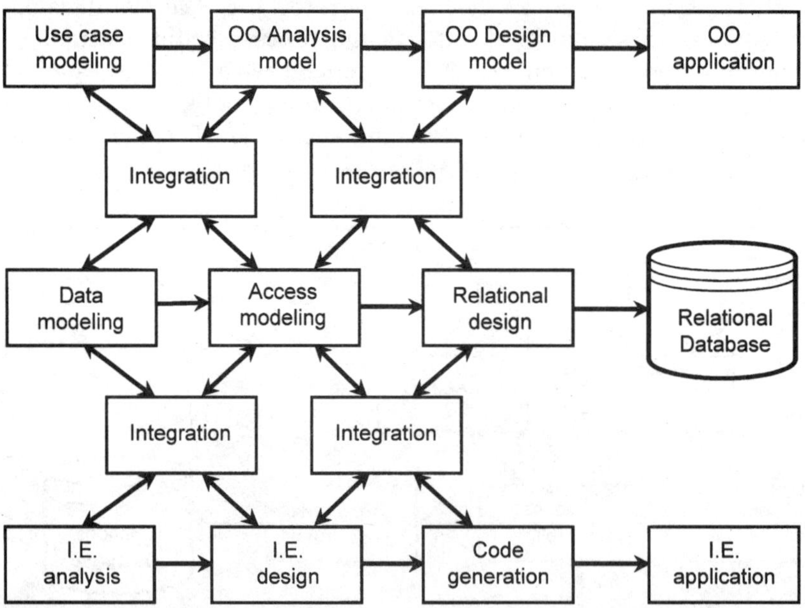

Figure 5.4   Data integration points for OO and IE development.

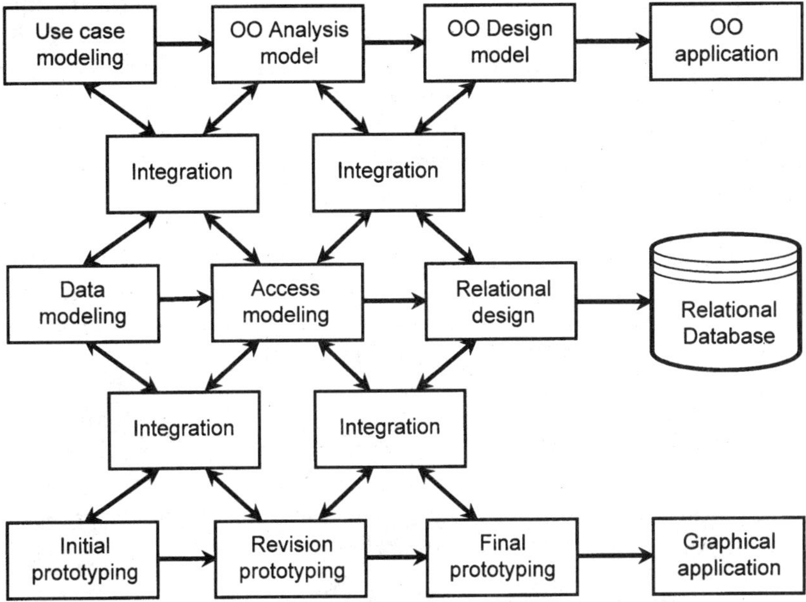

Figure 5.5 Data integration points for OO and graphical development.

whether stored in a relational table, expressed as attributes of an entity type, displayed on a screen or instantiated as attributes within an object, is still a customer's address. It represents the same thing, and it has the same meaning to the business. This similarity does not hold true for business requirements.

To understand why, along with the host of problems that are the inevitable result, we must first do some exploration into the nature of business requirements. We can't understand the differences between the way different development paradigms tackle requirements if we aren't really sure about what business requirements are.

Business requirements for a computer application, in the most basic sense, delineate what the application must do to support the business so that it can satisfy a business need and provide value to the organization. At first, this definition might look OK. But it really isn't. An application that does what the business needs, but doesn't do it the way the business needs it done, isn't likely to provide its business users with a lot of benefit. An application that calculates bond yields, for example, won't be of much value if it is a UNIX application and its users are in a Windows NT environment. The yield calculation, no matter how correct, may not provide a lot of value to its users if they can't dynamically link it to the electronic spreadsheets they use for portfolio valuation. What is needed is not just functions (such as the yield calculation, or the types of bonds it can handle), but also features (such as how the results of the yield calculation are displayed, whether it is updated in response to real-time market feeds, or how the application will interoperate with other applications). In a changing, complex multiple-technology environment, with different sets of business users having different needs and utilizing different kinds of servers, networks, system software, and workstations, what an application does must be described not only in terms of functions, but also in terms of its features.

But specifying an application's requirements in terms of functions and features, although better than functions alone, is still inadequate. The reason is that functions and features don't address the way the application will have to respond to its environment—how it will handle business events, such as the arrival of an order, an irate customer questioning an invoice, an engineering change, or an unanticipated swing in the price of a bond. And nailing down requirements for how an application will handle these kinds of business events requires that we be able to specify the application's behavior—the "what happens when" scenarios with which:

- its users will be able to navigate through its interface to get what they need,

- other applications will be able to access it, so that the application can supply them with information and get the information it needs,

- devices, such as medical sensors, home televisions, or robots on a shop floor, can access it to exchange information, and

- it will handle different kinds of unexpected conditions and errors.

Our bond yield application, for example, might have to respond to events—recalculate bond yield and send an e-mail message to a set of users, in response to certain kinds of corporate actions. It might also have to notify a risk management system. The idea is that, in today's complex IT and corporate environments, functions and features alone are not sufficient to describe applications' requirements. Events and scenarios are also needed. But as we shall see, the addition of events and scenarios, although markedly better than features and functions alone, is still insufficient. The element that must be added to complete the picture is *data*.

Of all the ways in which we describe application requirements, it is hard to envision a topic that is more important—and more controversial—than data. Data, in the form of common identifiers for basics like customers, suppliers, inventory, and products, can facilitate or can place stringent limits on a company's ability to leverage them over its different business units. Examples abound. It is frighteningly common for large companies to miss cross-selling opportunities because the same customer—the person, household, or business that purchases different services and products through different channels or from different business units—is identified differently in each business unit's systems. Serious problems caused by inconsistencies stemming from poorly defined data requirements are not limited to external data, such as suppliers or customers.

Significant data-related problems can easily be manufactured from within, as was the case when the CEO of a worldwide manufacturing company was asked by a Wall Street analyst to explain the origins of the financial results that the company had just reported. When the CEO went to the two divisions that generated the results in question, to confer with their Presidents, they were at a complete loss to explain the numbers. While each could easily explain the origins of his division's "management reporting" results—the results that they generated, were measured by, and were held accountable for—they couldn't explain the shareholder reporting results, the (different) set of results that the Wall Street analyst was calling about.

The CEO, who was not pleased and didn't intend to find himself in that position again, launched a task force to find the origin of the differences, and to implement corrective action. The conclusion of the 9-month, 11-person study was that the management reporting and shareholder reporting differences were the result of data-related issues among the systems and procedures utilized to roll-up, consolidate, and report the company's operations.

The simple truth is that data are an important element of application requirements, and if not taken into account, situations such as the one our CEO found himself embroiled in—or worse—are the inevitable result. Specifically, data-based requirements help to ensure that:

- common business basics, such as products, suppliers, and customers, can be commonly identified as such,

- the information used to manage the business is consistent, supportable, and correct, and that

- applications developed and run at different times, utilizing different technologies, can integrate and interoperate with each other.

Taken together, features and functions, events and scenarios, and data become a three-dimensional "requirements space," in which each dimension contributes a different, orthogonal, and critically important view of application requirements. (See Fig. 5.6.) Keep them all together, and you have a holistic view—a balanced set of

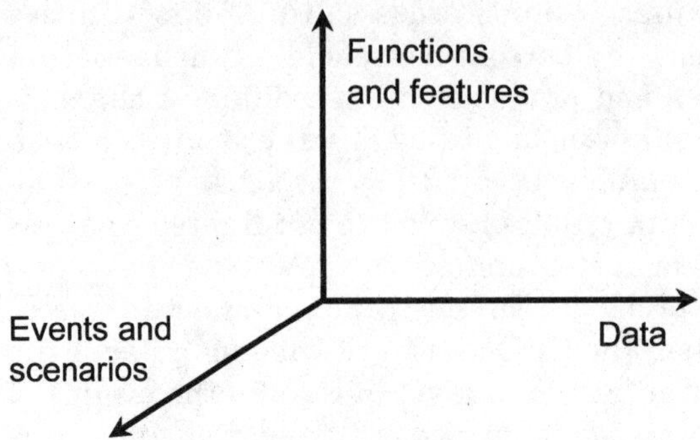

Figure 5.6 Requirements space.

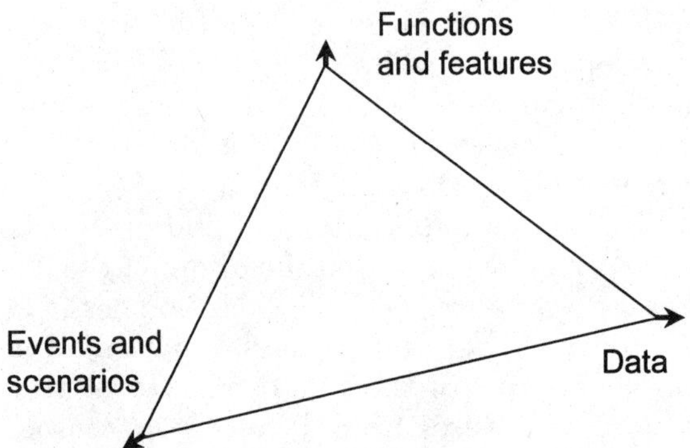

Figure 5.7 Requirements space ideal: a balanced set of requirements.

business requirements. This is the requirements space ideal, in which all aspects of requirements are fully taken into account. (See Fig. 5.7.) Take one or more away, and you run the risk of developing an application that does "what it's supposed to do," but that doesn't fully consider one or more important component of its requirements and consequently contains flaws that can seriously constrain its ability to function as an effective business tool in its complex corporate environment.[7]

The time compressed technology problem, and a serious application development issue in many of today's companies, is that each of the three dimensions of requirements space are development paradigm-specific. Depending on the approach and tools utilized for application development, one or more of the dimensions—one or more basic elements of requirements—may not be fully addressed. Indeed certain development paradigms don't address some dimensions at all. To see how this situation comes about, let's explore how requirements, in terms of our three-dimensional requirements space, are addressed by each of our development paradigms.

As IE utilizes the relational data model as its prime metaphor for developing, documenting, and communicating requirements, the data dimension is fully addressed.[8] IE's implementations—in CASE tools such as Texas Instruments' IEF—provide mechanisms to ensure that data within each application are internally consistent and that data between different applications—at least, IEF-based applications—are consistent with each another. The problem of identical customers, with different and inconsistent identifiers, doesn't occur with applications developed utilizing IEF.

In terms of our features and functions dimension, IE doesn't fare quite as well. IE's utilization of data, along with functions and processes, forms an excellent vehicle for documenting an application's functions: what's in and what's out. But features such as imaging, real-time analysis, or linking and embedding are typically not addressed until late in the IE development process, when expectations have been set and misunderstandings are difficult and expensive to correct.

When it comes to expressing event and scenario requirements, IE does even worse. While business events are sometimes acknowledged (in the form of process logic diagrams), they're neither fully developed or rigorously enforced. As with features, scenarios are addressed late in the development process, and then only in terms of dialog flow diagrams that tackle them from an application-centric view. There is no place in IE-based tools for fully developing events and scenarios from a business perspective, as they often are in OO development. Information engineering-based development therefore forms a lopsided triangle on our three-dimensional requirements space, revealing its heavy emphasis on data, partial treatment of functions and features, and limited acknowledgment of events and scenarios. (See Fig. 5.8.)

Addressing the three dimensions of our requirements space through graphical design presents a different, but equally frustrating, picture. As graphical design develops requirements through construction of successive prototypes, the developing application's features and functions become quickly evident. Not only do the application's business users get to see its functions first hand, in terms of what's in and what's out, but they also get to see its features—such as imaging and real-time updates—along with what they do and how they work. Functions and features that are missing, or misinterpreted by the application's developers, become visible in the prototypes for everyone

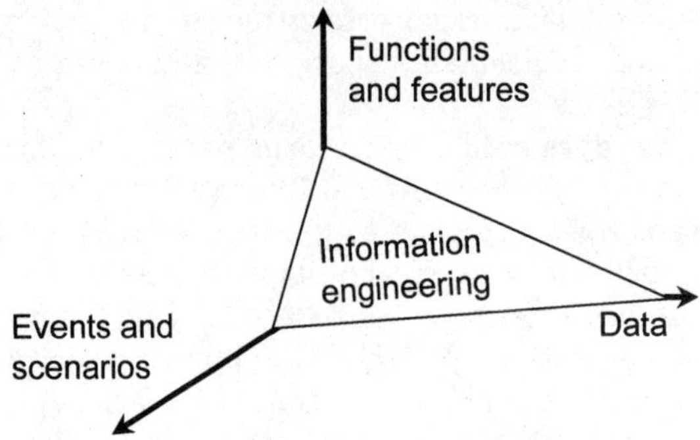

Figure 5.8 How information engineering addresses requirements space.

to see, so that they can be corrected, and the corrections are validated through the next set of prototypes.

Graphical design does less well as a vehicle for identifying requirements in terms of events and scenarios. Although graphical design's successive prototypes are a good vehicle for analyzing the scenarios through which users and applications interact, graphical design methodologies and tools tend to lack formal mechanisms for identifying business events and for ensuring that all scenarios associated with each business event are adequately addressed. Identification of business scenarios, and validation that the developing applications are robust enough to handle them, is the responsibility of business users, who unfortunately don't always have the training and experience to know what to cover, or even what to look for or where to look for it. For applications that are large and complex, and where a number of different groups of users are involved, important events and scenarios can easily fall through the cracks, with all-too-familiar results.

A mixed set of issues becomes apparent when graphical development tools and approaches are used to develop requirements in terms of our third dimension: data. The underlying problem is that the graphical design process doesn't really develop requirements in terms of data at all—at least, not directly. When the graphical development process begins with an existing data model or database, and is used to develop an application within the constraints imposed by the data requirements that it began with, everything is fine. Most graphical development tools—PowerBuilder, for example—ensure that the graphical objects used to develop the user interface conform to the data-based constraints.

The problem is that graphical development doesn't always work that way. When new data are defined as a result of the iterative prototyping process, their definitions are typically created as an after-thought, as indirect by-products of graphical development. With no processes within graphical design methodologies to analyze such data, and no mechanisms for ensuring integration of the design with data, it's easy to develop data-based requirements—such as customer or product identifiers and attributes—that are right for the application being developed, but wrong for everything else. This kind of de facto data requirements development is a rich source of data-imposed constraints that prevent companies' systems from being able to recognize business basics such as common customers, suppliers, or products, and that wreak havoc on data warehouses and decision support systems.

When plotted on our three-dimensional requirements space, graphical design forms a triangle showing high function and feature content, moderate events and scenarios, and weak data. (See Fig. 5.9.)

Object-oriented development, when viewed in terms of our three-dimensional requirements space, presents a highly skewed result, in which function, feature, event, and scenario requirements are all well developed, and data requirements—from perspectives that are external to the application—are hardly developed at all.

Object-oriented development's well-developed event and scenario requirements owe their origins to the wide employment of use cases, that were first applied as part of Ivar Jacobson's Objectory methodology and CASE tool, and that have since gained wide acceptance as a staple of mainstream OO development. Developing requirements in terms of use cases, in which business events and detailed "what happens when" scenarios are developed from the perspective of "actors" (people, systems, and devices that exchange information with the application) is a good mechanism for identifying, analyzing, and documenting events and scenarios. As use cases describe each scenario in

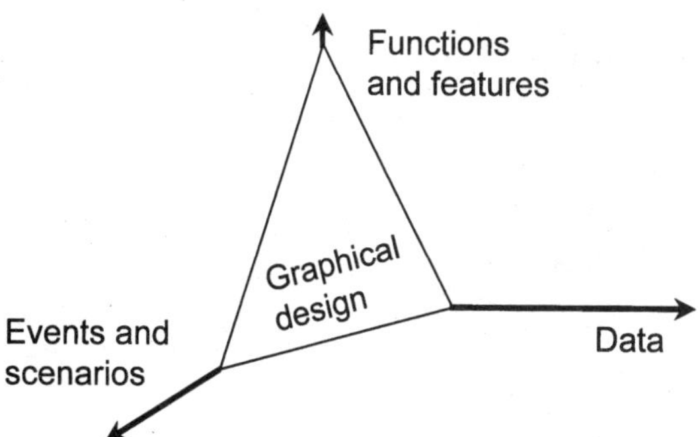

Figure 5.9 How graphical design addresses requirements space.

terms of sequential steps expressed in business English, they're easily understandable by business users as well as by developers.

When supplemented by prototypes and combined with business object modeling, use case analysis presents a clear and understandable picture, in which applications' functions and features become quickly apparent. As in graphical development, features—such as imaging, application embedding and real-time updates—show up clearly for everyone to see. The result is that when they are missing or wrong, the errors can be quickly corrected, and the corrections validated, utilizing successive use cases and use case-based prototypes.

The problem with OO, in terms of our three-dimensional requirements space, is the inability of OO methodologies and tools to express requirements in terms of data. Although data are addressed by virtually all OO methodologies and tools as variables encapsulated within persistent objects, the view of data that they capture is totally OO- and application-centric. The resulting problem is that data requirements, such as common identifiers, consistent domains, or mandatory relationships, that are external to the application and external to OO, but that are critical to its being able to function as part of a company's integrated IT infrastructure, are not addressed. Nor are data-centric performance requirements that extend beyond object technology, which is a shame because performance requirements and volume metrics can easily be added to use cases and traced through object models to the relational databases, hierarchical databases, and other kinds of data stores that must be accessed.[9] In an integrated business environment, in which data requirements can come from applications and data stores that are external to the application, as easily as from the application's business users, OO development misses the boat. (See Fig. 5.10.)

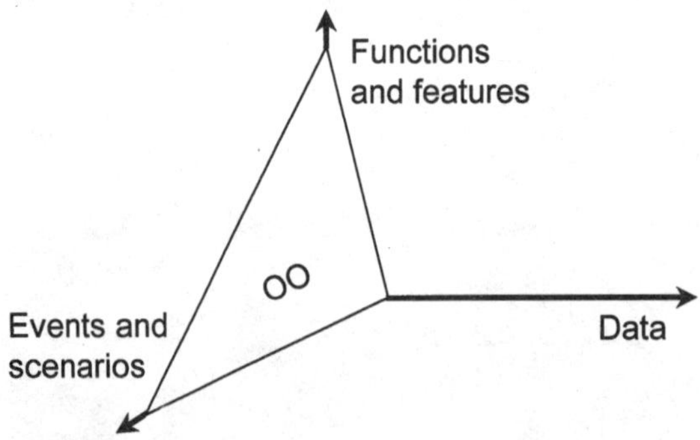

Figure 5.10 How object-oriented development addresses requirements space.

The real problem—the IT problem that ultimately impacts the business—is not that individual development tools and approaches exhibit shortcomings in terms of one or more dimensions of our holistic requirements space, but the incompatibilities and artificial barriers that are erected when multiple tools and approaches are utilized within the same company to develop business requirements. The result is a continuation of development paradigm-specific shortcomings, along with lost opportunities, in the form of:

- software development assets—IE data models, for example, that contain important business requirements and compatibility information that aren't leverageable by OO developers;

- analytic techniques, such as OO use case analysis, that could rectify significant IE shortcomings in enabling business users to visualize features or developers to understand events and scenarios, but which aren't supported by IE development;

- recognition of diversity in technology environments, so that OO applications integrate with applications developed in other paradigms, and perform well in non-OO database environments; and

- coordination, so that graphical applications developed from successive prototypes don't produce applications that propagate incompatible data into the company's IT infrastructure.

The inability of our development tools and techniques to successfully tackle these problems is the product of the jagged interplay between our slow-moving cultures and fast-paced time compressed change. The cultural component is the result of two primary forces within the IT community. The first is the combination of the dogma, substantial learning curves, and insular cultures that surround each approach. The second is the business pressures resulting from the cohesive and lucrative markets for tool developers and consulting firms that these insular and slow-moving cultures represent. The time compressed technology component is the result of accelerating advances in development, approach, and execution technologies, unfulfilled business needs, and the potential, in terms of fulfilling the needs, that new technologies and approaches represent.

Conflicting Participation and Support

Differences and shortcomings among today's paradigms for developing applications are not limited to requirements. Indeed, they can span surprisingly large cross sections of a company's IT and business communities, impacting the majority of those who come into contact with its application development processes. Much of the resultant mayhem and confusion shows up as direct products of the diversity of approaches employed by today's companies. A good deal more shows up as a result of the inadequacies and inappropriateness of the narrow sets of tools, methodologies, and support infrastructure utilized to support today's range of application development. This leads to a late-1990s paradox in development participation and support: as companies seek to gain control over their system development confusion and rising development costs through consolidation of participants, development tools, and support infrastructure, they actually make it worse.

To gain some insight into how this situation comes about, consider the impact that the analysis function in each of our four development paradigms exerts on business users, management, and their support infrastructure as they manage goals and requirements, activities and progress, risk, and development project support. (See Fig. 5.11.)

The process of identifying and analyzing a business application's goals and requirements is, to a great extent, a product of how the development paradigm addresses our 3-dimensional requirements space. If, for example, the paradigm is OO development, the business users who become involved in developing their application are likely to find themselves spending their time developing and validating the stream of business objects, use cases and interface prototypes that

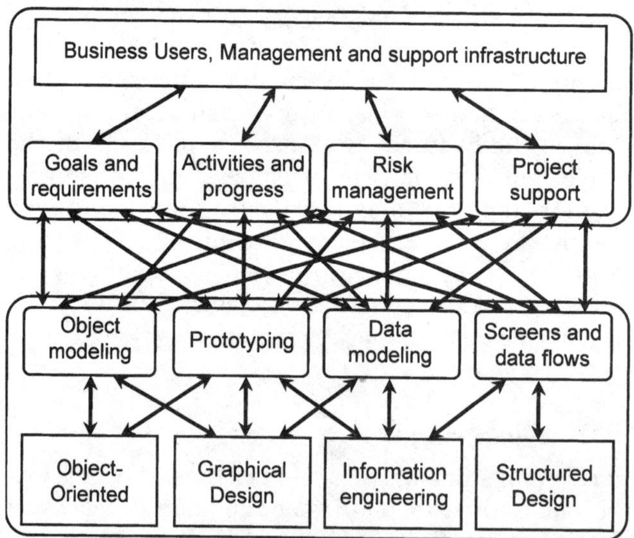

Figure 5.11 Different development paradigms require conflicting participation and support.

OO developers use to represent their application's goals and requirements. So far, so good. This view of goals and requirements is consistent, not terribly difficult to master, and relevant to most business environments.

But for business users who have been involved in IE-based development, who have developed (or directly managed the development of) their own graphical applications, or who have participated in traditional structured development, things can become confused and development can suffer as a result. For such people, expressing equivalent business requirements in terms of object models, detailed IE-based data models, series of iterative prototypes, and activity-oriented specifications requires that they become conversant with a number of different and conflicting metaphors for documenting their requirements. And, if the resultant applications are to be successful, it also requires that they become sufficiently competent in each to be able to identify the seemingly small, but critically important, problems and inconsistencies that the different metaphors contain so that their IT peers can correct the errors and present them with yet another set of equally disparate requirements models. As there are no tools to automate this process and help them by:

- quickly and accurately translating business requirements from one metaphor to another,

- comparing requirements across different kinds of models, so that discrepancies can be brought to light, or

- translating the requirements contained in each model into a common business-oriented "requirements-speak,"

business users and developers are left to their own devices to cope with the awkward and incomplete translations as best they can.[10]

The result is that requirements modeling, where different development paradigms are involved, remains very much a manual, confusing, inconsistent, and error-prone process. This is especially true for an increasing number of business users who are being focused on business process reengineering fundamentals, such as customer needs or integrated logistics, and whose business involvement therefore spans a number of traditional organizational units.[11] For such business users, simultaneous involvement in application development projects, that are based on the different development paradigms that were in use at each traditional organizational unit, is the order of the day, and mass confusion is the typical result.

To management these disparate views of application goals and requirements can appear even more confusing, and a lot less complete. The principal reason for the confusion is that the extent of the differences between current paradigms for application development is neither understood nor expected. From a management perspective, differences in applications are expected, in the same sense that differences in other business infrastructure components—such as advertising campaigns, distribution channels, buildings, and labor contracts—are expected. The catch is that for computer applications, the key differences are more likely to show up in the process (of application development) than in the applications themselves. The reason for the confusion is that to managers who are not conversant with the development technologies that underlie the key process differences, in the way that they would be conversant with process differences in other (nontechnical) areas, significant differences in application development are perceived as meaningless variations of the same technology gobbledygook.[12] Meaningless or not, differences in numbers of business and technical application development participants, the nature of their participation, and the diversity of rumors and facts that bubble up to the top, are real. And if they cannot be understood and dealt with, they can become important factors in thwarting development and implementation of the applications that the business needs in order to remain competitive.

Another significant underlying problem, and a cause of much of the mayhem and confusion surrounding development technologies and approaches, is the absence of consistency among the tools, methodologies, and infrastructure utilized in development support. Object-oriented, IE, and graphical development tools and techniques, for example, are based on OO-, IE-, and graphical development–centric models of application development that don't include acknowledgment of—or processes for coming to terms with—the other approaches. The result is a dearth of anything that can help business users or management understand and resolve these differences. (See Fig. 5.12.)

A similar set of approach-dependent disparities must be dealt with in terms of participation in day-to-day activities and tasks associated with the planning, execution, and reporting of application development projects. Lots of misunderstanding and confusion are almost always the result.

When this happens, the culprits are usually the methodologies that supply the different and confusing sets of work breakdown structures, project deliverables, and management reports that are used to support the different paradigms, tools, and techniques in use for application development. The underlying problem, however, is not the methodologies but the contradictory requirements placed on the methodologies by the multiple-technology environments that they support. Consider the conflicting demands on coupling between the methodology and the activities that the methodology supports.

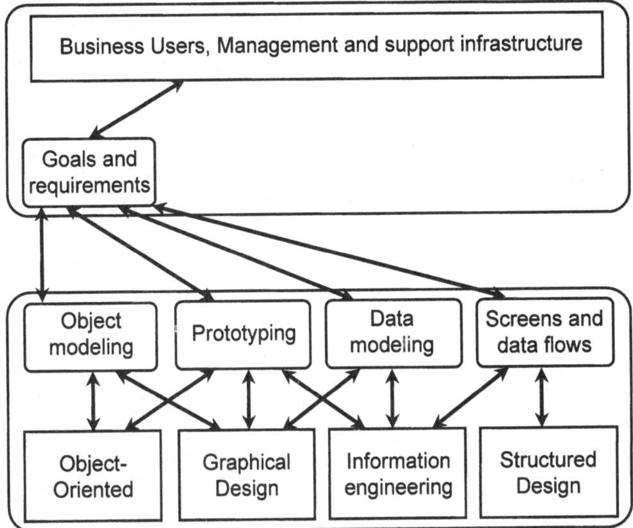

Figure 5.12 Business user, management, and support infrastructure views of goals and requirements.

For a methodology to be useful—so that it adds real value to development teams working to deliver applications against tight deadlines, and doesn't end up as shelfware for project leaders like Russ—tight coupling between the methodology and the team's day-to-day tasks and activities is an absolute requisite. If the team is utilizing an IE-based tool [such as High Productivity System (HPS) or Information Engineering Facility (IEF)], the methodology must be detailed and explicit in guiding development teams through their data modeling activities and in producing the entity relationship diagrams, domains, properties, and attribute lists that are required to make these tools perform. If the development team is using an OO development-based tool (such as Select Enterprise, VisualAge, Smalltalk, or C++), the methodology has to be just as detailed and explicit in guiding its developers through dividing the required functionality between application layers and frameworks, and in constructing class hierarchies for each with the proper methods and variables in each class.

But in a multiple and changing technology environment, the same kind of tight coupling that serves IE and OO technology developers so well can quickly lead to confusion when it's applied to progress reporting and project management. For management, the kind of detailed and explicit guidance that developers thrive on, and that tight coupling enables, is neither relevant or important. Nor are the detailed differences between development paradigms that tight coupling highlights.

What is important to management is veracity, accuracy, and consistency in reporting needs, issues, and progress. To management, detailed information on the number of entity types modeled by HPS developers, or the number of classes reused by VisualWorks developers, is unimportant compared to the fact that critical resources shortly needed by one of the teams may not be available, or that one team is making satisfactory progress while the other is not. Getting management the information it needs, while filtering out the information it doesn't, requires loose coupling between the methodology's detailed activities, tasks, and work products and what's reported to management. In management and reporting, the tight coupling (one-to-one) relationship between the methodology and activity at the development team level must be replaced by loose coupling (many-to-one) summarizations and roll-ups. (See Fig. 5.13.)

Risk management in a multiple-technology environment presents a new and unique set of problems that our current tools and infrastructure are also ill equipped to address. Consider the following three examples.

As IE is based on a relational view of application development, IE-based tools, such as IEF and HPS, are well equipped to address performance in a relational environment—through denormalization, for example. Object-oriented tools typically do an equally admirable job of object modeling. But there's little among the current crop of tools or methodologies that adequately addresses data modeling and object

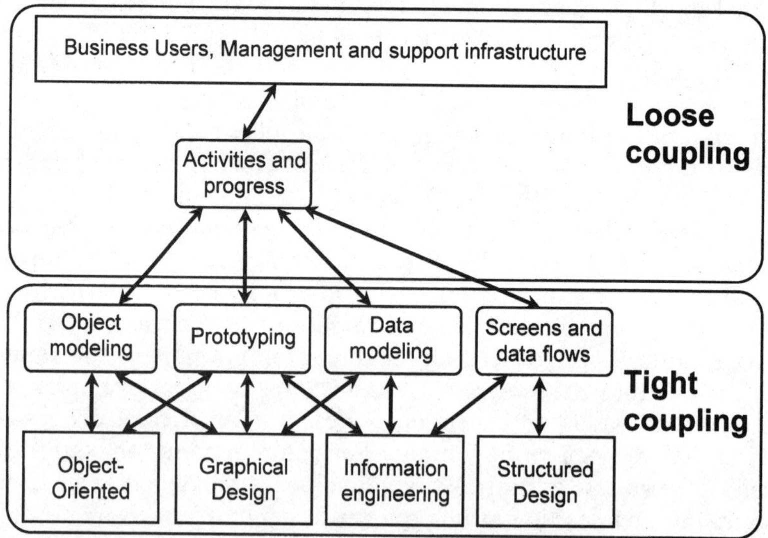

Figure 5.13 Activities and progress views of goals and requirements require loose coupling.

modeling. There are also no tools for modeling and optimizing performance across technologies, such as Smalltalk and C++ in a relational database environment.

There are also no tools for trapping warning signs—such as disparities among analysis, design, and code models—and displaying the results for project developers and managers to see and act on. Although good project leaders identify and address these kinds of disparities as part of their day-to-day management, doing so requires a base of experience with the development and execution technologies, along with the way they're being applied. The problem is that where multiple and changing development and execution technologies are involved—for example, multiple development languages, middleware layers, or a execution technology environment involving different workstations, operating systems, and databases—there are fewer and fewer people with sufficient breadth of experience to make these kinds of judgments.

The third problem is a lack of forecasting tools for estimating time and effort to develop projects in multiple and changing technology environments. The reasons for the problem are twofold. The first reason is that the newness of the early work products associated with many of the technologies, and lack of a large empirical experience base, makes development of such tools difficult. At a recent Object-Oriented Program Systems Languages and Applications (OOPSLA) Metrics Workshop, for example, there was only one paper on forecasting that was backed up with real results, even though OO development was already in wide use as a paradigm for development. The second part of the problem is that the numbers of multiple-technology combinations—each representing a viable development and execution architecture, and each exerting a significant impact on time and effort forecasts—are hard to cope with. The increasing numbers of development and execution technology combinations decrease the size of the already small samples of empirical data, making the already daunting task of accurate project estimation even harder to address.

The result, in our time compressed environment, is that developers of estimation tools must develop more and more tools (or more versions of the same tools) that must be sold into an increasingly fragmented market. The difficulties associated with achieving acceptable returns on the research and development investments required to bring these kinds of tools to market is a significant factor in the lack of multiple-technology tools, even though the need for them is great.

A final area in which multiple and changing technologies wreak havoc on application development is in the infrastructure, tools, and techniques utilized for project support. Traditional development support organizations—such as Data Administration, Database

Administration, Quality Assurance, and Standards—are finding themselves increasingly ill equipped to deal with the multiple and proliferating development and execution technologies that comprise today's application development environments. The reason why this happens is that these support organizations are finding themselves in the confluence of two powerful forces, one related to technology and the other to business, each pulling them in opposite directions.

The technology force is time compression. The accelerating proliferation and diversification of development and execution technologies and the reality of inadequate tools and techniques call for staffing these infrastructure functions with people who are knowledgeable in broad spectrums of technologies and approaches. Without the ability to muster data administrators, database administrators, and Quality Assurance(Q/A) personnel who understand and have experience in the diversity of technologies employed for application development, projects are left to develop applications on their own, with no safeguards against proliferation of redundant and inconsistent data, inadequate performance, and outright failure.

The business force is organizational and economic in nature. In an era of increasingly intense competition and business reengineering, there is well-founded business pressure to keep non-value-added costs to a minimum, reduce the roles of administrative and support organizations, and lower head counts. As these pressures often come from finance, accounting, and Human Resources—functions that typically don't view IT as strategic—they aren't always as sensitive as they might be to the increasing diversity of technologies that the company's development support infrastructure must be prepared to address. In the eyes of these business organizations, development support infrastructure is a rich source of cost reduction targets.

The result, all too often, is an application development support infrastructure that cannot support its company's application development needs.

References

1. Some OO development practitioners may take exception to exploration of OO compatibilities in terms of data, as object technology deals very effectively with data by encapsulating it. However, encapsulation of key data in large organizations is not always possible, or even desirable, as many systems that are not OO must often access them.
2. John Stone, "CASE Plays A Role In Visual Development," *Application Development Trends,* January 1994.
3. John Stone, *Inside ADW and IEF: The Promise and Reality of CASE,* McGraw-Hill, 1993; Ivar Jacobson, *Object-Oriented Software Engineering: A Use Case Driven Approach,* Addison-Wesley, 1993.
4. The assumption here is that the data for the OO application are stored in a relational database. For OO applications that are small and self-contained—word processors,

graphics tools, or workstation-based reporting environments, for example—this need not be the case, as objects can be stored directly in an object database. However, this is not an option for many business applications for which data must be sharable with other applications developed in other paradigms. Indeed, for such applications, the data are often owned, created, updated, and modified by the non-OO applications that make up the company's application infrastructure—a situation that, in large organizations, can be expected to persist for many years.

5. The data, along with the methods that access the data, may be somewhere in the object's parentage, in a class from which they are inherited by the object. For a simple, clear, and concise explanation of how this works, see David Taylor, *Object-Oriented Technology: A Manager's Guide,* Addison-Wesley. For a more detailed explanation, see Rebecca Wirfs-Brock, Brian Wilkerson, and Lauren Wiener, *Designing Object-Oriented Software,* PTR Prentice Hall, 1990.

6. For a good overview of the problems encountered in storing persistent objects on relational databases, see Ivar Jacobson, *Object-Oriented Software Engineering: A Use Case Driven Approach,* Addison-Wesley, 1993, Chap. 10.

7. This does not hold true for tactical applications that are small, isolated, and self-contained, and that do not have to function in an environment larger than their own workstation.

8. For a good overview of how information engineering addresses data, see Clive Finklestein, *An Introduction to Information Engineering,* Addison-Wesley, 1989; and James Martin, *Information Engineering,* Prentice-Hall, 1990, Books I, II, and III.

9. The assumption here is that the data are stored in a relational database architecture. Although this may not be the case for individual, self-contained workstation-based applications—such as word processors, drawing tools, and CASE—it is generally true of companies' business data that are typically shared, sometimes in real time, by applications developed using many different architectures.

10. There are a number of tools that utilize information in one model (a data model, for example) to seed the development of another (such as a domain object model). I have not come across any tools that can make the kinds of detail translations or comparisons that would be useful to developers and their business users.

11. See Michael Hammer and James Champy, *Reengineering The Corporation,* Harper Business, 1993; and Don Tapscott and Art Caston, *Paradigm Shift,* McGraw-Hill, 1993.

12. This unfortunate situation is a common mid-1990s problem. I continue to come across significant numbers of high-level executives who are so put off by IT that they have difficulty bringing themselves to discuss the subject.

6

Sources of Time Compressed Technology Proliferation and Change—Why They Can't Be Stopped

"Our management made a total commitment to HPS, which we'll be using for all of our development." "I've standardized on Visual Basic and Microsoft Visual C++ for new systems." "This company's applications are all done in PowerBuilder." No CASE or object-oriented development in this division...." "Ours is an IBM shop, so a lot of our development is going to be in VisualAge. I don't really see object technology playing a significant role in our future."[1]

Sound familiar? These application development refrains—along with many others just like them—have marked our application development landscape for more than a decade, as IT organizations seek to retain some control over their development environments. In an age of time compressed technology change, the idea of erecting a "fire wall," to fend off approaches and technologies that aren't consistent with a strategic development direction is a beguiling concept. It keeps things simple, makes order out of chaos, and allows us to plan. It also provides us with the opportunity to accurately predict and to succeed—if we know which development technologies are coming and manage them correctly.

The problem is that, in today's business and IT environments, this kind of fire wall management doesn't work. In fact, it can't work. There are too many sources of development technologies, too many reasons for bringing them in. And there are too many new technologies and approaches that become part of our development and execution architectures, whether we want them to or not. Indeed, in most organizations, the increasing flood of new development approaches and technologies can neither be throttled nor stopped.

To understand how this situation comes about, and to gain some insight into how it's underlying mechanisms work, let's examine the forces that drive it. We'll explore 10 primary business and IT drivers that make development technology micromanagement into a myth—an unattainable goal. And we'll see that, although some of the drivers can be managed some of the time, when taken as a whole, they act to ensure the inevitability of time compressed technology change. (See Fig. 6.1.)

Business Sources

Let's begin with the five primary business drivers—the corporate origins of application development diversity and change over which IT organizations have little governance, and almost no control. In most large organizations, the combination of software packages acquired by business units, the move toward decentralization and empowerment, extreme delivery and operational requirements, mergers and acquisitions, and increasing needs for closer business-to-business communications, act to ensure that this is the case.

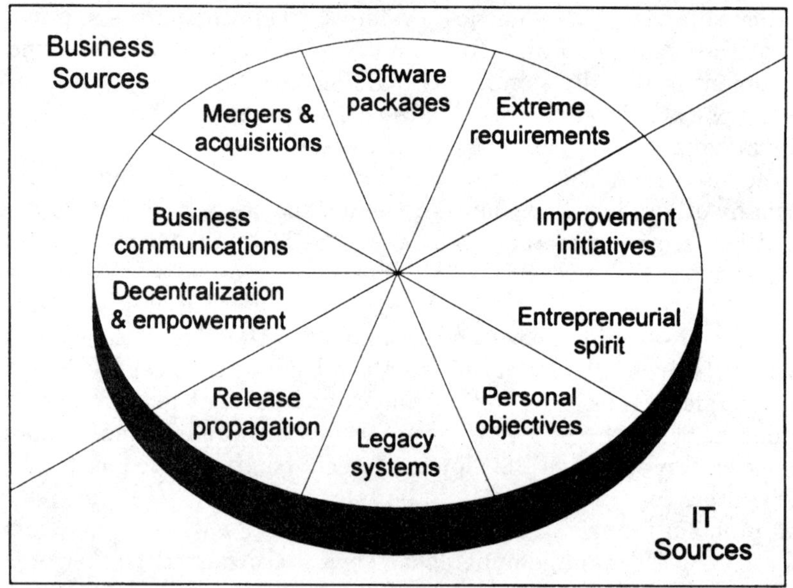

Figure 6.1   Ten primary reasons why we cannot control time compressed technology change.

Software Packages

In a time of stiffening competition from businesses operating in low-cost environments halfway around the world, and increasing dependence on information systems for business to operate competitively at home, packages are becoming an increasingly attractive option for acquiring information systems and containing application development costs. At companies with less than stellar track records for on-time delivery of applications that work, utilization of packages can also represent an attractive business strategy for quickly implementing reliable functionality when and where it's needed. This is especially true in areas—such as funds management, trade processing, MRP, shop floor management, and accounting—in which there is significant business exposure in not getting it right, and little perceived business benefit from the potential differentiation offered by custom software development.

Packages also represent technology architectures, and sometimes significant shadow development and execution technology commitments as well. Business users who purchase software packages must include the package's suite of execution and development technologies along with their own—whether they, or their IT departments, want to or not. Companies that purchase packages that run under UNIX, must learn to live, not only with UNIX, but also with the implementations of UNIX that the packages they purchase were developed to execute under. Companies that acquire packages written in PowerBuilder must learn to live with the advantages and disadvantages of PowerBuilder. The same thing goes for COBOL, HPS, C++, and Smalltalk. With every new package comes the possibility of additions to the company's expanding suite of development and execution technologies.

Consider Imis, a popular package for insurance company fund management that was sold to Texas Instruments. It wasn't long before Texas Instruments rewrote the package (in IEF, their IE-based integrated CASE tool) and renamed it "Maximis." Although Texas Instruments improved on the original Imis, and continued to make enhancements available to the companies that represented the package's installed base, the enhancements were provided in the form of IEF models. Maximus users, whose companies were also users of IEF, were in luck. To them, the package's new model of distribution was appropriate and convenient. The rest had to acquire IEF, adding Texas Instrument's integrated CASE offering to their suite of development tools, and information engineering to their suite of development paradigms.[2]

Other examples abound, with similar scenarios in every sector of our economy, from trade processing systems (written in Seer Technologies' HPS), to independent vendor-developed MRP systems (written in Smalltalk to run under Hewlett-Packard's UX), to graphics tools (that are available only on an Apple Macintosh), to internally developed general ledger systems (written in Software AG's Natural to utilize ADABAS). In each case, a specific business need was served. And in each case, a new suite of shadow development and execution technologies was introduced.

The obvious impact is an accelerated increase in the numbers of new development and execution technologies. Companies must cope, not only with the suite of technologies that they choose, but with the shadow suite of technologies introduced by applications that were purchased in the form of packages. Such are the obvious and unavoidable impacts. There are additional development and execution technology impacts resulting from utilization of packages, some of which are less obvious and take longer to surface. Obvious or not, they can still exact substantial tolls. The reason is that seemingly innocent commitments, represented by packages' development and execution technology architectures, can turn up as significant technology constraints—sometimes months or years after the purchase and implementation of the package, and sometimes in surprising ways.

This is what happened to a Midwest manufacturing company when one of its plants purchased a shop floor management package based on a Client/Server architecture in which the Client software was written in a popular rendition of Smalltalk. The whole thing was a sound business decision. The package, which was selected and purchased by the business users, and implemented by the vendor that wrote it, quickly began providing the plant's managers with an accurate and up-to-the-minute picture of each lot's status as it made its way through the plant's labyrinth of manufacturing and finishing operations. At Systems' insistence, the vendor even supplied the plant with the package's source code, so that their programmers (who were Smalltalk literate) could modify the package's functionality when required, and integrate the package into the company's new desktop Management Workstation—an important strategic objective of the its division and corporate management. As the package's Client workstation was Intel- and Windows-based, no one foresaw any significant problems. The purchase was a textbook example of IT being harnessed for fast, cost-effective, business support—an example that was quickly picked up by the plant's management to help support the case they were making for greater autonomy and empowerment.

But there were also latent problems that came crashing to the surface 6 months after the package's installation, when Systems tried to integrate the package into the rest of the Management Workstation, which was written in Visual C++. While the package and the workstation software would execute side by side, the package's icons and visual controls existed only within its Smalltalk image, and could therefore not be placed in the Workstation's "Shop Floor" window along with the other shop floor icons. In spite of valiant efforts to correct the situation, the best that Systems could do was to provide a "hot key" that allowed the workstation's users to toggle back and forth between the shop floor management package and the rest of their plant management software.

The company's corporate and division management, who were touting the Management Workstation as the first visible symbol of the company's new technology initiatives, weren't impressed. They saw the workstation's visibly flawed interface as a prime example of what happens when plants go off on their own, exercising their own prerogatives and judgment. And "to ensure that the debacle wouldn't be repeated" they seized the opportunity to decrease plant autonomy and "rein them in."

The point is that from a business perspective, utilization of packages can represent a sound strategy for fast and reliable acquisition of business functionality. But packages can also represent shadow development and execution technology architectures and commitments, that from a multiple and changing technology development viewpoint, can add to (bottom line) costs, increase risk, and produce unforeseen constraints.

Decentralization and Empowerment

This kind of scenario isn't limited to packages. In most organizations, it's the unavoidable by-product of all applications that are developed, purchased, or contracted for by business units and their IT support organizations—in divisions, departments, and plants. It's therefore also an unavoidable side effect of the trend toward empowerment and decentralization, in which local business and IT organizations are increasingly free to purchase, contract for, and develop the applications they need, without being encumbered by corporate constraints.

With stringent business requirements, local funding, their own experiences and beliefs, and lots of autonomy, it is not surprising that local business units and their IT organizations seek to develop and acquire their own applications utilizing the technologies and approaches of their choice. In addition to acquisition of packages representing disparate technology architectures, they can contract with independent software vendors to develop the applications they need. As a result, much of the application development backlog of the 1980s is a problem of the past, along with the monolithic technology architectures of the past. From the perspective of managing technology diversity and change, packages are a problem, but in many ways, decentralization and empowerment are the real culprits.

Figure 6.2 was taken from a manufacturing company at which decentralized and empowered business units were free to acquire and develop their own applications; it shows that a business can wind up with almost as many development and execution technology architectures as it has business units. The same thing, of course, holds true for companies in other sectors, such as retail, publishing, and financial services.

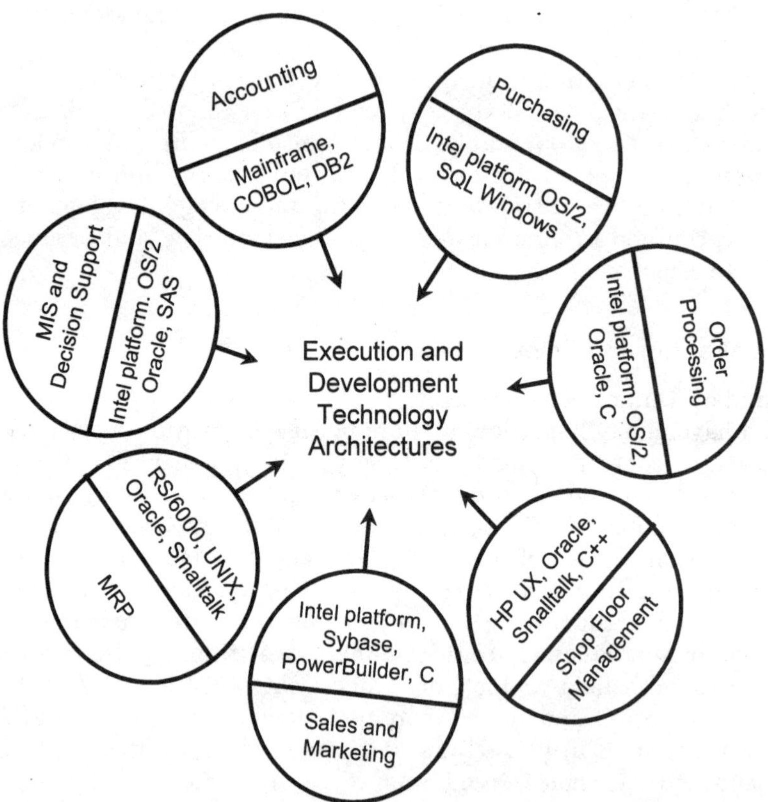

Figure 6.2 How development and execution technology architectures can vary over business units.

Extreme Delivery and Operating Requirements

Business delivery and operating requirements, in which applications can be developed over consistent amounts of time to operate in a consistent set of business environments, are not drivers of technology diversity. The suite of applications that serve a midsized distribution business, for example, in which new development can be carried out over a period months to years, and in which the systems all operate in office environments, can include a wide band of development and execution technology architectures. Mainframes will do, as will Client/Server architectures based on UNIX or Windows. Development can take place in traditional COBOL, IE-based CASE, or OO technology. From the perspective of business development and operations environments, a single set of consistent technology architectures, selected from this broad suite (IE-based CASE, for example), will do the job.

The same idea holds true for companies that support front office trading in financial instruments. For such companies, all development must be extremely rapid and flexible, so that a continuous stream of new financial instruments can be supported, and the operations environment must be fault-tolerant so that it can provide continuous support on a 7-day, 24-hour basis (a loss of service for only a few minutes' support somewhere in the world can put positions worth hundreds of millions of dollars at risk). Although the band of appropriate technologies might be somewhat narrower (such as Client/Server and UNIX for execution technologies and OO technology-based Smalltalk for development), the actual technologies selected for development and operations need not be diverse. In each of these examples, a single suite of development and execution technologies can do the job. Technology diversity and change are not issues, at least from development and operations environment standpoints.

When development and operating requirements are not uniform and consistent, this no longer holds true. And when nonuniform and inconsistent development and operations environments also include a number of extremes, the combination of extremes can drive technology diversity very hard. Consider our trading company. As long as the applications only had to support front office trading—a specific set of analytics for its trader workstations—there was no problem. But if the same company must support not only front office trading, but back office trade settlement as well (this is often the case for trading companies or trading business units of brokerage firms or investment banks), diversity can quickly become part of the development and execution technology equations. The reason is that back office settlement processing involves an entirely different set of high-volume batch processing requirements that are the products of less stringent, slower-paced, development. The suite of optimal technologies for these kinds of business requirements might include mainframes, COBOL, and integrated CASE. If the trading company's suite of applications also includes software for risk management that must interface in real time with the UNIX-based front office trading systems and with the back office settlement and accounting systems, things get even more complicated. Here, the advantages of an OO environment might be needed, but Smalltalk isn't the optimal solution, as these systems require two-way communication with non-OO platforms. The risk management software might therefore be written in C++. And, if the suite is expanded still further to include account management workstations with analysis, e-mail, spreadsheet, graphics, and word processing capabilities—technologies that are most prevalent in Windows environments—numbers of, and conflicting requirements among, competing development and execution technologies can become a real challenge. (See Fig. 6.3.) We utilized a trading company as our example, but similar scenarios, with comparable results, can be found in every sector of our economy.

Mergers and Acquisitions

Mergers and acquisitions represent a rich source of diversity for development and execution technologies in today's organizations. Although the idea of combining two organizations in similar or syner-

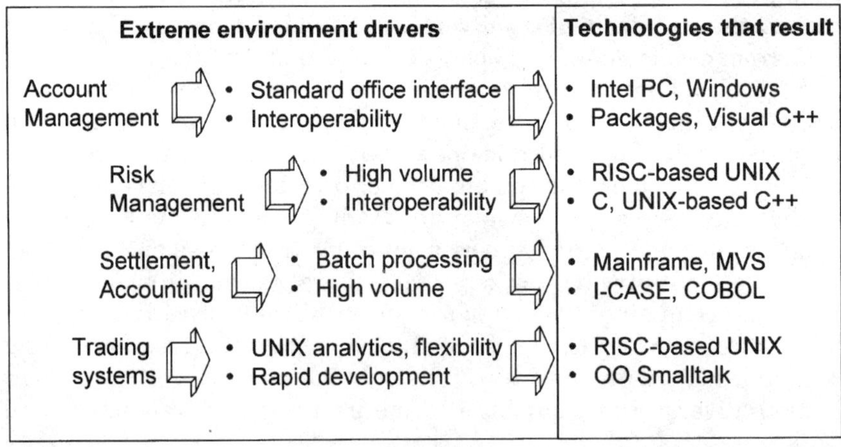

Figure 6.3 How extreme environments can drive technology diversity.

gistic businesses and supporting them with a single combined IT infrastructure is beguiling, it doesn't always work out that way in practice. When two companies or organizations merge, the likely and anticipated result is commonality and savings resulting from single applications and architectures supporting similar functions in both organizations. An equally likely, and often unanticipated, result is an increase in the numbers of development and execution technology architectures in use at the new combined organization.

The reasons for the increase in approach and development technology architectures, that vary with organizations, their businesses, and their IT infrastructures, typically include their:

- development personnel, along with their skills and competencies in the development technologies in use;

- policies and business rules that are embedded in specific development technology architectures (such as data models, object models, expert systems, and use cases);

- existing development support infrastructure (such as methodologies, development tools, data administration, database administration, configuration management, and class library support); and

- business users, who are at ease with the suite development approach technologies already in use.

The drivers of corresponding increases in execution technology architectures include each organization's:

- installed base of PCs, notebooks, PDAs, workstations, and other input and output devices (such as point-of-sale devices, process logic controls, and robotics);

- network infrastructure between it and other organizations (e.g., suppliers, customers, distributors, and agents) with which it does business;

- legacy applications (some of which may be the only remaining repository of the business policies and rules under which the organization operates); and the

- extreme delivery and operating requirements associated with business functionality that is added by one or more of the merging organizations.

Business Communication Requirements

The need for increased business-to-business communications is becoming an increasingly common, if unexpected, driver of time compressed technology change. Although businesses-to-business communications has been a reality for a number of years, today's increasing requirement that the communications integrate with, and more significantly, interoperate with, suppliers', customers', and intracompany plants' applications can drive technology in surprising ways.

Consider what happened to a Southwest fabric manufacturer when its largest customer, an offshore clothing company that was reengineering its business operations, demanded that its cutting operations (the initial set of operations in its clothing manufacturing process) be included in its supplier's manufacturing process. From a business perspective, the fabric manufacturer had no real choice, as two offshore competitors had already offered to supply precut product, and it couldn't afford to lose the business.

From an IT perspective, things were a bit more complex, as the clothing manufacturer was demanding not only that its supplier provide precut product, but that the cutting process be fully integrated into its UNIX-based process logic control and shop floor management systems. As a result, the material manufacturer's development and execution technology architectures, which had been carefully planned and crafted around Windows and Visual C++ for workstations, and Microsoft NT servers, were suddenly expanded to include Hewlett-Packard's Distributed Smalltalk and UX. Its IT personnel found themselves not only learning how to come to terms with technologies that they weren't prepared to adopt, but figuring out how to integrate them into its current manufacturing environment.

Although this example involved manufacturing companies, similar scenarios are played out over and over in the retail sector. This happens as buyers need to communicate with different chains that have disparate distribution and point-of-sale technologies; in insurance as companies seek to provide higher added value to agents that already have an installed technology architecture; and in financial services as deregulation forces providers to integrate with correspondent companies that can expand their offerings. The point is that in each of these instances, the need for closer business communications among different companies and organizations that didn't plan for it has expanded technology architectures and increased the rate of time compressed change.

Information Technology Sources

Though significant amounts of proliferation and change among development, approach and execution technologies have business origins, over which IT has little control, much of the time compressed technology changes being experienced by IT organizations have their origins within IT itself. Although this isn't unexpected, what is surprising is the breadth of its IT-based sources, the disparities between many of its sources and business needs, and the resistance that they can exhibit to attempts at planning and control. Although we'll examine a number of examples, in terms of different IT sources of technology proliferation and change, let's begin with improvement initiatives, an altruistic source over which IT does have control.

Improvement Initiatives

In the discipline that many of us chose because we have faith in, and enjoy working with, technology, and in which management is typically culled from its technical ranks, the phenomenon that many IT managers look to technology as a source for implementing needed improvements should not be surprising. To such individuals, introducing new technologies is quicker, easier, and far more satisfying than addressing the cultural, organizational, and personnel problems that prevent our IT organizations from being more effective than they are, and paradoxically, that thwart the adoption of many of the technologies being introduced. The result is a seemingly never-ending series of improvement initiatives built around new technologies, some of which work well, and stick, but most of which do not. Either way, the diversity of development and execution technologies that they leave in their wake accelerates the onslaught of technology change.

A West Coast financial services company provides a poignant example of how this can work, as its IT management brought the chosen developers from structured COBOL, through CASE, and on to graphical design and object technology—all with the laudable objective of improving the company's dismal track record in application development. As we shall see, a large contributor to their problems was their obvious success.

In the early 1990s, when their Director of Application Development, an astute young executive with a strong background in computer science, was promoted to be the company's CIO, he was struck by the poor perception of the company's IT organization by his business peers. Although the IT organization delivered applications on time, and generally within budget, the applications rarely did what the business units they were meant to serve really needed. Consequently, his organization was spending substantial amounts of time correcting their applications after they were delivered, with maintenance comprising over 80 percent of their work.

He knew that the discipline and rigor associated with IE-based CASE would do the trick. It would not only force his organization to model the business's requirements, so that his developers would get it right the first time around, but it would generate their code, adding immensely to the quality of the applications they produced. His assessment proved to be correct. Despite objections from a number of businesspeople, who had to learn data modeling so that they could participate in their own application development, he was able to demonstrate a substantial return on his investment. The CASE-generated applications that his development organization produced were well received, and their maintenance was less than 50 percent of what it would have been, a success underscored by the fact that the maintenance staff assigned to them were "sitting on their hands with nothing to do."

What his move to IEF didn't accomplish was a substantial reduction in development time, especially for small, tactical, applications. What his CASE initiative didn't do was make a substantial dent in his company's application infrastructure which consisted of millions of lines of COBOL that had been written by hand over the past 25 years. The net result was therefore significantly reduced maintenance for a couple of new applications, and two development paradigms where there had previously been only one.

Our CIO wasn't dissuaded. The year was 1993, and for development of tactical Client/Server applications, PowerBuilder would be the answer. Once again, his decision was correct, and his PowerBuilder development initiative took off. It wasn't long before no less than 20 tactical PowerBuilder-based applications were in production and two large-scale PowerBuilder applications were in the works. While the tactical applications functioned flawlessly, the two large-scale PowerBuilder applications had to be supplemented with generous amounts of code written in C. Once again, our CIO's technology initiatives were successful and correct. And once again, the numbers of development technology paradigms multiplied as a result, this time to four: hand-coded COBOL, IEF, PowerBuilder, and C.

Although each of his initiatives had met its objectives, the IT organization's development and maintenance staffs had fragmented into four separate camps with little overlap, and severe restrictions on his managers' ability to redeploy personnel from one discipline to the next, to balance workload and assignments. Also, despite each vendor's predictions, his managers were experiencing very little reuse.

The answer would be OO technology—a choice that could not only fulfill the roles currently occupied by PowerBuilder and IEF, but a technology that was also built on, and actively fostered, reuse. Although he went ahead with his OO technology initiative, his developers were split on how to implement it. His staff's computer science contingent went with Smalltalk, based on its enforced rigor and elegant approach. His C contingent, which was by this time maintaining the two mission-critical applications that were written largely in C, and who had the total support of the business units they were servicing, was far more comfortable with C++. As a result, the company's IT organization moved ahead with two parallel OO initiatives, one using Smalltalk and the other utilizing C++. (See Fig. 6.4.)

Although the outcome of their OO technology initiatives was still not certain, what was certain was that company's four development paradigms had now expanded to six.

Entrepreneurial Spirit

Somewhat less altruistic, but just as effective as a source of new and different development technologies and approaches, is our entrepreneurial spirit. Indeed, utilizing a company's resources to create new development technologies that can not only support its business's requirements, but can also be sold as a general product on the open market, is as alluring as it can be profitable. One of the best examples of an entrepreneurial initiative that did both is a very successful CASE tool known as HPS. The tool started life as a code generator that First Boston Corporation developed in order to meet the demanding requirements of the new set of trading applications that couldn't be fulfilled with the conventional technologies of the day. Having done the job at First Boston, the tool was then launched into the commercial marketplace by Seer Technologies, a company that was started for that purpose. In the years that ensued, HPS went on to become one of the most successful integrated CASE tools on the market.

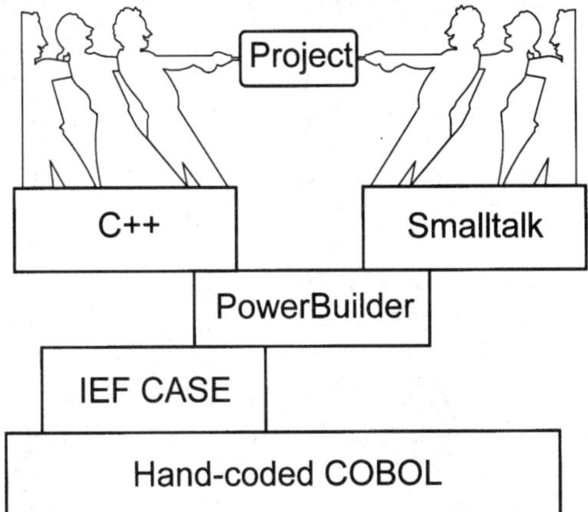

Figure 6.4 Improvement initiatives can cause technologies to proliferate.

There are similar, albeit less successful, examples of this kind of development from many other companies in almost every sector of the economy. The point is that the combination of:

- specialized development needs,

- the lack of commercially available development technologies that can satisfy the needs,

- an application development market hungry for new and promising technologies, and

- bright developers with innovative solutions,

has led to the development of many such products. And, successful or not, the entrepreneurial initiatives that lead to their creation, represents a rich source of new development technologies—for the companies at which they are developed as well as for the companies that purchase them on the open market.

Personal Objectives

Promotion of new technologies to further personal objectives is hardly altruistic and rarely successful in serving company needs, but it is surprisingly potent as a source of time compressed change. Although personal objectives for introducing new and divergent technologies can potentially take as many forms as there are employees and consultants with personal objectives, they most commonly include introduction of development, approach, and execution technologies that:

- they are personally taken with, or sometimes merely comfortable with, having utilized them at a previous company,

- position them to further their careers and increase their worth in the application development job market, and that

- restrict company options and influence decisions so that other (nontechnical) personal objectives are served.

The most common—and in many respects, most benign—form of technology introduction as a result of personal objectives, is promotion of technologies with which people are personally taken, or simply comfortable with. As many new development technologies—IE and OO technology, for example—require substantial learning curves, many months of hard work and failed attempts are often required before the light goes on and developers become productive with them. Therefore, it is beguiling indeed to work with a technology that one has already mastered, that one knows—with 100 percent certainty—

that he or she can be successful with, that can produce a working application on time and within budget, and that will cause the developer to stand out as a knowledgeable and competent individual.

It's easy to understand why, when an application being developed is important and visible, time is short, and a lot is at stake, technology selection often degenerates to individuals promoting what they are confident in and know best. When a number of such individuals follow one another from one company to the next—a common phenomenon in the world of application development, in which development projects quickly come and go and demand often outstrips availability—the arrival of a group of developers from a common technology background often results in the adoption of the suite of technologies with which they're most familiar.

Whether such development technologies result in the most cost-effective solutions, or whether they turn out to be the most appropriate for the job at hand, is debatable. It is *not* debatable that this kind of technology introduction adds to the diversity of development technology portfolios.

While introduction of new development technologies to further career objectives may be more sinister, it's a common path through which new development approach and execution technologies are introduced. As salaries, bonuses, and consulting rates for application developers can be driven to a greater extent by technologies than by companies, profitability, economic sector, or even individual talent, the fact that programmers seek to program their careers by promoting high-paying technologies should hardly be a surprise. By giving developers incentives to promote hot new technologies this way, we, as an industry, are sowing the seeds for diversity and change among technologies our companies utilize for application development. As the following figure indicates, we're also promoting technologies that are in the early portions of their life cycles, where they don't provide the highest ROI to our businesses. (See Fig. 6.5.)

Similar pressures become evident during the latter portion of technology life cycles, where compensation levels tend to rise again, as technologies pass beyond their useful lives and developers who are competent in their use become scarce. They too add to technology diversity, in this case by exerting pressure to stick with existing technologies, while other developers introduce new technologies. Although this rise in compensation for older technologies tends not to reach dizzying compensation levels that people get for technologies that are promising and new, such incentives to developers can still be significant.

If the promotion of new development technologies over old resulted in an equal number of new technologies displacing an equal number of older technologies, there would be no problem. No net gain in num-

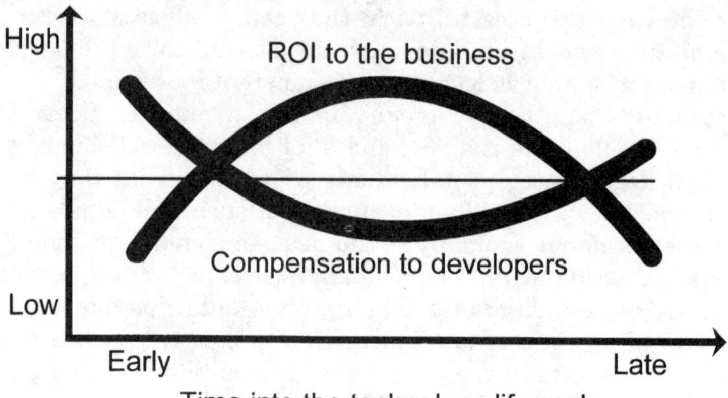

Figure 6.5 Inverse relationship between compensation and ROI for many development technologies.

bers of development technologies resulting from these kinds of personal objectives would result. There are, however, two additional factors that act to ensure that the net gain is real. The first is the acceleration in the number of development technologies that arrive on the scene each year. There are simply more new development technologies than old development technologies. The second factor is that the applications that development technologies are used to create tend to outlast the technologies utilized to build them. Although the technologies utilized to develop an application 5 years ago may no longer be current, the chances are that, with the exception of small tactical applications that can be quickly redeveloped, the application will still be around. And provided that the application is doing its job, the money and effort that could be allocated to its redevelopment in newer, more current, technologies, will be allocated instead to developing new applications to support business requirements that are not yet being served. A thumbnail survey of the information technology landscape of almost any large company, counting the applications built on 10- to 20-year-old technologies, but that are still in production, will quickly verify just how effective this scenario can be.

Deployment of development, approach, and execution technologies to restrict business and IT options, in order to influence decisions that promote personal objectives, is certainly the least altruistic channel through which personal objectives add to our technology mix. That this occurs at all is a paradoxical tribute to the extent to which applications and application development can influence today's' businesses. But it does occur, and in the hands of skilled individuals, it can be surprisingly effective.

As an example of how this works, consider what happened at a Midwest service company that had experienced 3 bad consecutive years, each resulting in a significant business loss. While revenues remained high, and the company retained the prominent position that it had held in its industry for many years, the company's CFO was concerned that his company was becoming a takeover target, with its leading competitor in a prime position to purchase it. He knew the competitor and its management, and he also knew that if the takeover became a reality, his job would almost certainly be lost. While he was powerless to directly stop the takeover, he was able to implement an ingenious plan that derailed it. And at the core of his plan was his company's IT infrastructure.

By outsourcing a number of his company's mission-critical business applications to a second competitor—one that he was far more comfortable with—he was not only able to buy his way out of the development costs (that had accounted for over a third of the company's losses), but was able to make his IT infrastructure fully compatible with that of the second competitor. Although the second competitor's applications worked, the fact that its applications had been developed in technologies that were nonmainstream and difficult to integrate with made his new IT infrastructure incompatible with that of the first competitor. His plan worked. The technology barrier that he erected raised the cost of the unwanted takeover to the extent that it couldn't take place. What did take place was the introduction of a suite of new and diverse development, approach, and execution technologies into his company's IT environment—a legacy that the company still has trouble coping with.

Legacy Systems

Even where there are no personal objectives to influence technology decisions, legacy systems can still represent an expanding source of development and execution technologies because the production applications that are based on them have longer lives than the development, approach, and execution technologies that were utilized in their development. The culprit is legacy systems. While newer and better development, approach, and execution technologies come on the scene, and are adopted by companies for their new applications, legacy systems become the primary force that helps ensure that the older technologies upon which they are based remain in the mix. This is especially true for legacy systems that are:

- large, so that they would be time-consuming and expensive to redevelop in newer technologies,
- extensively deployed, so that many users and lots of hardware over a wide geographic region are involved,

- utilized by, or that themselves utilize, other applications throughout the organization, and that are

- interfaced with specialized technologies—such as proprietary databases, robotics or Point Of Sale(POS) devices—that other technologies cannot access.

There's an additional and compelling business reason why legacy applications tend to outlast the technologies with which they're built. The reason is that, as a result of downsizings, attrition, and inadequate documentation, many of the policies, procedures, and business rules under which our companies operate exist only in the form of our company's legacy systems. With the people who understood the myriad of business details that went into their development long gone, redeveloping core legacy applications in newer technologies not only represents a considerable expense, but also the substantial business risk that the new developers may not get it right.

As a result, many of our company's mainstream business applications have been developed in, and for the foreseeable future will continue to run in, older technologies. The resultant impact, and a significant challenge for today's developers, is that applications developed using newer technologies (such as C++ Java, and Smalltalk) will have to run, accurately and efficiently, in environments riddled with older technologies (such as COBOL, DataBase2(DB2), and Information Management System(IMS).

Release Propagation

If uncontrollable proliferation of execution, development, and approach technologies is a problem, interactions among technology releases can make things even worse. Seemingly innocent changes in a single application—an upgrade to a new release, for example—can propagate through significant portions of a company's production and application development infrastructures, leaving in their wake inconsistencies and unplanned-for changes, and the need for new development and execution technologies. At the root of the problem is the combination of the growing numbers of different technologies required to develop and run today's applications and the interdependencies among different releases of each technology.

To illustrate how this works, consider what can happen when a business unit upgrades a purchased application to a release that provides additional functionality that it now requires, to handle a new type of product, or to satisfy a new regulation. (See Fig. 6.6.) So far, there's no apparent problem, except that the upgrade was developed around a newer version of the middleware product it utilizes to access

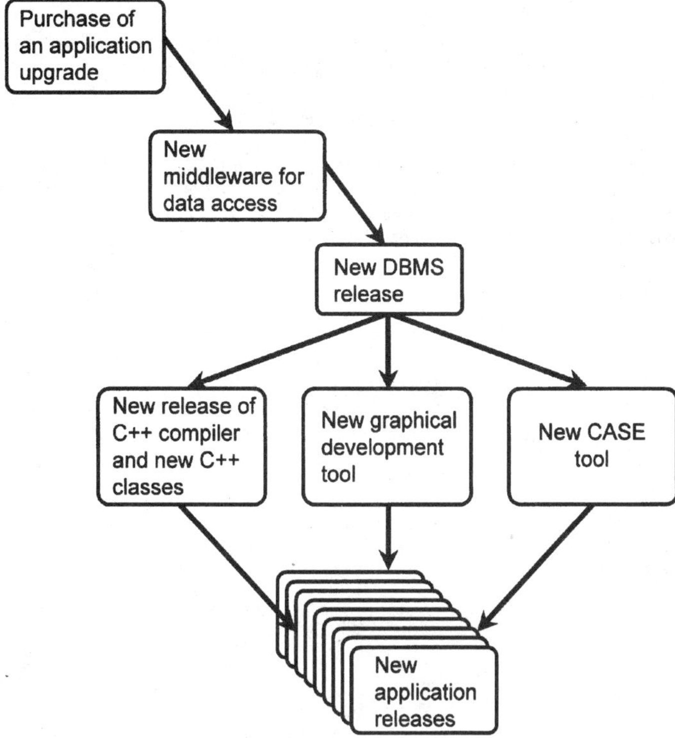

Figure 6.6 How release propagation increases technology proliferation.

its database. The new middleware product can, in turn, require an upgrade to the database, which may not be fully compatible with existing releases of C++ compilers, class libraries, graphical application development tools, CASE-based code generators—or even the existing applications that they were used to develop.

But the company may have neither the time, resources, or business justification to redevelop the existing applications utilizing the new C++ compiler, graphical tool, or CASE-based code generator. And it may not be prepared to withstand the additional risks and delays in current application development projects that would be encountered if the projects switched, in midstream, to new versions of their development tools. When this happens, the typical result is simultaneous implementation of multiple versions along with the multiple technologies that they represent. The impact is that application developers must simultaneously deal with more development and execution technologies, which aggravates the effects of time compressed change.

References

1. Although this statement is contradictory, as VisualAge is IBM's implementation of Smalltalk—a thoroughly OO language—I have heard it many times. I believe that this statement personifies a common misperception that a company can seek refuge from the time compressed onslaught of new approaches and technologies by casting its lot with a single, dominant, vendor.
2. Maximis has since been sold to Premier Solutions, Ltd., a company that, although not part of Texas Instruments, has retained the product's IEF-based development and execution technology architectures. For other products that are similarly built around IEF, see Texas Instruments' "Software Referral Catalog."

Time Compression Management—A Framework of Strategies and Techniques for Developing Successful Applications in a Time Compressed Changing Technology Environment

Time Compression Management

In the first six chapters, we explored many reasons why application development, despite its increasing criticality to late-1990s business and significant advances in information technologies, has tenaciously remained an uncertain and error-prone process. We also examined the ravaging effects that time compressed changes have had on the application development process in today's rapidly expanding and evolving development, approach, and execution information technologies and on the increasing numbers of people whose corporate lives are impacted by application development. Indeed, it is my firm belief that companies that are not able to successfully master large-scale application development within the harsh realities that today's time compressed business and technology environments represent, and are thus not able to make application development a reliable business process, will become less and less competitive as we close out the 1990s and push forward into the twenty-first century.

But solving the multitude of problems that accompany time compressed application development is neither simple nor certain. Nor can such problems be quickly addressed by business units, or the IT organizations that support them. This is especially true in large-scale corporate environments, in which business needs are subtle and complex, entrenched organizations and infrastructure are resistant to change, the development process has become politicized, and cultural conflict is rampant. Nevertheless, the job must be tackled.

For companies to make it into the next century as vital organizations in an increasingly competitive world economy, their ability to develop business applications must be improved. And, if they are to be effective in our time compressed business and technology environments, the improvements that are made must be as viable as they are far-reaching in what they accomplish.

TCM and Its Four Components

Time Compression Management is a simple, holistic approach for helping managers to successfully address the multitude of problems associated with today's application development. TCM is not a "silver bullet." TCM doesn't provide pat answers. Nor does TCM offer easy solutions. TCM does present a comprehensive set of strategies and techniques that are implementable by business and IT managers in their real-world large-scale corporate environments. Its objective is reliable and predictable application development for large-scale business systems, fortified to withstand the sometimes radical changes and shifts that mark today's changing technology environments.

Each of the TCM components address a different facet of today's application development challenges, so that the following five CSFs are achieved[1]: (See Fig. 7.1.)

- *Broadness:* TCM must be broad enough to address application development within each of the company's environments that will be impacted by it.

- *Business Focus:* TCM must be business-focused, so that its results have a measurable and positive impact on the business that IT is chartered to support.

- *Cohesiveness:* The initiatives in each TCM component must function together, as a cohesive whole, so that they don't conflict with one another or lead the organization in inconsistent directions, and so that the entire effort makes sense to business and IT management.

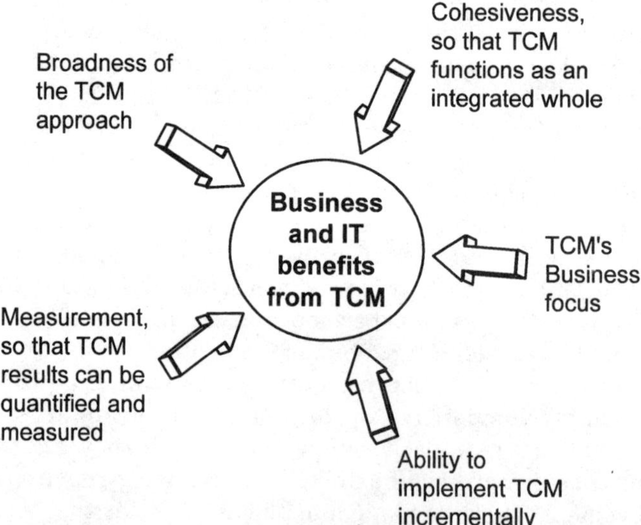

Figure 7.1   The five CSFs for TCM's business and IT benefits.

■ *Incremental Implementation:* TCM must be implementable in phases—a little at a time, so that obvious problems with big payoffs can be picked off early, risk can be managed, and that the entire initiative can be made self-funding so that each phase can provide incremental ROI to the business.

■ *Measurement:* TCM initiatives must be measurable, so that their impact can be quantified, and the quantified results utilized to optimize TCM for the organization's specific needs.

Business Focus

It's tempting to believe that introduction of new and better technologies will have a positive business impact commensurate with their added capabilities and reduced costs. But experience shows that this isn't always so. Although the benefits and reduced costs that new technologies bring are generally real, their impact often stops within IT, never making it across to the business. As we saw in Chap. 6, technology orientation resulting from a combination of personal objectives, technical improvement initiatives, and entrepreneurial spirit can all too easily get in the way.

For TCM to be effective as a corporate framework for channeling the benefits of new technologies, along with the multiple-technology environment they create, to benefit business, it must have a business focus. For this to become a reality:

■ TCM's objectives must be couched in terms of demonstrable business benefit—TCM's, and hopefully IT's, ultimate goal,

■ TCM must be broad enough to address not only IT's composition, in terms of parameters such as organization, process, and infrastructure, but business's composition as well, and perhaps most importantly,

■ TCM must address the complex interactions between IT and business.

If these CSFs aren't achieved, TCM runs a strong risk of joining a host of other thoughtful and well-meaning initiatives, that may have helped IT but did little for business.[2]

Broadness

Today's large-scale companies are complex entities, in which many parts of their organizations and infrastructures can be impacted by changes in application development. Seemingly isolated changes in development technology, for example, can impact not only the IT developers who use the technology, but also the company's IT and business cultures, their processes and infrastructures, and the way they interact. In some cases, introduction of new development, approach, and execution technologies can impact the way an entire business unit conducts (or can't conduct) business. Introduction of an OO technology, such as C++, without an appropriate infrastructure—such as reusable object administration, OO methodology, development tools, standards and reporting procedures—that are capable of supporting high-productivity OO development, will not yield good results. Nor will the applications it produces be successful unless they can function within the company's business and production technology environments. Even with a robust and appropriate infrastructure in place, and applications capable of functioning flawlessly within their intended environments, the initiative stands a good chance of failing if the company's IT and business cultures aren't open to accept it, or if the initiative can't demonstrate sufficient ROI to the business.

Consider what happened to a West Coast software company, when it tried to utilize object-oriented Smalltalk as the development technology for its new product's user interface. The concept was right. By going to Smalltalk, they would not only develop their user interface more quick-ly, but their user interface software would run on Windows and OS/2 workstations—an important requirement, based on the diverse array of workstations installed at their customers' sites. Their management bought into it, the project was funded, and a staff of 10 Smalltalk designers and programmers went to work on the new user interface.

The initial prototypes were quick and good, bolstering everyone's confidence in their decision to go to Smalltalk, a decision that a substantial number of their staff was proud to have played a part in making. But when 6 months had gone by, with nothing to show but the initial prototypes, their management became concerned that something might be wrong. And 3 months after that, with half of the project's Smalltalk programmers having left "to seek better opportunities," the remaining half looking to leave, a horde of furious customers at the company's doorstep, and still no interface to show for the project's effort, management became convinced that they were in deep trouble. In the frantic atmosphere that ensued, everything was questioned, especially the competency of the project's manager, his future with the company, and their collective decision to go to Smalltalk—a decision that, at the moment, not a single person was willing to own up to. Tempers flared, and irate managers stormed out of meetings. In short, they had a full-scale application development disaster.

Although their disaster was real, it was not caused by the decision to go to Smalltalk—which was, in fact, the optimal implementation technology for developing the company's new multitechnology user interface. Nor was it caused by the programmers who had abandoned the project, or the project's manager. At the root of the problem was a set of chasms between the Smalltalk developers' needs and the rest of the company's organization, culture, and infrastructure, that no one was able to cross. Many of the user interface's requirements, for example, were expressed in terms of a detailed data model that had been painstakingly refined over many years to support development using information engineering-based CASE. Requirements not expressed in the data model were represented as static interface prototypes that looked good on paper, but provided little insight into the *behavior* of the visual objects they contained. As the project's Business Analyst, who had never developed an OO event-driven system with a graphical interface, didn't understand the need for detailed interface requirements, and had no OO methodology to guide him in performing the necessary analysis, it simply wasn't done.

The result was a baffled team of programmers, who had been imported from the Philippines to implement the application "at a greatly reduced cost," who had considerable Smalltalk expertise, but who knew little about data models and even less about how the ill-defined visual objects should behave. As stopping progress to ask detailed questions about what they were expected to do was not a part of their culture, they silently charged ahead on a best-guess basis, filling in the gaps as well as they could by making the necessary business decisions along the way. Although the team delivered working programs, what they delivered contained only a fraction of the interface functionality that was expected, and the functionality that was delivered wasn't usable by the company's customers.

The point is that narrow, sharply focused approaches don't work. Without taking new requirements, infrastructure, and culture into account, the introduction of new technologies—such as event-driven programming and Smalltalk—almost universally leads to disaster, even though the technology choice might be right. In today's complex business organizations, with lots of sources for technology and application development, and with copious amounts of political capital tied to each, introduction of development, approach, or execution technology can be a fragile and uncertain endeavor. In an era of rapid time compressed technology change, for TCM to work, it must be broad enough to take the issues and needs of each of these areas are taken into account.

Cohesiveness

TCM's broadness, while necessary, is not without risk. Indeed, a significant risk resulting from TCM's broadness, a risk that must be addressed for TCM to add consistent value over time as a business tool, is that TCM's different components have the potential to lead a company's IT and business organizations in different and conflicting directions.

A robust development support infrastructure, for example, is an important requisite for application development involving new and multiple technologies to work. The same infrastructure, however, can become an insurmountable problem if it isn't consistent with business cost cutting objectives, or if the business cannot see a near-term return on the investment that it represents. Propagation of project personnel with recently acquired new technology skills throughout IT and business organizations so that the technology can spread and a broad cross section of the company can benefit from it is also important. But for the new technology to be successful, its propagation must not conflict with the equally important requirement that the developers who are learning the technology be able to complete a number of development projects with it—so that they can climb the S-shaped technology adoption curve and technology initiative can be made to pay off.[3]

TCM can be effective in a large-scale corporate environment only to the extent that it addresses and resolves these kinds of conflicts between its components and their constituents.

Incremental Implementation

Among the harsher corporate realities of conducting business in today's increasingly competitive global economy, are that initiatives are being subjected to increased levels of scrutiny. Consequently, of the many worthy initiatives presented to business and IT management, only a few are funded. A corollary to this sometimes unwelcome truth is that during business down turns, when times are tough, only initiatives that are obviously successful and that give back more than to the business than they take are likely to be left intact. Indeed, there's little tolerance among today's businesses for initiatives that require substantial investments over long periods of time before they (hopefully) come to fruition and pay their sponsors back. This is especially true among initiatives involving IT, as they have a collective history of questionable payback, high cost, and substantial risk.

For TCM—a complex, long-range, and costly IT and business initiative to succeed—and in many organizations, just to be seriously considered TCM must provide its sponsors with incremental return on the substantial political, cultural, and monetary investments that it represents. The obvious solution is for TCM to provide fast incremental return on these investments, and to the extent it is possible, be made self-funding so that most of the investment that TCM represents can come from the business and IT benefits that it generates. By dividing TCM's implementation into a series of incremental initiatives, and targeting problems that provide a high ROI first, each successive TCM initiative can be made to require less investment than the initiative that preceded it until no incremental investment is required at all. (See Fig. 7.2.)

Measurement

For TCM's incremental ROI to work, the benefits that it generates must be demonstrable to its business and IT sponsors in terms of predictable, measurable and understandable results. Without the means to predict, measure, and compare the outcome of TCM initiatives, measuring the benefits of each TCM initiative so that it can be applied to offset the cost of the next would not be possible. Neither would organizations be able to make rational decisions regarding which TCM initiatives to implement, or how best to implement them in their companies. Indeed, without the ability to predict and measure TCM's impact, implementation of its initiatives would, in most organizations, be left to intuition and happenstance.

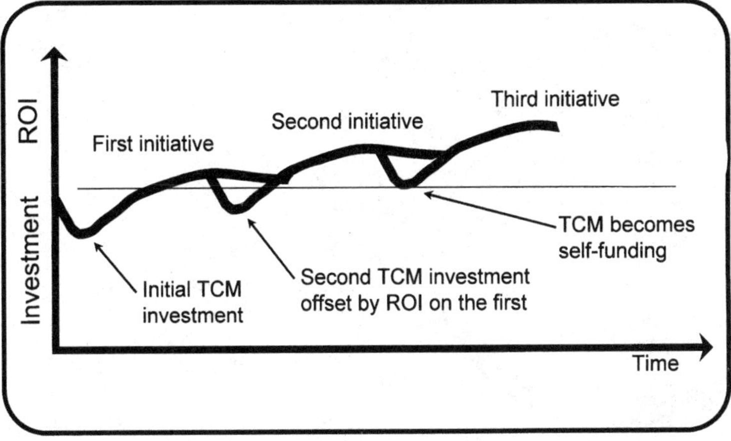

Figure 7.2 How TCM can become self-funding through a series of high-ROI initiatives.

But implementing TCM measurement implies that organizations have a consistent understanding of what application development effectiveness means, that they have metrics and procedures to measure it, that they have consistent and reliable baseline data so that they can make before and after measurements, and that IT and business stakeholders in the development process believe in the measurements and their results. Achieving this kind of measurement isn't easy. For example, complications, such as rapidly evolving organizational, business, and IT environments thwart the process. Making consistent before-and-after measurements, in a world of changing business practices, reorganizations, business process reengineering, and wildly changing new and legacy technologies would be like making sense out of baseball statistics over a period of years while the numbers of players on teams is changing, various kinds of bats and balls are used by different sets of players in different games, and the umpires are constantly changing the locations of the bases.

Although this CSF is not an easy one to address, and is especially difficult to achieve in most large-scale corporate environments, its achievement is necessary for TCM is to be a success.

TCM Components

TCM is comprised of the following four basic components: (See Fig. 7.3.)

- a culture that can deal effectively with multiple and changing development, approach, and execution technologies,

- an IT infrastructure fortified to cope with a time compressed technology environment,

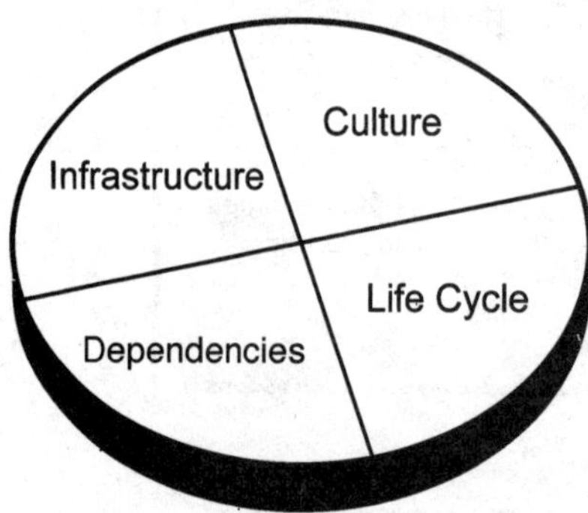

Figure 7.3 The four components of TCM.

- a component that insulates critical application dependencies from the effects of time compressed change, and

- an IT life cycle that's optimized for change rather than for a fixed suite of technologies.

TCM Culture Component

A colleague, and one of the most successful application developers that I know, when asked to name the top three problems causing the high rate of failure that continues to plague large-scale application development projects, replied "people, people and people."[4] He went on to explain that, in his experience, development projects didn't fail because the technologies didn't work, because the approaches weren't appropriate, or because the problems weren't solvable. They failed—and continue to fail—due to a combination of underlying problems involving organization, expectation, orientation, skills, objectives, compensation, motivation, and management. These are, of course, cultural issues—issues that are among the most recalcitrant, time-consuming and difficult to address. This is especially true for IT organizations, that tend to be technology- rather than people-oriented, and that therefore have a tough time grappling with these cultural and people-oriented issues.

For TCM to add real value to large-scale application development in today's time compressed changing technology environments, so that it has a positive and measurable impact on the way application development supports our businesses, it must address these kinds of cultural issues. Indeed, TCM must address them in such a way that the culture that results helps fortify our IT organizations against the havoc wreaked by our constantly evolving multitechnology development environments. This is a significant task—one that requires a distinct component comprising a full quarter of what TCM is, what it does and how it works.

The objective of this component is to help companies to reorient away from cultures that have been carefully optimized over many years to support centralized development utilizing a fixed set of technologies to support a static set of business requirements, to new cultures that are optimized to support decentralized development utilizing multiple and constantly evolving sets of technologies to support today's changing business requirements. To accomplish this objective, TCM's culture component will address a wide variety of people and cultural issues, including:

- reorientation away from away from technology and toward business,

- broad competencies in many different development, approach, and execution technologies,

- dual career paths, fostering combinations of business and technology skills,

- better collaboration among developer and business peers, and

- a framework for technology empowerment to ensure that the numbers and kinds of ITs don't get out of hand without throttling the autonomy of our empowered business users.

TCM Infrastructure Component

A prime consequence of developing applications in a multiple and evolving technology environment is the need for a constantly evolving development support infrastructure. As development, approach, and execution technologies evolve and change, so do their support requirements, in terms of things like:

- project management strategies and techniques, that are geared to multiple development projects, each with an evolving set of technologies,

- methodologies that are built around changing technology environments,

- CASE tools that are designed to support methodologies that are built around change, and

- a reuse infrastructure that's optimized for multiple and evolving technologies.

When viewed as a whole, the infrastructure required to support successful development in today's time compressed technology environments is expensive and difficult to implement. It's also given short shrift by many technology vendors and consultants, who aren't prepared to allow this nasty bit of reality stand in the way of a sale, and new technology pundits who aren't fully acquainted with the vagaries of large-scale application development and the critical roles that infrastructure components play in addressing them. Approaching management, less than a year after spending several hundred thousand dollars on a new methodology and CASE tool, telling them that an equivalent amount of the company's capital must be spent yet again on this year's newer and better development technologies is, at best, a tough sell. At worst, it can cost jobs and damage careers. But developing applications without the benefit of an appropriate infrastructure, or developing the infrastructure in parallel with the first set of applications that utilize it—an alarmingly common practice—can be even tougher. It too can cost jobs and damage careers. The purpose of the TCM infrastructure component is to help businesses and their IT organizations to address this pervasive "catch 22" dilemma.

The infrastructure component, like the culture component, makes up a quarter of the TCM approach. And like each of the other TCM components, the infrastructure component tackles the problem, not from the vantage point of technologies or their vendors, but from the vantage point of IT and business units that have to utilize multiple and evolving technologies to develop large-scale applications that fulfill their business's mission objectives.

TCM Dependency Component

One of the areas in which time compressed change exacts its largest, and least expected, toll is in the way it impacts dependencies among application development infrastructure and process components. Developing successful large and mission-critical applications in a multiple and changing technology environment requires, not only that the components of our development environment be right, but that they be able to function together as a cohesive whole. This is difficult to achieve in a traditional monolithic development environment, and a lot harder when the many of the technologies are in a constant state of flux. The dependency component, which also takes up a quarter of TCM, addresses critical dependencies among:

- application layers (the layers with the user interface and business logic) and support layers (the layers containing the common services—such as data access—that support the application);

- life cycle phases—the subtle and far-reaching effects that different development, approach, and execution technologies that are in different portions of their life cycles have on each another; and

- horizontal dependencies—dependencies between applications, that show up as systems that don't fully interoperate with one another, and as systems that encounter trouble accessing each other's data.

TCM Life Cycle Component

The final TCM component addresses the technology life cycle—the process that defines how we identify and acquire new technologies, how they we manage them as they run the course of their useful lives, and eventually, how we discard them. In the relatively static technology environments of the past three decades, our technology life cycles were carefully optimized to manage the constant trickle of new development, approach, and execution technologies of an earlier era. Now, if we are to manage in our current and future environments, in which new ITs come and go at ever faster rates, we must reengineer our technology life cycle process so that they're once more optimized—to handle time compressed change.

In this component, we examine what the new, reengineered life cycle has to do, along with the CSFs that must be in place for it to succeed. We then explore a new life cycle, based on acquisition, communication, management, and connectivity components, that are optimized to support time compressed change.

Implementing TCM

Understanding and buying into TCM is easy. Implementing TCM in a real-world organization, so that it's successfully adopted and provides measurable benefit, can be a lot more difficult. In terms of implementation, perhaps the most important thing to understand about TCM, is that *TCM is not an all-or-nothing approach*. Although presented as a whole, so that its components can be seen together and understood as a comprehensive and holistic solution to time compressed change, it is not necessary that TCM be implemented all at once. Indeed, doing so would be too wrenching for most large-scale organizations to accept, and in some cases, too risky for their management to even try.[5]

The strategies and techniques contained in each of TCM's components should therefore be adopted, as required, commensurate with the organization's needs, ability to change, and tolerance for risk. Some components may be implementable as wholes. Others may be utilized as concepts and approaches to be included in development reengineering initiatives that are already under way. This approach will provide a framework for fitting TCM into each company's individual needs, and provide its management with an incremental return on its TCM investment.

References

1. For an in-depth discussion of CSFs and their application, see Nancy S. Foster and John F. Rockart, "Critical Success Factors: An Annotated Bibliography, "MIT CISR (Massachusetts Institute ofTechnology, Center for Information System Research) Working Paper No. 191, June 1989.
2. Many such initiatives have been tried over the years. For a couple of good examples, along with insight into why technology-oriented solutions don't work, see James Martin's trilogy, *Information Engineering*, Prentice-Hall, 1990; James Martin, *Rapid*

Application Development, Macmillan, 1991; and Paul Strassmann, *The Business Value of Computers,* The Information Economics Press, 1988.

3. Chris Kemerer, "How the Learning Curve Affects CASE Tool Adoption," *IEEE Software,* May 1992.

4. Interview with Steve Fogarty, President of Sextant Business Solutions, Ltd. who related and underscored this concept, which was introduced to him by Bernard Donefer, CIO of DKB Data Services USA, Inc.

5. As time compressed technology change cannot be throttled or stopped, there are often more adoption problems and risks in not implementing TCM in many organizations than in implementing it. Although implementing TCM represents a proactive approach to an inevitable problem, the fact that it is a proactive approach gives it more visibility—and with the visibility, perceived cost and risk—than limiting technology management to damage control as time compressed change runs its inevitable course.

8

Reengineering Culture for Time Compression Management

It was early May, and as far as Donna was concerned, it was going to be a glorious Northwest spring. For the fifth month in a row, each weekly status report had conveyed the same unmistakable message: that her C++ implementation team was holding its own, still slightly ahead of schedule. They were midway through acceptance testing of her project's second phase—the critical phase that her business users were counting on for an important initiative—and her system was passing each test. Although her implementers were still putting in over 10 hours on a typical day, there was no animosity or discontent. Each knew that the team was headed for a successful on-time finish, and with it, his or her share in the substantial economic benefit that would result from their company being first to market with an innovative new product.

Things hadn't always been so glorious. Indeed, it was just a little over a year ago when three of her remaining six C++ programmers stormed into her office to deal the death blow to her already crippled project, letting her know that they would be leaving in 2 weeks for greener pastures at a near-by competitor. They were fed up with the project's "sophisticated OO-framework" that handled all the interesting work, leaving them with the mundane and unrewarding tasks of "wiring prefabricated objects together" to produce their application. What was particularly galling to the group's leader—a bright and talented programmer with extensive experience in Windows and C—was that the project's "sophisticated" infrastructure was holding him back, preventing him from building the highly touted interfaces and slick algorithms that he knew he could develop, that he had so successfully developed in the past, that were the venue through which he could show his stuff. He had taken the position to learn object technology and expand his C expertise into C++, so that he could command more money in the burgeoning OO job market. But in less than 2 weeks, the three programmers would begin plying their newfound skills in a less sophisticated environment, where their prerogatives would be respected and their user interface and design expertise would be put to "more productive use."

What transpired between the tumultuous time when the last group of sophisticated but disgruntled programmers stormed into her office to leave her troubled project, and the project being brought to a successful conclusion by a group of uniformly enthusiastic developers? Where does the cultural strife, that seems to go hand-in-hand with our rapidly evolving and proliferating information technologies, come from? How can it be managed? or better yet, turned into a positive force? How can management deal effectively with the frenzied developer job markets that our hot new technologies create? How can an IT organization develop and maintain a business focus?

The answers to these questions, along with strategies for dealing with their underlying route cause cultural issues, are the subjects of this chapter. But before we proceed, we need to take a closer look at the differences between the rapid rate of time compressed technology change and the comparatively slow rate of cultural change, along with their implications in terms of how we can address these issues.

Technology Proliferation and Cultural Change

One of the most striking facets of late-1990s IT is the juxtaposition of the rapid rate of time compressed technology proliferation and change, and the ponderous pace at which our cultures struggle to respond. The resulting conundrum, and a major challenge to those who must manage our IT functions during the late 1990s and into the next century, is that:

> While new and multiple technologies, which arrive at an exponential rate, demand cultural changes at an exponential rate, cultural changes in real-world companies take place ponderously slowly—at a linear rate.

The natural and predictable result is that many IT functions find themselves moving swiftly through several generations of new and evolving technologies while their organizations' cultures struggle in vain to respond to the first. Although a number of the required cultural changes, such as abstract modeling, evolutionary deliverables, and increased business user involvement, may be common to a number of new technologies, many cultural changes are not. And, as the numbers of new technologies increase at exponential rates (an inevitable by-product of time compressed change), the resultant multiple-technology environments can easily wind up vying against each other to pull already strained cultures in different and inconsistent directions, at exponential rates commensurate with the technologies that are the sources of the impact.

For example: Graphical Client/Server development tools, such as PowerBuilder, are built around data, and consequently pull their developers and business users toward a combination of data models and series' of interface prototypes as metaphors for describing business requirements. But equally graphical Client/Server tools, such as VisualAge Smalltalk, that are built around objects, pull their developers and business users away from data and toward a combination of object modeling, interfaces, and use cases as their metaphors for expressing business requirements. The objectives are the same, but the business user involvement and cultural impact could hardly be more different.

The underlying problem is not so much that different technologies pull our cultures in different and inconsistent directions, but that the exponential rate at which the pulling takes place. Our IT, business, and management cultures simply can't respond to these forces at anything like an exponential rate. The management result is a technology culture gap between the exponential rate at which technologies impact our cultures and the slow linear rate at which our cultures can respond—a gap that itself increases at an exponential rate, and that managers find extremely difficult to control. (See Fig. 8.1.)

My experiences in working with companies, as they grapple with this technology culture gap, my belief, and the major theme of this chapter, is that our most effective recourse is to reengineer our cultures so that they're less sensitive to, more open to accept, and more inclined to support the coming technology changes, regardless of their origins or rates. To the extent that this can be achieved, the result will be a markedly reduced need for cultural change brought about by new and proliferating technologies. Although the culture gap in most organizations cannot be made to disappear, and the exponential-to-linear relationship of technology to cultural change will remain a late-1990s through early 2000s fact of life, the magnitude of the gap can be decreased so that it becomes manageable in terms of achievable rates of cultural change. (See Fig. 8.2.) To the extent that this can be made to happen, everyone wins.

To make it happen, we'll address cultural reengineering in terms of five key management, business, and IT cultural elements that are

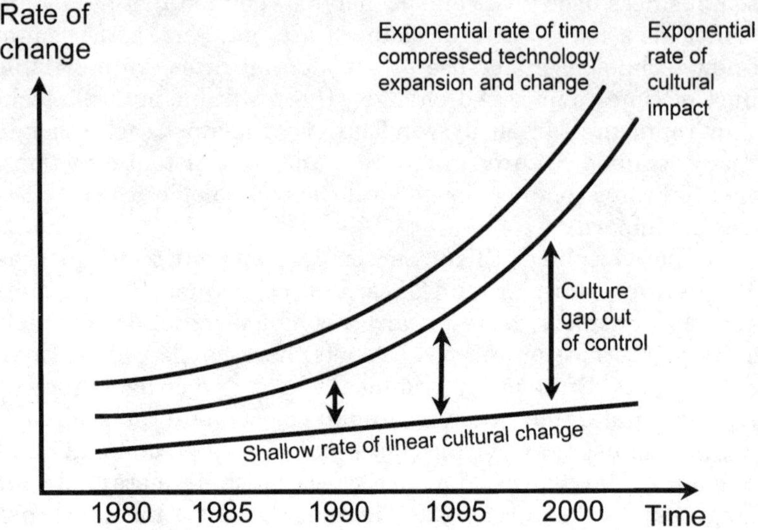

Figure 8.1   Need for time compressed cultural reengineering.

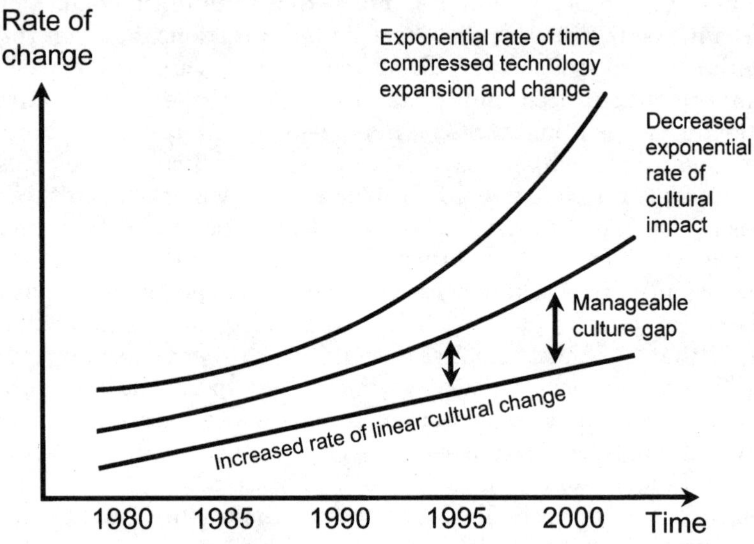

Figure 8.2   Result of time compressed cultural reengineering.

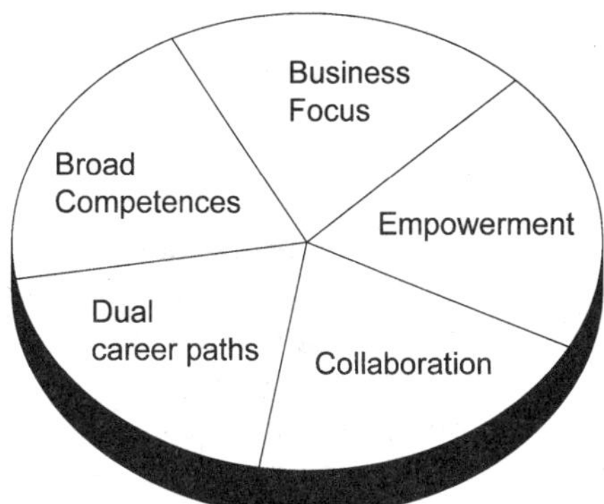

Figure 8.3 Five key cultural elements that are
required to lower sensitivity to time compressed technology change.

required to lower sensitivity to time compressed technology change.
(See Fig. 8.3.) The TCM's cultural CSFs are:

- *Business Focus:* Reorienting IT culture away from technology, so
  that technology prowess becomes secondary to business results;

- *Dual Career Paths:* A career path for people with combinations of
  business and IT skills and who want to focus on applying IT to
  solve business problems and opportunities, and a smaller highly
  technical career path for those who are more oriented toward the
  technologies themselves;

- *Better Collaboration:* Promoting meaningful collaboration among
  all business and technical individuals who are associated with
  application development; and

- *Technology Empowerment:* Ensuring that individual business units
  remain empowered to choose the best information technologies for
  their needs.

We'll examine each of these elements in terms of what it is, why it's
important for lowering our cultural sensitivity to time compressed
technology change, and in terms of what's required to achieve it.

Business Focus

It's ironic and unfortunate that although many of our newest development technologies are pushing IT cultures away from technology and
toward business—a trend that's acknowledged by the numerous articles and books on business focus and alignment—many of our deepest

and most disruptive disputes arise over technology. And when IT factions focus on and clash over the merits of one information technology versus the next—OO versus Data, CASE versus manual analysis, Smalltalk versus C++, Windows 95 versus UNIX—the loser is almost always the business, regardless of who may be wrong or right. If we are to support our businesses, so that IT reaches its potential as a meaningful contributor to competitiveness in our global economy, we must be able to rise above these kinds of concerns, and the turf wars that they fuel. Ultimately, the extent to which we'll be able to extricate ourselves from these kinds of issues will depend on our IT organizations' ability to implement cultures that are business-oriented and that focus most of their efforts on business support instead of on technology.

At the most basic level, a business-focused culture is one in which the primary focus of IT practitioners is oriented toward business, so that the development technologies, execution technologies and approaches we employ are means to ends rather than ends in themselves. Although implementation of such a culture can take as many forms as there are companies, business cultures, organizations and needs, for a business-oriented IT culture to succeed, the following basic characteristics must be present:

- broad-based business and technology skills,

- communications tools, along with interpersonal and communications skills,

- identification with, enthusiasm for, and knowledge about, the company and its business, and

- loyalty to the company, long-term commitment and low turnover.

For IT to contribute as a full business partner, the employees who populate our IT organizations must develop proficient business skills along with a good understanding of their company's business and the forces that affect it. Information technology practitioners who have an interest in, and grasp of, the business that they seek to support, will be much better positioned to harness the correct technologies to address the right business problems than those who don't.

The reverse of this basic principle is also true. For business users to derive substantial benefit from IT, they must become discerning consumers of IT, so that they can play active roles in ensuring that the right suite of technologies are brought to bear on their specific suite of problems—just as they do when dealing with manufacturing plants, distribution, financial instruments, or logistics. To illustrate why things go wrong when IT and business personnel aren't at least partially conversant in each other's disciplines, consider the following two examples, one from manufacturing, and the other from financial services.

Fast MRP can be an extremely effective business tool for optimizing a manufacturing company's logistics management in real time, as its business environment changes. It permits the company to quickly run alternate planning scenarios in response to sudden unforeseen events—such as an extremely large order, a late delivery or a product change—and to choose among the scenarios for the optimal response. But the benefits of real-time logistics management can be achieved only if the company's business users understand, and are comfortable with, the underlying technologies (fast, very large memory, RISC-based processors) that are required to decrease day-long MRP runs down to a few minutes, so that the alternate scenarios can be completed quickly enough to be of use.

If the company's business users are sufficiently comfortable with IT and have enough understanding to actively champion new software on RISC-based processors over older tried-and-true mainframe-based MRP systems, and to enforce the common data definitions and stewardship, fast MRP—and with it, real-time enterprise logistics management (ELM)—can work. Without this kind of understanding and active sponsorship, fast MRP and ELM are likely to remain interesting technical and strategic concepts; unimplemented, and with the business receiving no real benefit.[1]

Successful implementation of ELM also depends on the company's IT organization's ability to understand the importance and depth of the supply chain problems that ELM addresses, so that they are willing to seek, learn, and implement the suite of new technologies that are often required to interface the RISC-based servers and software to the rest of the company's logistics systems. Business and IT personnel must possess good interdisciplinary skills if ELM is to work.

Although the industry couldn't be more different, characteristics-based trading software presents a strikingly similar picture for companies that deal with constantly changing financial instruments. Although software that treats financial instruments as composites of financial instrument characteristics has been around for some time, and has been leveraged to great advantage in a number of companies, the idea continues to meet with substantial resistance from business and IT organizations.[2] Business users, who don't understand software engineering processes in which applications are developed from business models, and who are uncomfortable with the abstract nature of the models that characteristics-based software is based on, often kill such projects out of fear that they're too risky and won't work. Information Technology practitioners, who don't fully grasp the nature of the business data and transactions that make up the business problem, kill the projects out of unfounded fear that characteristics-based applications won't perform. I've personally witnessed each of these problems in three different companies, with the same set of fears and frustrations, and with the same results.

Regardless of the industry, or the specifics of its needs, the message is substantially the same. Companies will leverage time compressed information technology change for their late-1990s businesses only to the extent that a good mix of business and technology skills are present. As business challenges increase, and demand IT solutions that are more subtle, far-reaching, and complex, the IT solutions become implementable only to the extent that: business users understand and are comfortable with the technologies, and that IT practitioners understand and are more comfortable with the business.

As by-products of this kind of bilateral understanding, two significant changes occur. The first is that the range of technology solutions broadens to include not only the tried and true technologies that may have served the company in the past, but new and innovative technologies—such as fast RISC-based servers and characteristics-based modeling—that once mastered, can provide better solutions for the business. The second important change is that the company's business users become desensitized to the merits and risks associated with specific technologies for satisfying their business requirements. This change enables them to regard information technologies as a level playing field so that each technology can be evaluated on its merits as an enabler of business solutions. Without reasonable amounts of technology skills and competencies, business users don't have a basis for objectively evaluating the increasing numbers of competing information technologies that, as the century comes to a close, will profoundly impact their ability to remain competitive, and in some cases, even conduct business.

The result is a cultural change; a shift in focus, away from specific technologies that people might favor, that may have worked at a previous company, or that may might have caused problems in the past, toward the business, its challenges, and the suite of IT that can best meet them. An important key to achieving a business focus, so that time compressed changes in development, approach, and execution technologies can be harnessed to support the business, is a reasonable mix of business and technology skills on everyone's part. (See Fig. 8.4.)

Given the criticality of this CSF, how can it be achieved? How does one go about developing a reasonable mix of business and technology skills among IT practitioners and business users in a real-world corporate environment? Although this question probably has as many answers as there are companies and cultures, there are a number of fundamental initiatives that can go a long way toward helping a company to achieve a good business and technology skill mix. They are:

- training and individual mentoring programs for IT professionals in business skills, so that IT personnel can acquire the business

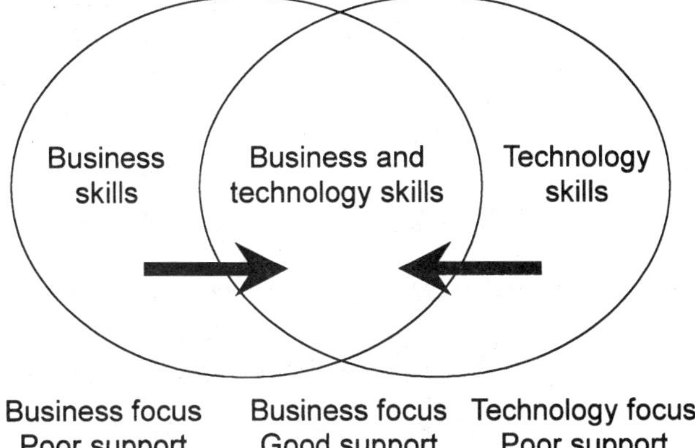

Figure 8.4 A mix of business and technology skills on everyone's part for good business support.

knowledge and terminology needed to understand their business peers and the origins of the pressures that they face;

- rotations of IT practitioners through the business units they serve, so that the people who analyze business requirements and develop applications gain first-hand experience with the business's objectives, problems, strategies and constraints;

- seminars and workshops for business users, in information technologies, emphasizing their strengths, weaknesses, requirements, scalability issues, and the learning curves required to put them to use; and

- implementation of project-oriented application development teams composed of business users, business analysts and technical members, with singular sponsorship and continuity throughout the development process.

But broad-based competencies in business information technologies on everyone's part, however necessary, isn't sufficient. Achieving an understanding of, and comfort level with, the increasing array of ITs that we find at our doorsteps will do little to help achieve a business focus unless we also learn to communicate. To achieve a business focus, in which the right suite of technologies are harnessed to support our businesses, two communications CSFs must be achieved. The first is that the ideas, initiatives, needs, sensitivities, and constraints that make up what we loosely refer to as "business requirements" have to be on the table, so that the business and IT personnel who are involved with application development have an accurate and consistent understanding of what must be accomplished. The second communications CSF is open and accurate discussions on the constantly changing technologies, initiatives, requirements, and constraints that make up our IT environments.

Achieving these communications CSF, and developing the necessary skills so that business ideas, needs, sensitivities and constraints can be communicated in a ways that everyone can understand them, requires that:

- application developers become conversant with the vocabulary of the business units they support,

- technology-independent metaphors be adopted for expressing business requirements and IT solutions,

- business-based metaphors be adopted for communicating technology requirements and constraints to the business, and that

- IT practitioners increase their competencies in listening, and in making themselves understood.

In an era of increasing business complexity and specialization, application developers can expect to experience corresponding increases in problems communicating with the businesses they support. Indeed, many will not be able to communicate consistently and effectively with their business peers unless they're able to understand and adopt the working vocabulary of their business units. For example, developers of applications for financial services companies will need to understand the terminology associated with portfolio management, trade processing, money transfers, and financial instruments. Developers of manufacturing applications won't be able to fully understand their business peers if they cannot converse with them in terms of the same manufacturing processes, logistics, and total quality terminology that the company's manufacturing people use to plan and run their operations.

Achieving competency, among application developers, in their business's vocabulary requires the following three basics: business terminology training, low turnover, and industry experience. Although they seem obvious, their implementation in most companies remains as elusive as the communications that they are required to facilitate. Indeed, the hiring and downsizing policies in many companies thwart, rather than promote, their achievement.

The good news is that facilitating the adoption of a business vocabulary isn't difficult. Courses for IT practitioners in business terminology, supplemented by hands-on exposure to business practices can provide IT organizations with a business perspective that most do not have today. By altering downsizing policies, so that they promote retention of application developers who have experience with and understanding of the business, instead of making it attractive for such people to leave, far better communications will almost always result. The gains provided through more appropriately targeted downsizings can then be supplemented by reengineering hiring policies so that industry knowledge, communications skills, interpersonal skills, and business experience are given priorities, along with technical capabilities, for prospective employees who will be developing business applications.

Metaphors for expressing requirements that are business-oriented and technology-independent can also be an effective means for fostering good business to IT communications. Consider use cases. Although use cases have their origins in object technology, they can be effectively utilized to analyze and document requirements for all types of event-driven applications, regardless of their development, approach, or execution technologies.[3] Entity relationship-based data modeling, an outgrowth of relational databases, is useful in analyzing requirements for many types of applications, including OO applications that have to run in relational data environments, and can be employed to similar ends.[4] A third example of a technology-independent metaphor that can aid in communicating business requirements are the same association matrices that have been extensively utilized in information engineering-based information systems planning to analyze relationships among features, functions, data and a host of business objectives, CSFs and critical assumptions, but that have been conspicuously absent from non-IE-based development.[5] Although each of these examples represents a technology-independent tool, from a different origin, the underlying principal of a business-oriented metaphor that isn't tied to a specific technology is essentially the same.

For communicating technology initiatives, along with their benefits, requirements, issues, and constraints in terms that are understandable to the business, financial statements—in the form of income statements and balance sheets—represent valuable yet almost universally underutilized tools. The idea behind the conceptual pro forma income statement, based on the S-shaped technology adoption model presented in Chap. 4, is simple and straightforward. (See Fig. 8.5.) The basic concept is the utilization of a vehicle that business people understand and are comfortable with to express the investment and ROI associated with harnessing new technologies for productive application development.

This conceptual pro forma income statement can be easily translated into a tabular income statement, such as the pro forma OO technology adoption income statement presented below. This statement is, of course, a management income statement. It's therefore neither consistent with nor compatible with accounting income statements, and it won't do much for financial reporting. What it does do is present a

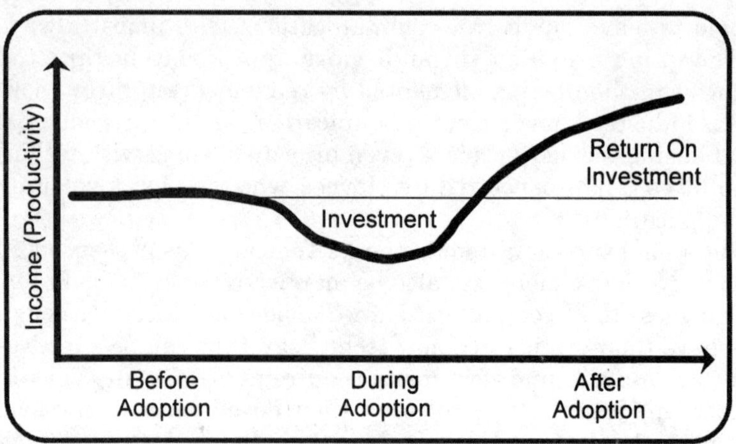

Figure 8.5 S-shaped productivity adoption curve reflected to management in terms of ROI.

quarter-by-quarter management view, in income statement format, of the most significant investment and ROI associated with adoption of an application development technology, such as OO technology, to serve the business.

Pro Forma Income Statement for OO Technology Adoption

	Q1/97	Q2/97	Q3/97	Q4/97	Q1/98	Q2/98	Q3/98	Q4/98
Development income								
Reused analysis objects								
Reused application objects								
Reused infrastructure objects								
Development costs								
Analysis objects								
Application objects								
Infrastructure objects								
Maintenance income								
Reused analysis objects								
Reused application objects								
Reused infrastructure objects								
Maintenance costs								
Analysis objects								
Application objects								
Infrastructure objects								
Gross profit from								
OO technology adoption								
Object depreciation								
Object administration								
Training and mentoring								
Monitoring and assessment								
New infrastructure								
Earnings from								
OO technology adoption								

There are many different, and equally valid, ways to utilize this tool, depending on the goals and sensitivities of the business and the specifics of the technology being adopted. In this rendition, "income" is expressed in terms of reused analysis objects (use cases and business domain objects, for example), reused application objects (such as C++ application classes and frameworks), and reused infrastructure objects (such as infrastructure frameworks that serve applications—by providing persistence, transaction processing services, security, or fault tolerance). The development income is therefore a business measure, in dollars, of OO benefit from reuse.

Development "costs" are represented as the cost of developing new analysis, application, and infrastructure objects that will be reusable by others. The quarterly figures under "development costs" therefore reflect the costs of adding the additional robustness and stability required to make objects and frameworks reusable by people who didn't develop them. "Maintenance income" and "Maintenance costs" include similar figures, but they reflect costs for maintenance of OO technology applications instead of OO technology development. The final expense items in our OO technology adoption income statement accounts for "Object depreciation" over objects' useful lives. "Object administration" includes the costs associated with maintaining and administrating the company's library of reusable objects, training, and mentoring in OO technology adoption and development, and acquisition of new infrastructure components required for OO technology, such as special CASE tools, testing tools, and an OO technology methodology. "Monitoring and assessment" accounts for the costs associated with locating and proving (or not proving) new technologies. "Earnings from OO technology adoption," the pro forma income statement's bottom line, shows the investment and ROI, associated with OO technology adoption on a quarter-by-quarter basis.

Creation of reusable objects can also be reflected as "Software assets" on a proforma OO adoption balance sheet. The idea here is that the cost and benefit of reusable analysis, application, and infrastructure objects should be amortized over the development and maintenance projects that utilize them throughout their useful lives. Depending on the company, its business needs, and its IT environment, application objects might be depreciated over a 3-year period, while longer-lasting analysis and infrastructure objects might be depreciated over 4- or 5-year periods. To complete the balance sheet, and to provide a realistic picture of how time compressed technology change can impact costs, the pro forma balance sheet might include accruals for technology evaluation and for acquisition of new technologies, so that the "Retained earnings from OO technology adoption" bottom line reflects these very real costs.

Pro Forma Balance Sheet For OO Technology Adoption

	Q1/97	Q2/97	Q3/97	Q4/97	Q1/98	Q2/98	Q3/98	Q4/98
Software assets								
Analysis object inventory								
Application object inventory								
Infrastructure object inventory								
Software liabilities								
Accrual for technology evaluation								
Accrual for next technology								
Retained earnings from OO technology adoption								

Regardless of the extent to which business and technical competencies are shared across projects, or how well business and IT peers might communicate, a business focus on the part of IT is difficult to achieve, and almost impossible to sustain, without identification with, enthusiasm for, and knowledge about the company and its business. As long as application developers consider IT to be their domain, their profession, and their primary field of expertise, the business and its needs will be relegated to second-class status. One need only look at the alarmingly high IT turnover figures on difficult and problem-filled development projects—the projects on which IT loyalty and skills are needed most—to bear this out.

The issue is that in a time compressed technology environment, lack of company loyalty and long-term commitment creates a cultural vacuum that is all too often filled by the latest whiz-bang technologies, without regard to their business benefit, but with substantial regard to the personal benefit they can bring to those developers who are expert in them. A glance at the classified ads in the employment section of most national newspapers will verify just how rewarding experience with the latest ITs can be compared to technologies that were popular just a few years before.

Although there are a number of useful tactics for addressing this problem—such as extracting personal commitments from staff to remain for the duration of a project in return for recommendations, or increased utilization of consultants—that sometimes permit managers to retain staff long enough to complete projects, the real solution is to bring compensation levels in line with market value. The key here is to tie developer compensation levels, not to whatever the latest technologies might be, but to a combination of business understanding, interpersonal and communications skills, competencies in current technologies, and ability to leverage these skills to utilize the right technologies to support the business; in other words, to reward business focus. Although compensation levels for such individuals may be higher than those of their IT peers at other companies, I believe that the difference will, in most cases, be more than offset by the combination of:

- increased business understanding among IT developers,
- better communications among IT and business peers,
- faster and more accurate analysis,
- utilization of technologies that are more appropriate for each project, and
- better continuity and lower turnover

that will result. The net cost of such individuals will be lower than the cost of their peers, who may not be paid as much, but who provide less value to the businesses they serve. We'll take a closer look at these issues when we examine dual career paths.

Broad Competencies

Although most of today's IT organizations fall short of the culture described by these TCM elements, they're critically important, and as we shall see, they're also achievable in most companies. Without broad competencies in a number of different development, approach, and execution technologies, for example, IT organizations are constrained to renditions of "one size fits all" approaches to equally broad ranges of business needs. During the 1960s, 1970s, and through the mid-1980s, this worked because there was relatively little choice. The only viable technologies for producing and running large-scale industrial-strength applications were mainframes, along with standard languages such as COBOL or C along with a few well-supported data stores. It should therefore not be surprising that our IT organizations and cultures—the organizations and cultures that, in many companies, persist today—are legacies of organizations and cultures that were developed and carefully optimized around the restrictive development paradigms of those stable decades when IT came of age.

The diversity of today's development, approach, and execution technologies stands in sharp contrast to the "one size fits all" technologies of that era. Substantial amounts of computing capacity can now be achieved through many different means, from traditional mainframe-style computers to massive parallel processors, to networked servers, to personal workstations coordinated through Linda networks. And in terms of what is to come, these different arrangements barely scratch the surface. Industrial-strength development and approach technologies are becoming equally diverse. Successful large-scale business applications are now being built by a variety of tools, from COBOL and C, to code generators, application generators, graphical development tools, and various renditions of Smalltalk, Java, and C++. And, by using object request brokers (ORBs), these diverse paradigms can be successfully mixed and matched.

If this all sounds a bit too good to be true, the reason is that it is too good to be true—not because the technologies aren't real, but because our IT cultures aren't ready to harness them or to confidently apply the right suite of technologies to the right business problems. To a large extent, the reasons why we can't do so are that we lack sufficient competencies in these diverse technologies, along with how and where each should or should not be applied to solve specific business problems. And to an equally large extent, the reasons why we lack competencies in applying the broad range of technologies available today to solve business problems is that our "one size fits all" IT cultures of another era continue to persist, throttling our efforts to do so.

The principal cultural traits that inhibit attainment of broad technology competencies include:

- lack of development organizations that are chartered to, capable of, and rewarded for, applying the right technology to the right business problem;

- lack of technology-neutral adoption paths, through which IT practitioners can become acquainted with, trained in, and experienced with new and multiple technologies on series of successively more challenging projects;

- lack of the means to identify and disseminate information on which technologies are best—and least—suited for different kinds of business problems;

- compensation structures among IT practitioners that reward deep technology expertise, but do little to recognize broad expertise, or the valuable topsight that accompanies it; and

- lack of broad competency career paths for IT practitioners, so that once having attained a broad range of competencies, people can leverage their competencies to build their careers.

Given this daunting set of cultural inhibitors to attaining broad competencies in our increasingly diverse array of development, approach, and execution technologies, our propensity to continue to pursue monolithic technology solutions to broad ranges of business opportunities and problems should not be a surprise.

The challenge is to reengineer our IT organizations and cultures so that they can attain competencies in ranges of technologies that are appropriate for the sizes and complexities of the organizations and the businesses they support, and having done so, to give incentives to IT practitioners to successfully apply the right suite of technologies to the right business problems and needs. The answer to the challenge lies in how well we can address each of these points, so that our IT organizations and cultures can leverage technological diversity to support our businesses.

But reengineering application development organizations so that they're chartered to, capable of, and rewarded for applying the right technology to the right business problem is a tricky business. For one thing, what the right technologies are for each business problem that the company has to address may not be crystal clear. Indeed, for many business requirements, more than one development, approach or execution technology may be correct, with differences representing sets of subtle tradeoffs among the complex alternatives that each represents. What can be made crystal clear are the following factors that work together to empower development organizations to utilize the right development technologies to address the right business problems. They are:

- willingness to attain competency and experience in different information technologies, along with mechanisms to propagate the competencies and experience throughout their organizations to where it's needed,

- extensive use of proof-of-concept pilot projects to test new technologies and approaches,

- utilization of technology-independent metaphors for analyzing business requirements,

- analysis and presentation of tradeoffs among alternate development, approach, and execution technology architectures for each business problem, and

- willingness to invest time, effort, and funding to explore and harness new technologies and approaches for developing better applications.

Although not all IT organizations can, or should, attain each of these traits, they do represent a good cross section of the cultural attributes that are required for companies to successfully develop applications in a changing technology environment. When compared to the amounts of time and effort required to implement other cultural changes, they are also not especially difficult to achieve.

Willingness to attain competence and experience in multiple technologies, for example, can be promoted through a program of briefings, training courses, and hands-on workshops designed to meet the needs of business and IT management, project management, and project personnel. The important factors in this approach are to ensure that the material is available when and where it is needed, that it's appropriate for each group that it has to reach, and that it's presented by credible and experienced individuals. People at all levels need to be able to probe, challenge, and ask their own pointed questions about new technologies that they don't know well and aren't yet comfortable with. Proof-of-concept pilot projects are still one of the best means available for proving new technologies, for learning about their strengths and weaknesses, and for understanding how and where they should (and shouldn't) be used. And if they're large enough, pilot projects can also be used to bring developers through a number of cycles with new technologies so that they can become more productive more quickly.[7] Finally, pilot projects are good mechanisms for developing peer champions among developers and business users of new technologies, so that word about what the technology can do spreads throughout their respective organizations. Utilization of technology-independent metaphors, such as use cases, for identifying and analyzing requirements helps to postpone development and implementation technology decisions until later in the application development cycle when more is known about the application and the technologies that might be utilized to develop and run it.

Although the following two traits can be somewhat more difficult to implement, they are nevertheless important. Analysis and presentation of alternate technology tradeoffs can be promoted by including it in the application development life cycle in the form of formal tasks and reviews that developers must complete, and as part of the development management and funding processes. Willingness to make the investments needed to broaden a company's IT base can be effectively sought through communicating the need and the payback to the business in terms of pro forma technology business plans with appropriate balance sheets and income statements.

Dual Career Paths

For organizations to attract and retain IT professionals in today's time compressed technology environment, so that the right combination of business and technology skills are available for application development, and so that each project's staff remains committed through implementation, two conditions must be met. The first is that project personnel with key technology skills are compensated commensurate with the market value of their technical skills. The second condition is that project personnel with key business skills, and who have knowledge about the company's industry and its business, are compensated for their contributions to the business in terms of the applications that they help develop.

To gain some insight into what this means, consider an OO development organization that's properly leveraging object reuse.[8] Although the exact numbers depend on the complexity of the business, the technologies used and the maturity of the organization in terms of its adoption of OO technology, my experience is that, in such organizations, 25 percent of the development personnel are typically involved in technology evaluation, development, and management of reusable components, and in developing the frameworks on which OO applications are built. These are technical activities that require a high degree of competency in specific object technologies and their use. The remaining 75 percent are typically involved in utilizing the infrastructure frameworks and leveraging the reusable components to develop applications that support the business. (See Fig. 8.6.) If the frameworks and components are properly developed, leveraging their use need not involve lots of highly-technical activities. They are, however, business-centric, and can require a copious amount of business and company knowledge to successfully execute.

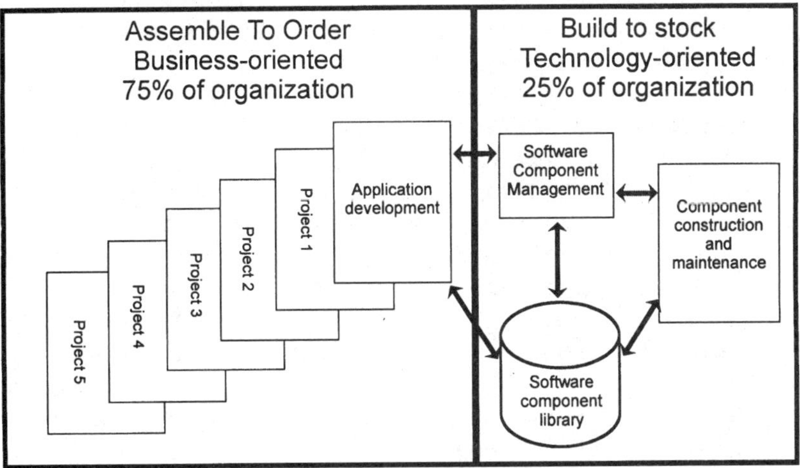

Figure 8.6 Competency requirements for high-productivity development projects.

For high-productivity OO technology, and for many other current approaches to application development, two distinct groups of individuals are needed: one oriented to technology, the other oriented toward the business. In addition to their very different orientation, these groups have different needs, they respond to different pressures, and retention of individuals within each of these groups can affect companies in different ways.

The worth of technology-oriented people on the consulting and job markets, for example, is highly dependent on their competencies and experience with technologies that are new and hot. In this high-tech market, differences of only a few months in key technology experience can lead to compensation differentials of over 100 percent—differentials that stretch far beyond what most companies' compensation models can cope with. By comparison, the companies at which one might have learned a new technology or gained implementation experience, along with the sectors of the economy that the companies might represent, are relatively unimportant. The predictable result of this dichotomy is our highly fragmented development technology job market, in which individuals move from company to company in order to gain the most experience with the latest technologies as quickly as possible, and with little regard for the well-being of the development projects they leave in their wakes.

The worth of individuals in the business-oriented group lies not as much with particular technologies as it does with their industry knowledge, experience with the company, and ability to harness new technologies to support the business. But in a time compressed technology environment, their worth on the job market is often driven more by the technologies they're experienced in than by the business knowledge and experience that they possess. Like their more technical brethren, their compensation levels can increase dramatically as a result of a few months of experience with key technologies, with the same predictable result. But unlike their more technical counterparts, their disappearance extracts a toll, not only in terms of the project they might be working on, but in terms of the organization's "corporate memory"—the company's collective understanding of its policies, procedures, and business rules that is an absolute requisite for successful application development. The problem, and the business impact, is that business knowledge takes longer to acquire, and people with detailed knowledge of their business and its needs are a lot harder to replace.

Our TCM solution for addressing this problem involves dual career paths, in which all IT personnel can advance, and are compensated, based on the business contribution of their efforts, with technology-oriented employees career paths also based on harnessing relevant

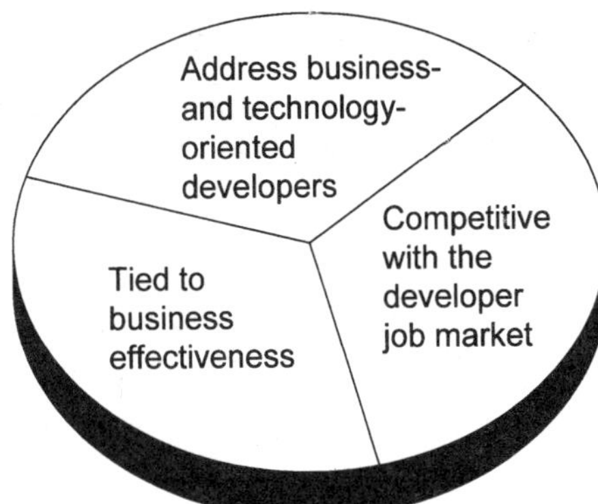

Figure 8.7 Human Resources policy requirements for development in a time compressed environment.

technologies to support the business, and business-oriented employees' career paths also based on company and business expertise. This solution is predicated on three basic requirements for developing applications in an environment fraught by time compressed change. (See Fig. 8.7.)

The first is that, for such policies to be effective, so that the right numbers of people with the right skills and competencies are available for developing applications when and where they are needed, so that development projects can be completed with a single set of participants (rather than three or more sets, as many do now), career paths and compensation levels must be competitive with the open market. The second requirement is that, to help ensure that application development effectively supports the business, Human Resources policies must tie individual career paths and compensation levels to individual performance—measured in terms of contribution to the business based on the applications they help to enable and create. The third basic requirement is that for modern approaches to application development, such as OO technology, to be effective, Human Resources policies must accommodate two sets of individuals—one oriented to technologies, the other oriented to the business.

To gain some insight into how this can be applied, let's examine how technology-and business-oriented application development participants might be promoted and compensated consistently with these requirements. Technology-oriented application development participants, in a TCM environment, would be promoted and compensated based on a combination of:

- the quality of the applications that their technologies, frameworks, and reusable objects help to create,
- the business effectiveness of the applications they help to develop and implement, and

- the value of their technology skills on the open job market.

Business-oriented application development participants, in a TCM environment, would be promoted and compensated based on a similar combination of attributes that include:

- the quality of the applications that they help to create,

- their industry and business knowledge, along with the business effectiveness of the applications they help to develop and implement,

- the value of their business and technology skills on the open job market.

Measuring the "quality" of the applications that each group of developers helps to create need not be a daunting task. Although there are a number of views concerning what software quality means, the following traditional software engineering-based quality attributes, defined by William Perry, represent a good place to start.

- *Correctness:* The extent to which a program satisfies its specifications and fulfills its user's mission objectives.

- *Reliability:* The extent to which a program can be expected to perform its intended function with required precision.

- *Efficiency:* The amount of computing resources and code required to perform a function.

- *Integrity:* The extent to which access to data by unauthorized individuals can be controlled.

- *Usability:* The effort required to learn, operate, prepare input for and interpret output of a program.

- *Maintainability:* The effort required to locate and fix an error in an operational program.

- *Testability:* The effort required to test a program and ensure it performs to its intended function.

- *Flexibility:* The effort required to modify an operational program.

- *Portability:* The effort required to transfer a program from one hardware configuration to another.

- *Reusability:* The extent to which a program can be used in other applications related to the packaging and scope of the function that the programs perform.

- *Interoperability:* The effort required to couple one system with another.[9]

These quality attributes set the general direction. The specific attributes that comprise the quality measurement, along with the weights given to each, should be set such that the quality result that they promote meets the specific requirements of the company's business and culture.

Like quality, measuring the business effectiveness of the applications that each group helps to create is neither simple nor straightforward. But it is doable; and as with quality, there's a fair amount of guidance available on business performance, the effectiveness of IT as a means for achieving it, and on metrics suitable for measuring it. The first and most important consideration in measuring the business effectiveness of applications is to agree on the set of business performance metrics that will be used.

The main problem in doing so is that traditional accounting metrics—such as revenue, cost reduction, profitability, and ROI—don't reflect what many of today's applications do.[10] Indeed, a compelling case can be made that such measures fall precipitously short of today's business's needs.[11] One good candidate is Kaplan and Norton's "Balanced Scorecard," in which business effectiveness is evaluated as a combination of:

- internal business perspectives ("What must we excel at?"),

- customer perspectives ("How do customers see us?"),

- innovation and learning perspectives ("How can we continue to improve and create value?"), and

- financial perspectives ("How do we look to our shareholders?").[12]

By settling on a set of these kinds of metrics, the business effectiveness of each of these groups, in terms of the applications they develop and implement, can be identified, measured, and disseminated for everyone to see.

In today's time compressed technology environment, it's inevitable that at least some application developers in most large-scale businesses will gain competencies in the hot new technologies of the day. And having done so, many business- and technology-oriented employees will leave to seek career opportunities based on their newfound worth. This phenomenon wreaks havoc on application development projects—especially strategic projects that are large and complex, and that can take a long time to complete.

For this kind of application development to be successful, it's imperative that employment for each group be competitive with the job market. And for such application developers to provide business value to their companies commensurate with their higher compensation, they will have to maintain sharp competencies in broad ranges of technologies instead of only a few.

Sharp competencies in broad ranges of current development, approach, and execution technologies will enable developers to achieve technology topsight, so that they can leverage time compressed technology change for their company's benefit. Although Smalltalk programmers may be able to command higher compensation than C programmers, their increased business value to a company may not fully justify the difference. But with the addition of skills in C, C++, graphical design tools, 4GLs, and relational databases the worth of the same Smalltalk programmers can more than justify the difference. The reason is that developers with the ability to see the big picture, from technology and business perspectives, will be able to make critical tradeoffs among alternative development, approach, and execution technologies so that the businesses they support get the most benefit. In a time compressed multiple-technology environment, it's broadness that really counts.

Human Resources policy in a time compressed environment should therefore promote a well-rounded combination of business skills as well as development skills in numbers of competing current technologies, so that the result is optimized for the highest return to the business. Those who successfully develop these kinds of competencies, and can demonstrate the result in terms of the business effectiveness of the applications they develop, should be compensated commensurately with their increased worth. The hot new technology job market will take care of those who do not.

Better Collaboration

For applications that truly support our businesses to become a commonplace reality, a culture that promotes collaboration among application developers and between developer and business peers will be required. Indeed, without a culture that fosters close collaboration among requirements analysts, application developers, framework developers, data administrators, and system architects, these functions will almost unerringly forge ahead in different and incompatible directions, without regard to business needs or development process. This unfortunate characteristic is the natural result of opposing pressures placed on each of these functions; by the group's requirements for optimal performance (attainment of the objectives it is measured against), and the compromises required among all development-related functions for optimal application development (attainment of optimal business support).

This problem is aggravated in time compressed environments in which substantial effort must be expended on keeping up with business and technology change, so it can be a formidable challenge to marshall whatever resources are left to attain the basic objectives that each of these functions is measured against. All too often, the result is that business support—the principal mission of IT, in most organizations—gets lost in the shuffle. Although there are, as we shall see, a number of process, infrastructure, and dependency measures that can be taken to address this problem, they will not work if the company's culture doesn't promote the close collaboration that these TCM initiatives require. What's needed, therefore, is a culture in which each of these functions is supported through a combination of:

- the specific objectives that it's uniquely qualified to meet,

- joint application delivery objectives, based on their collective products, and

- business support through faster, less expensive, and higher-quality applications.

The idea is to set cultural priorities such that the pressures imposed by time compressed change on each of these groups to hunker down and concentrate on achieving its basic mission are offset by cultural imperatives to collaborate with their peer groups in supporting TCM initiatives for the betterment of application development and for supporting the needs of the business.

There are also a number of process and cultural initiatives that will help build upon the incentives fostered by these objectives, so that collaboration among IT and business stakeholders in the application development process becomes an entrenched part of the company's collective culture. Among the easiest to implement is concurrent engineering of applications on the part of each of the IT functions, so that the impact of development, approach, and execution technology architectures on each other, as well as on the company's production environment, can be taken into account. Inclusion of joint design and review sessions in the application development process will get concurrent engineering going in most development organizations. Additional initiatives for promoting concurrent engineering in application development include common cross-functional objectives and measurements and the presence of each organization's management at common development project reviews.

Somewhat harder to implement, but also critically important, is elimination of interface organizations that separate business units from the application development organizations that serve them. It's hard for business users, and those who develop applications for business units, to collaborate if they cannot meet face to face. And it's hard to meet face to face if communication between these groups takes place through intermediaries whose continued existence depends on keeping business users and developers apart. There is no place for such organizations in the late 1990s, an era in which business users are becoming increasingly comfortable and familiar with computer systems, and in which modern development and approach technologies (such as OO technology, application generators, and 4GLs) place a premium on requirements and analysis.

A third initiative that can foster collaboration among developers and business users is rotating analysts and developers through "tours of duty" in the business units that they support. Working side-by-side with business practitioners will enable developers to attain a first-hand understanding of what their business peers need and what they face—from their own business perspectives. This initiative will also help to foster the kinds of personal relationships between development and business peers that cut through organizational and work-load-related barriers, so that business and IT needs can be directly communicated and specific questions can be understood and answered.

Finally, taking measures to ensure continuity among the people who staff application development efforts—from requirements analysis through production—will help ensure that good communications and collaboration among developers, support personnel, and business users will take place. People who work together over time, who share common development goals, and who have stakes in, and ownership of, the same application development work products, will have a far easier time collaborating than people who must build applications based on the work of others, or who develop "requirements" that others might (or might not) eventually implement.

Technology Empowerment

A problem being faced by more and more organizations is finding a way to ensure that the numbers and kinds of information technologies don't get out of hand, without throttling the ability of empowered business units to exercise their autonomy in justifying, acquiring, developing, and running their own computer applications. While increasing numbers of empowered business units are purchasing the applications they need, when they need them, from local vendors at affordable costs, a substantial increase in the numbers of development, approach, and execution technologies that make up the company's IT infrastructure is almost always the result. To empowered business units, who are reaping the benefits of their newfound autonomy in quickly acquiring and implementing application, the increase in the numbers of technologies upon which they are based is of little consequence. To centralized IT organizations that came of age before the PC revolution and the advent of time compressed change that accompanied it, when mainframe applications based on a small number of technologies supported by an even smaller number of vendors, the same increase in numbers of technologies can be a lot less welcome. (See Fig. 8.8.)

The same set of technologies that enables a business unit to double its inventory turns and to substantially increase its profits can look to the company's corporate IT function as a new supplier, a number of new technologies, and lots of new problems in standardizing part numbers, tracking customers, and rolling up results.

To corporate IT functions that came of age in the 1970s and 1980s, the compelling response is often to solve the problem through standards that place limits on the numbers of technologies in use at the company. This is not an appropriate response for an empowered company operating in today's time compressed technology environment. The reason is that the problem can be much more effectively addressed through harnessing new technologies to achieve the corporate compatibilities that the company requires, leaving the business units with the autonomy they needs to take care of their own business affairs. As we shall see in the coming chapters, when coupled with guidelines and dissemination of technology information, the corporate IT function can take on new and important roles to help the company's business units leverage time compressed change for everyone's benefit.

- Management information
- Overall relationship with customers and suppliers
- Compatible technologies
- Consistent approaches
- Low cost

- Comfort with new information technologies
- Rapid time to market
- Local vendor relationships
- Optimal technologies for needs

Figure 8.8 Corporate and business unit perspectives on increasing numbers of information technologies can be very different.

References

1. For an explanation of ELM, along with many of the business and technical hurdles required to make it work, see Thomas Gunn, *In the Age of the Real-Time Enterprise,* Oliver Wight Publications, 1994.
2. For a telling example of a successful trading system based on financial instrument characteristics, see Richard Pawson, Jean-Louis Bravard, and Lorette Cameron, "The Case for Expressive Systems," *Sloan Management Review,* Winter 1995.
3. Ivar Jacobson, *Object-Oriented Software Engineering: A Use Case Driven Approach,* Addison-Wesley, 1993.
4. While the entity relationship data model certainly isn't appropriate for all business users, I have seen it utilized as an extremely effective tool for documenting, analyzing, and presenting how data-intensive applications interact with their environments. My experience is that this can be especially true for OO applications, such as those used in financial services, that have to interact heavily with a relational data environments. Although there are many good texts on data modeling, the first, and still one of the best, is Peter Chen, "The Entity Relationship Model: Toward A Unified View Of Data," *ACM Transactions On Database Systems,* 1976.
5. For a good introduction to association matrices, see James Martin, *Information Engineering* Book II, Prentice-Hall, 1990. Dennis Minium, *A Guide To Information Engineering Using The IEF,* Texas Instruments, 1st ed., App. B provides additional insight into the history of matrix-based clustering along with their implementation in Texas Instruments' IEF CASE tool.
6. A note of caution. In presenting these kinds of results, it's important for everyone to understand that significant increases in "earnings from adoption" can be masked by equally significant increases in application utility, flexibility, and complexity. The fact that, in an era of time compressed business and technology change, productivity increases can show up in terms of spending equivalent amounts for significantly better applications as well as lower amounts for applications that do about the same things. Where productivity gains result in significantly better applications, the benefit to the business should be measured in terms of statistics such as increased productivity or customer retention.
7. Chris Kemerer "How the Learning Curve Affects CASE Tool Adoption," *IEEE Software,* May 1992.
8. For a discussion of this kind of OO technology organization, and the origin of the following figure, see Ivar Jacobson, *Object-Oriented Software Engineering: A Use Case Driven Approach,* Addison-Wesley, 1993.
9. William E. Perry, "Quality Concerns In Software Development," *Information Systems Management,* Spring 1992. For a discussion of software quality attributes, see John Stone, *Inside ADW and IEF: The Promise and Reality of CASE,* McGraw-Hill, 1993. For a similar set of software quality attributes and definitions, first published 15 years earlier, see J. McCall, P. Richards, and G. Walters, *Factors In Software Quality,* 3 vols., NTIS AD-A049-014, 015, 055, November 1977.
10. Paul A. Strassmann, *The Business Value of Computers,* The Information Economics Press, New Canaan, CT, 1990.
11. Robert G. Eccles, "The Performance Measurement Manifesto," *Harvard Business Review,* January-February 1991.
12. Robert S. Kaplan and David P. Norton, "The Balanced Scorecard—Measures That Drive Performance," *Harvard Business Review,* January-February 1992; and Robert S. Kaplan and David P. Norton, "Putting The Balanced Scorecard To Work," *Harvard Business Review,* September-October 1993.

Reengineering IT Infrastructure for Time Compression Management

"Swarm soccer" were the words that a friend chose to describe the approach utilized by the grade-school team, to which his 8-year-old daughter was a member and he was the coach. Lacking a good understanding of the game's strategies and rules, the team's young players swarmed from one part of the field to another—to wherever the ball happened to be—as if the player who had the ball knew something that the others didn't and had the magic elixir that would enable them to win. Whether they won or lost didn't really matter; it was all for fun. Everyone got lots of exercise and had a great time.

"Swarm soccer" were also the words he used to describe his company's approach to OO technology. Although the players were older and the game was for real, their strategy was substantially the same. Members of his company's IT organization had been swarming from one approach to another, depending on which proponent was most eloquent, who spoke the loudest, or what someone happened to spot in the latest trade journal. In just over 3 years, they had worked their way through three methodologies, two CASE tools, and four approaches to project management—sometimes embracing several combinations at the same time!

In addition to the different venue, the reality of their endeavor, and the age of those who took part, there was another significant difference between his company and the grade school soccer team. No one at his company was having much fun. Indeed, several of his organization's most experienced members had already lost their jobs, the company's business management was eyeing outsourcing as an attractive alternative, and none of his organization's over 2000 IT professionals felt very secure. Although they had worked their way through lots of new and exciting technologies, spent copious amounts of their company's bottom-line dollars on development projects, and reorganized several times, they were unable to consistently harness any of the promising new technologies to do the one thing that would have made a difference: quickly and reliably deliver working applications to support their business.

Successfully harnessing new development technologies—such as OO technology, hypertext markup language (HTML), and graphical development (GD)—to consistently deliver timely and cost-effective applications on a large-scale to support a global business, requires more than people, energy, money, and a development support infrastructure that might have worked in the past. It requires an infrastructure that meets the needs of the many and disparate new development technologies that make up our late-1990s application development landscape, and that supports all of them as they undergo time compressed change. In this chapter, we'll examine the four major components of such an infrastructure, not in terms of their basics, but in terms of the key differences that are required for TCM—so that they can effectively support late-1990s and twenty-first century application development. (See Fig. 9.1)

Managing Multiple, Vastly Different, and Constantly Changing, Development Projects

Application development projects in today's time compressed business and technology environments present a unique set of challenges to those who must manage them, as well as to those who must make

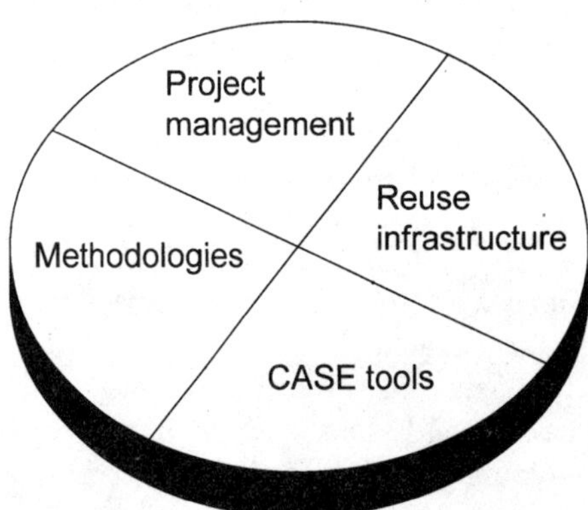

Figure 9.1 The four major TCM infrastructure components.

sense out of the disparate set of artifacts they produce. For one thing, large-scale corporate environments often contain many such projects at the same time, each representing a different set of development and execution technologies, and just as often a vastly different approach. Whether the technologies and approaches are the result of forays into new areas required to achieve a business objective, or dictated by a set of legacy development and execution technology environments that can't be changed or made to go away, they must be taken into account. And if development project's are to be successful, they must just as often deliver their product into a business environment in which goals, organization, work flow, and personnel are changing as fast as their technologies!

Although most of the good management practices that delivered successful results in the past still apply, successful development project management in today's time compressed environments also depends on:

- delivering results, in a series of short-term releases,

- managing progress, in terms of consistent and understandable milestones and tasks,

- communicating, in a consistent and meaningful way, to all development stakeholders, and

- rolling up the disparate infrastructure requirements of ongoing and future projects, so that appropriate levels of support can be planned for and provided.

Breaking up large-scale application development projects as a series of short-term development projects, instead of developing the entire application all at once, has been utilized by many organizations as a vehicle for providing incremental ROI and for managing risk. The same technique can also be employed to help fortify a development projects against technology and business change. Delivering functionality in a series of 6- to 9-month incremental releases, permits application development projects to complete while their technology and business environments remain relatively stable. Technology environment components, such as:

- desktop workstation configurations,

- local area networks, wide area networks, and web sites

- server and mainframe data stores,

- development and execution architecture technologies and releases,

- external systems, and

- internal systems that the application must interoperate with

represent common sources of technology-based requirements and constraints that can wreak havoc on application development projects when they change significantly during the development process. Yet each of these sources also represents a set of technologies that can usually be stabilized for a period of a few months. The same thing holds for business environment sources, such as

- the project's customers, along with their experiences, preferences, and needs,

- external business forces along with the system objectives that they drive, and the

- internal business policy and procedures that must be incorporated into applications as "business rules" but that can also undergo radical change as a result of changing needs and business reengineering initiatives.

The key to successfully breaking up large-scale development projects so that functionality is provided in terms of reasonable short-term delivery releases is to ensure that each release addresses technology needs, business needs, and release interdependencies. A simple strategy for accomplishing this is to complete a basic requirements analysis of the entire application prior to scheduling the initial delivery release, and to keep it current as the project proceeds. For large-scale OO development, this kind of analysis might involve high-level use case analysis and business object modeling, along with data modeling and data access modeling for each performance-critical use cases.[1] If kept to a sufficiently high level, the initial analysis can usually be completed within 6 months—even for large-scale applications spanning a number of delivery releases and several years of development. Revising and updating the analysis on a quarterly basis, should keep it sufficiently current to meet the changing requirements of most dynamic environments.

When the artifacts produced by this kind of analysis are associated with the application's objectives, features, and functions (via IE-style "association matrices") a clear picture of interdependencies will result.[2] Armed with this information, the interdependencies among objectives, features, functions, use cases, business objects, and data stores can be utilized to develop a set of short-term delivery releases that make sense from business and technology perspectives. By adjusting the impact of each release on each component of the high-level analysis, a picture of how each of these key sources is covered by each release can be developed. My experience is that a small number

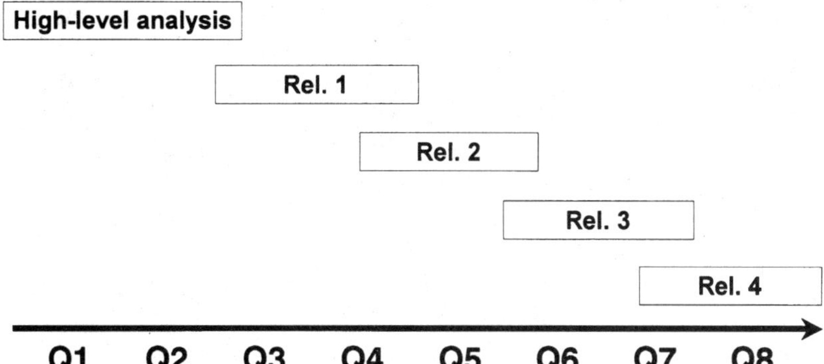

Figure 9.2 Completing a project through a series of releases following a high-level analysis.

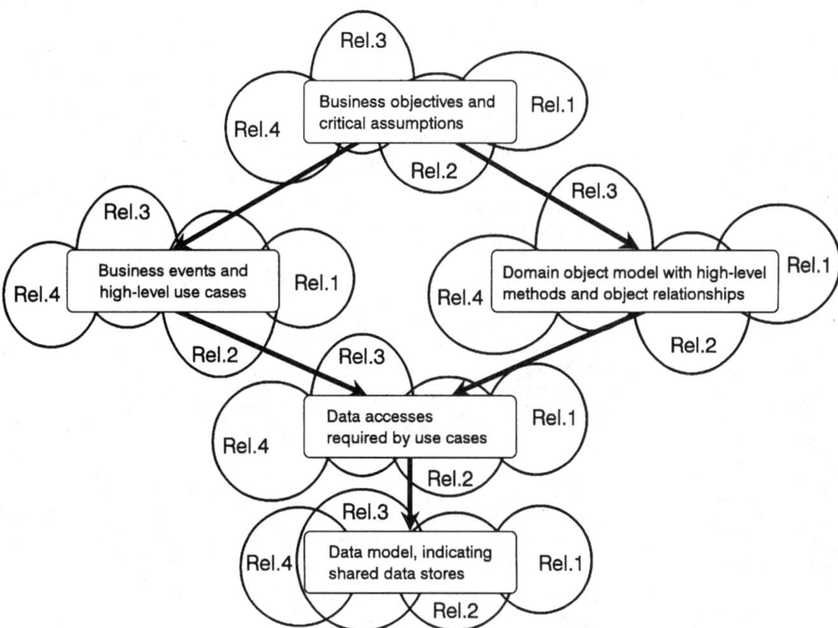

Figure 9.3 Utilizing a high-level analysis to develop a series of delivery releases.

of iterations will usually yield full coverage in terms of a logical sequence of releases, as shown in Figs. 9.2 and 9.3. If dependencies and staffing permit, the releases can overlap.

Development paradigms such as OO technology and GD, in which deliverables evolve and life cycle phases overlap, can become rich sources of consternation to project managers as well as to their business and IT management. This is especially true in companies with "one and done" cultures and that are used to traditional "waterfall" style development paradigms in which applications are supposed to progress toward completion as a series of head-to-tail tasks.[3] As the number of development paradigms increases—a natural consequence of time compressed change—IT's ability to demonstrate consistent progress over each of its development projects can be seriously impaired. Fortunately, this problem also has a solution that's not very difficult to implement.

The solution is to develop two views of each project's life cycle—a development team view that's consistent with the needs of the technology and paradigm utilized by the analysts and developers working on the project, and a management view that can be used to manage the project and report on progress. To illustrate how this works, consider the OO development project profile presented in Chap. 4 and illustrated again in Fig. 9.4.[4] The project's overlapping phases, which reflect the way OO development works, make a lot of sense to OO technology developers but can be a source of considerable frustration to those who are responsible for the project's management. Although the concept of convergence (also presented in Chap. 4) can be employed to help assess each phase's overall health, nothing in this view will be of much use to the OO development project's manager who needs to know exactly where the project is in its life cycle so that he or she can assess whether or not it will be completed on time and within budget.

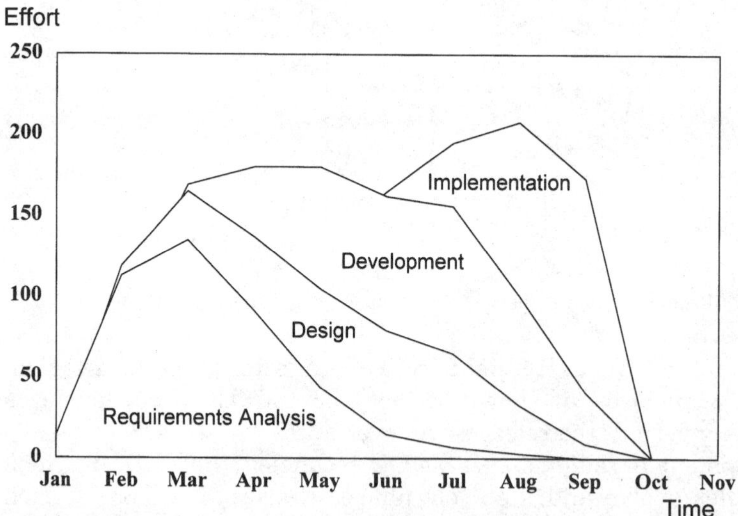

Figure 9.4 Object-oriented development project profile with overlapping phases.

From a management perspective, the project makes a lot more sense when it's seen in terms of discrete life cycle events. For example, a Requirements Analysis phase that runs from January through August isn't much use to management. But knowing when the Design phase starts, or when the Analysis phase peaks—life cycle events that occur at points in time, that are relevant to progress, and that can be measured and evaluated—can be of substantial use. (See Fig. 9.5.)

When the same project is viewed in terms of its life cycle events, a head-to-tail waterfall-style view of the project that's suitable for management and for reporting progress results. (See Fig. 9.6.)

In this form, the project can be compared to traditional development projects in terms that are meaningful not only to the project's management but also to IT and business management.

Although this example concerns an OO development project, the same principles can be applied to other development paradigms, such as IE and GD, with equal success. The point is that development projects employing vastly different paradigms can be viewed by each of their stakeholders in terms that make sense for his or her needs, and that regardless of the paradigm, or the nature of its deliverables and tasks, projects can and should be managed and reported in terms of sequential activities and completed tasks.

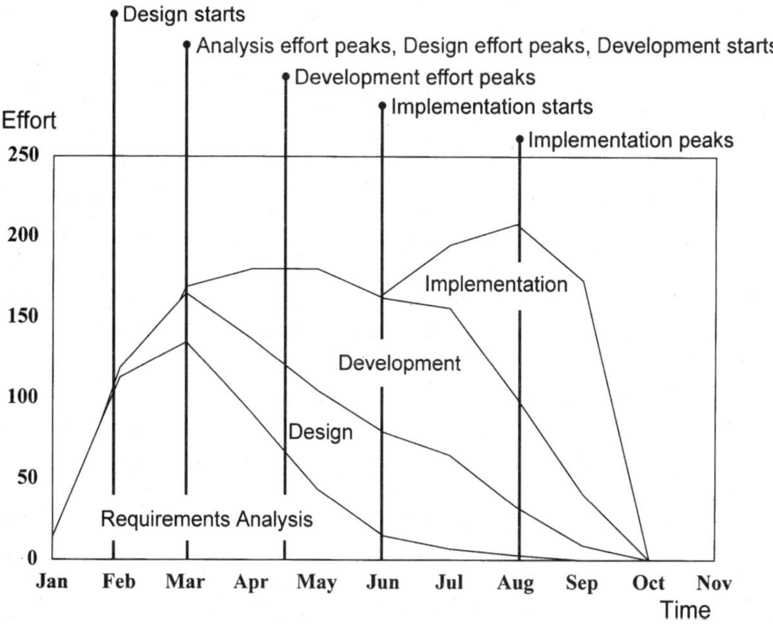

Figure 9.5 The same OO project profile mapped to life cycle events.

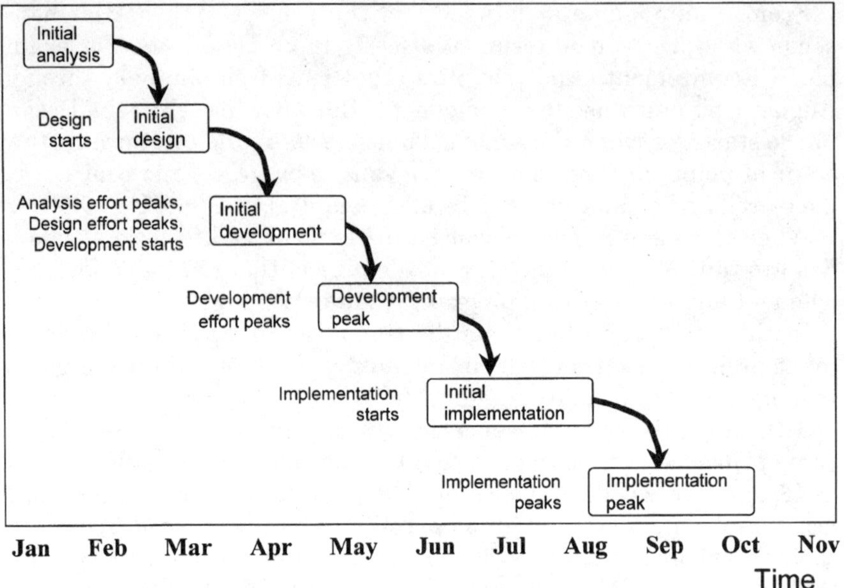

Figure 9.6 The same OO development project profile viewed solely in terms of life cycle events.

A consistent waterfall-style view of multiple projects representing different technologies and paradigms can also be used for developing a consistent roll-up of support requirements. Although requirements for infrastructure support will differ from project to project, and when they don't differ, will likely occur in different places, there are substantial advantages in being able to roll them up. In a large-scale environment, for example, structured development, IE, GD, and OO development projects will all require the services of subject matter experts, usability engineers, reusable asset managers, data administrators, database administrators, system architects, security specialists, and production personnel. When these requirements are not explicitly called for, their need can be masked by unfamiliarity with the vastly different paradigms that these approaches represent, and by the fact that some new approaches don't have large-scale development and implementation roots and therefore don't even recognize the need for many these services. When they aren't rolled up over all development efforts, the organization's total infrastructure requirements can't be forecasted and viewed from quarter to quarter and month to month—an all-too-common occurrence—and they may not be available to support all projects, even when they are identified! And when such requirements aren't available, troubled installations and failed projects are the inevitable result.

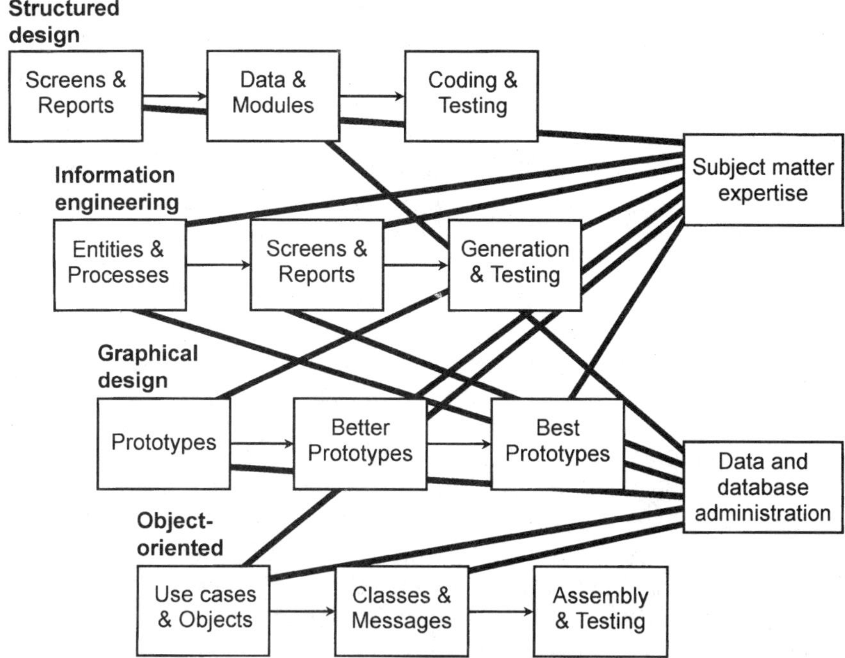

Figure 9.7   How common infrastructure requirements can be rolled up over different paradigms for development.

Figure 9.7 provides an example of how the need for three common types of infrastructure support—subject matter expertise, data administration, and database administration—are distributed over four common development paradigms.

While the need for these kinds of support should be—and often is—obvious within each development paradigm, what isn't always obvious is where, and in what quantity, they're needed. For example, the need for data administration and database administration in the early phases of GD—to design and stabilize the database—isn't always explicitly clear to development support organizations not familiar with the GD process. Nor are the data access requirements implied by high-volume response-critical use cases in OO development.

By mapping the life cycle phases of each development paradigm into a common waterfall-style format, associating each type of infrastructure requirement with each phase in the waterfall model, and rolling the results up so that full set of infrastructure requirements becomes available on a month-to-month basis, the most stringent and disparate set of infrastructure support needs can be understood and met.

Utilizing similar concepts, progress on multiple applications being developed in different paradigms can also be rolled up so that IT and business management can see a clear and consistent picture of how each project is doing. Building on the concepts of loose methodology coupling for reporting (introduced in Chap. 5) and mapping of development phases to waterfall-style models, a management "dashboard" capable of showing progress on a number of development projects, representing completely different paradigms, can be developed. (See Fig. 9.8.)

Although the three development projects represented in this dashboard prototype are being executed using OO, IE, and GD, and the differences in their life cycle phases reflect their different paradigms, the dashboard leaves little doubt about how each project is doing. As of July 31, the OO project has reached the correct life cycle phase, but has fallen behind, the IE project hasn't reached the scheduled phase and is 50 percent behind the phase that was scheduled for completion in June, and the GD project is on schedule.

There are many variations on this concept, and implementation of this kind of dashboard should be consistent with each company's projects, needs, and culture. The point, however, is the same. Mapping of disparate projects to a waterfall model provides a good basis for consistent reporting to management.

Methodologies and Time Compression Management

The common wisdom among large-scale application development organizations and their management is that process maturity is good.

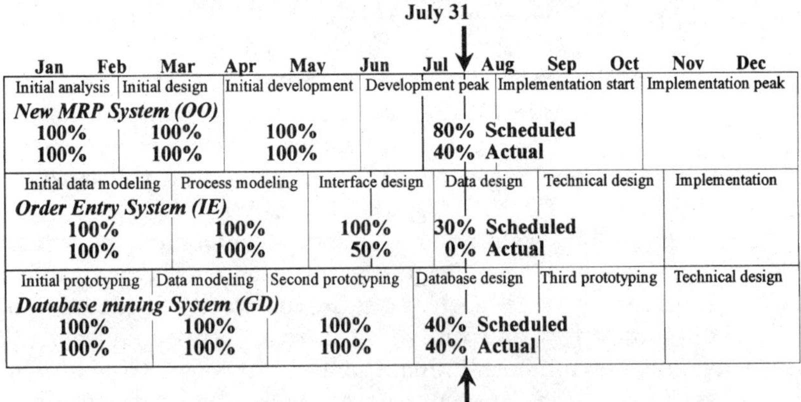

Figure 9.8 Management dashboard for multiple paradigm development.

Development organizations that utilize formal methodologies are better off than those that don't. And organizations are best off that are able to fully integrate a formal methodology into their organizations and cultures, so that each of their developers understands it, embraces its tenets, and utilizes it as an integral part of his or her development projects.

A stable and well-integrated development process sounds good—and probably is good—in a stable technology environment. During the 1970s and 1980s, when development, approach, and execution technologies didn't undergo radical change, and development organizations had the luxury of improving their processes over time to provide optimal support within their stable technology environments, a single, well-integrated and highly optimized methodology probably was indeed a good idea. But during the time compressed late-1990s and beyond, with multiple and revolutionary development technologies and business needs fostering continuous and radical change, what was a good idea during the 1970s and 1980s may no longer be appropriate.

To see why a well-integrated development process may no longer be appropriate, consider Kemerer's S-shaped technology adoption curve, presented in Chap. 2, in which productivity dips, as part of the adoption process, before it eventually increases.[5] Building on this concept, we found, in Chap. 4, that the rate of new technology adoption, in a time compressed environment, could be optimized for maximum return on technology investment. Change out development technologies too quickly, and your development organization thrashes. Stay with technologies too long, and you lose too, because you get shut out from new advances and the best talent. While this concept is correct from a general technology vantage point, it can be difficult to implement when the technology in question is a process—a development methodology. The reason is that, for methodologies to work, they must become an integral part of a company's development culture, and cultural change takes time—far too much time for today's time compressed rate of technology proliferation and change.

This results in a methodology "catch 22" in which we need methodologies that are mature and adopted by our development cultures to make our development technologies pay off, but the process of adopting methodologies and integrating them into our development cultures takes far more time than compressed change allows us. If we optimize for technology adoption, as we did in Chap. 4, our development process can't keep up. If we optimize for development process, we fall behind the productivity curve on the useful lives of our development technologies.

The answer to this dilemma is a methodology that can support multiple and disparate development technologies and paradigms, and that can support new and different development technologies without the imposition of time-consuming cultural change. To see how this can be achieved, let's take a look at the essential elements of a typical application development methodology, along with how each can be made robust so that it can withstand time compressed change. (See Fig. 9.9.) There are three basic concepts behind this approach.

- The first is that, for large-scale application development, much of the work tends to be pretty much the same, regardless of the paradigm, languages or tools.[6]

- The second is that many development paradigms and approaches can benefit from other paradigms' tasks and techniques.

- The third is that, by defining trajectories or "route maps" through the methodology, tasks that provide marginal value or that are irrelevant for a particular development paradigm can be skipped in favor of more germane tasks.

Some methodology phases and tasks will already be robust, or can be made so with little difficulty. For large projects, the tasks and deliverables that comprise Project Initiation will be largely the same, regardless of the paradigm or the technologies that the methodology

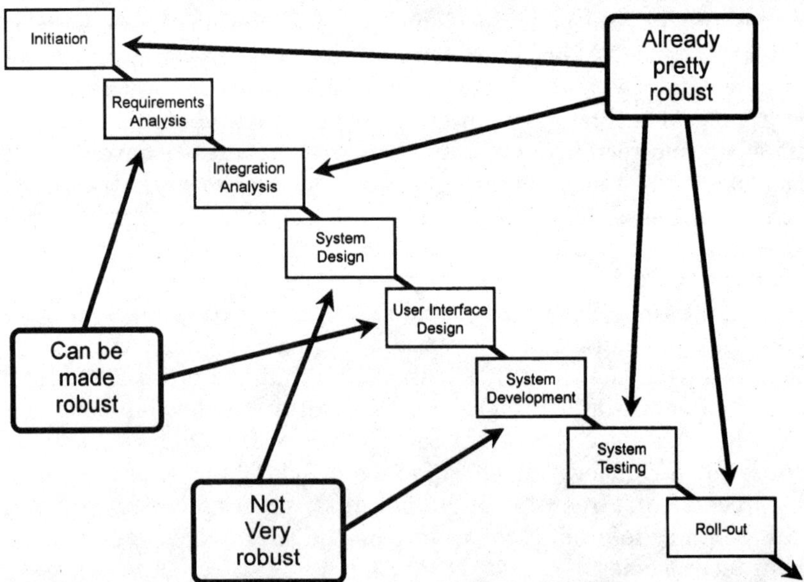

Figure 9.9 Robustness of development methodology phases.

supports. The problem needs to be defined, a project sponsor has to be identified, business users and IT professionals with the right skills and competencies have to be marshaled, and a project support infrastructure has to be put in place. With slight additions, a host of project precedents (such as a high-level use case analysis, an IE-based Information Systems Plan (ISP), or the work products of a business engineering effort can be called for and mapped into the methodology's initiation requirements.

Other phases, such as Requirements Analysis, can be broken down into robust and paradigm-specific components. Development of an entity relationship data model, for example, will—or should be—robust, regardless of the paradigm for development.[7] For OO projects, additional tasks for utilizing entity types and business objects to help identify one another, and for developing object to data associations can be added without compromising robustness. Early prototyping—embedded in use cases for OO development and on-screen for GD—can also be added to make Requirements Analysis more robust.

Requirements Analysis is also an example of a phase that for most methodologies can benefit greatly from cross-pollination of techniques from different development paradigms. Use cases, although an outgrowth of Jacobson's OO software engineering, can be an extremely effective metaphor for describing requirements for development of virtually all applications that respond to business events. Use cases are also good for helping business users and IT professionals develop a common vision of what the application will be like and how it will fit into their environments. State transition diagrams are another good cross-paradigm analysis technique, as is development of detailed data models when the data will be stored in a relational database environment. In addition to these direct benefits, including this kind of cross-pollination in a methodology phase makes the phase robust.

The methodology's Integration Analysis phase—something that has many aliases, but that is required for virtually all large-scale business applications—is another example of a phase that can be made robust. Data conversion—a task that can easily take up over 50 percent of the effort on a large-scale business application development project—will, in all likelihood, already be robust, as will be integration analysis. The means for achieving integration, however, will tend to be paradigm-specific.

User Interface Design is a methodology phase that's seen as being a lot less robust than it actually is, or should be. The reason is that business users, who have to deal with applications developed utilizing different paradigms and approaches, shouldn't have to deal with an equally different set of interfaces. Indeed, the development paradigm should be as transparent to application users as the application's internal design or the language in which it was implemented. If you accept this premise, then many of the tasks utilized to design user interfaces quickly converge.[8] The only tasks that remain different are those that develop the specific controls, visualizations, help, and agents that comprise the user interface.

Although design and development phases tend to be paradigm-specific, and therefore not robust, system testing—at least the integration, performance, and acceptance testing parts—can be robust. This is especially true when requirements are expressed in a consistent metaphor, such as use cases. Implementation and roll-out are a lot more dependent on network implementation, hardware availability, training, and change management than they are on the technology utilized in the application's development. Roll-out is therefore also robust.

What isn't robust is the order in which things happen, and as we saw in Chap. 5, CASE tools and the tight coupling that's required between the tools and the methodology's detailed tasks. The inclusion of phases and tasks, along with the order in which a methodology's phases and tasks are addressed, can, however, be substantially changed from one paradigm to the next without affecting the tools or their tight coupling to detailed methodology tasks.

Consider inclusion and order. There are two concepts that we can employ to help ensure that our development environments remain robust with respect to order, tools, and coupling requirements to detailed tasks. The first concept involves defining multiple route maps through our methodology. (See Fig. 9.10.) By developing consistent terminology for development phases and tasks, and by defining route maps through the methodology phases and tasks that are relevant for each development paradigm and approach, a consistent and efficient use of a single methodology can result.

Although the concept of a metamethodology, in which multiple "routes" or "trajectories" through methodologies are employed to optimize the development process for each project's needs, has been around for some time, and has been an effective means for ensuring that projects with different needs don't have to labor under a "one size fits all" approach, what multiple trajectories does is to expand the concept so that the needs of different development paradigms can be met. As Fig. 9.10 indicates, by defining three route maps through our metamethodology, the phase- and order-related needs of GD, OO development, and IE development can be served by a single development process.

When bolstered by a common lexicon for identifying and describing common work breakdown structure phases and tasks, a common understanding on the part of business and IT development stakehold-

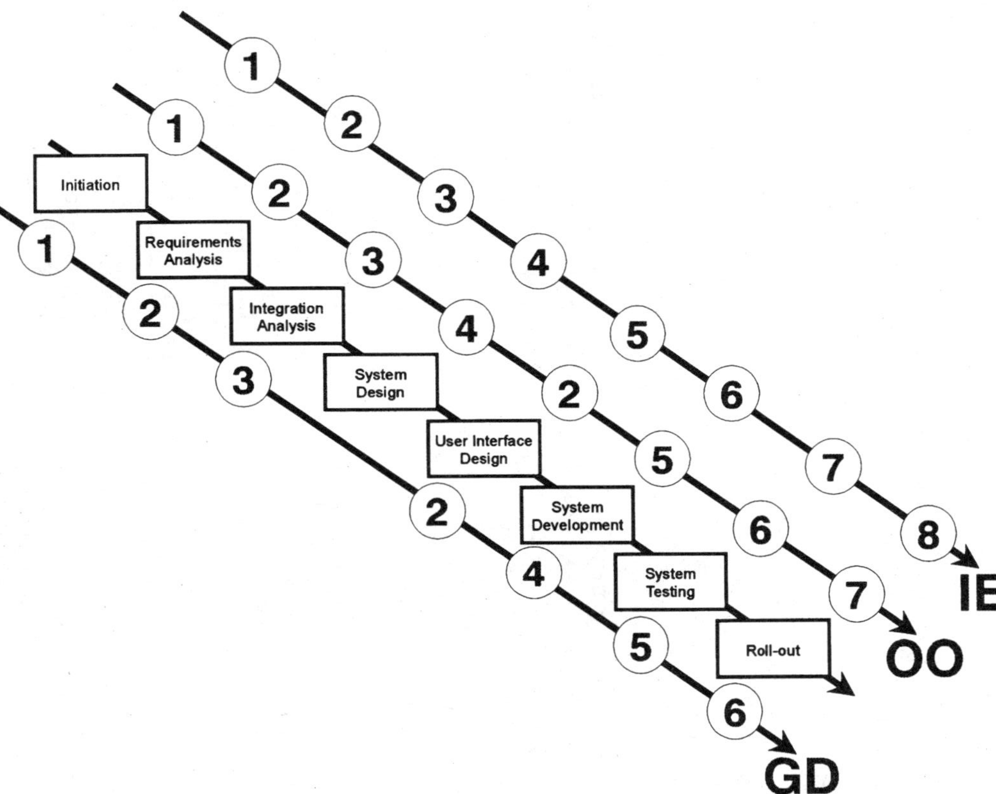

Figure 9.10 Multiple route maps permit a single metamethodology to support different development paradigms.

ers can also be developed. A secondary, but sometimes important, benefit of multiple route maps based on a single lexicon is that the single metamethodology eases restrictions on management's ability to redeploy scarce resources, as needed, on development projects utilizing new and different paradigms for development. The end result is that the combination of multiple route maps and a common lexicon helps to shift the methodology from a technology-centric process to a company-centric process that helps make time compressed change easier to assimilate.

CASE Tools and Time Compression Management

CASE tools can be made as robust as the methodologies they support, although the means for making them robust are somewhat different. This is true not only for the tools themselves, but also for their tight coupling to detailed methodology tasks through which they can add substantial value. To see how this can be accomplished, let's take a look at the current classes of CASE tools and explore the reasons why they are (and aren't) robust.

In terms of robustness, today's CASE tools can be roughly classed into the following four principal categories, in order of increasing robustness (see Fig. 9.11):

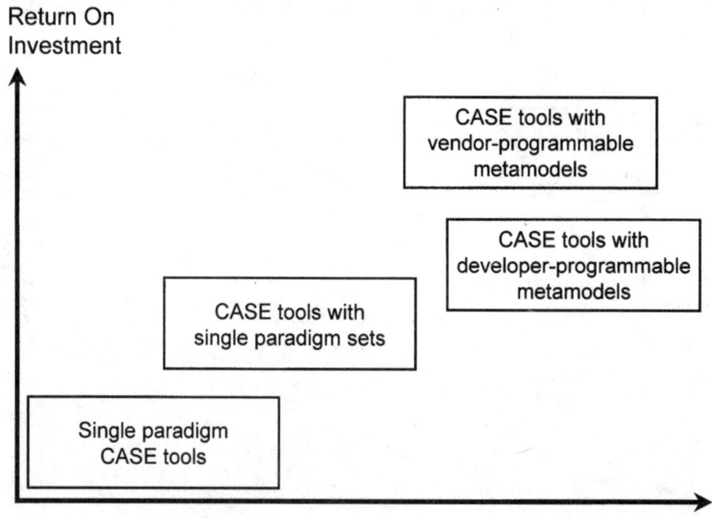

Figure 9.11 Robustness and ROI for CASE tools in a time compressed technology environment.

- tools with specific metamodels that support a singular and specific paradigm for development (the least robust),

- tools that support a bounded menu of specific methodology choices,

- tools with metamodels that support a mix of approaches and techniques, and

- tools that are based on programmable metamodels that can configured by their users to support the approaches they need (the most robust).

Tools, such as IEF or Objectory, that cover singular paradigms for development, are useful only to the extent that their developers' processes fit the paradigm of the tool. Although IEF is an excellent best-in-class CASE tool for IE-based development, it's based on a closed metamodel (the model of how the CASE tool's different diagrams and techniques fit together to support a development process). For example: IEF doesn't, and can't be made to, support use case-driven OO development. Although Objectory is an outstanding CASE tool for use case-driven OO, it doesn't, and can't be made to, support entity relationship data modeling and data-driven development. Both are excellent examples of high value-added CASE tools, but neither tool is robust. Neither tool will add significant value in terms of helping its users deal with robust methodologies that cover data and OO development, or time compressed change.

Other CASE tools provide their users with menus of discrete methodology choices—Booch, Jacobson, Wirfs-Brock, or Rumbaugh, for example—and are therefore more robust than their fixed paradigm counterparts.(9) Although these tools afford their users the opportunity of utilizing the same tool to support a range of fixed-methodology approaches, when viewed in terms of time compressed change, they too aren't robust. The reason is that cultural and adoption inertia prevent companies from switching from one methodology to the next in anything like the time frames that would be required to keep up with time compressed change. And even if they could switch back and forth across methodologies, this class of tools doesn't provide enough latitude to optimize the development process based on a combination of approaches and techniques that span more than one of the predefined methodologies that they support. Users of this class of CASE tools, who want to combine use cases and entity relationship data modeling in a single development process, for example, are also out of luck.

The third class of CASE tools on our robustness scale does provide for mixing and matching approaches and techniques from different methodologies to form a single robust development process. These

CASE tools differ from the others in that they can support multiple metaphors and techniques from a number of paradigms at the same time and tie them together via their metamodels. Such tools provide their users with the flexibility to include use cases (from Jacobson), object and state transition modeling (from Rumbaugh), and entity relationship data modeling (from Martin) in the same development process—a significant advantage for developers who must deal with a time compressed technology environment. One vendor, Select Software Ltd., has developed its CASE tools around a two-tiered metamodel that enables the user to modify and enhance the "metameta model" as required to ensure that the relevant tool's (already robust) metamodel keeps up not only with diagrams and techniques from different paradigms, but also with entirely new paradigms for development. In terms of dealing with time compressed change, this is perhaps the most robust approach, since it permits the CASE tool's basic architecture to take time compressed proliferation and evolution into account.

There is another class of CASE tools that are potentially the most robust in terms of keeping up with time compressed change. These tools, sometimes referred to as "metaCASE tools," are based on metamodels that can be programmed by their users to support the sets of paradigms, diagrams, and techniques of their choice. As technologies and needs evolve, and needs change, these tools can be reprogrammed to keep up. While they are clearly very robust, I have two concerns regarding these tools. The first is that most companies development organizations aren't—and probably shouldn't be—engaging in this type of programming. My second concern is that even if they can and do correctly alter their CASE tool's metamodel to keep up with time compressed change, the time and cost that it takes to make and test the changes may be too great to provide a sufficient ROI to the business that these organizations must support.[11] Although user-programmable metamodels can provide substantial robustness, the additional robustness comes at a cost that cannot be leveraged over many development organizations, since each development organization that uses the MetaCASE tool must pay it. From a business perspective, programming CASE tool metamodels may therefore not represent an optimal investment.

Although there are a number of different approaches and solutions to the problem, with an equal number of different results, specific examples—such as Select Software's "Enterprise"—show that the problem can be solved. CASE tools can be made robust, and the robustness can be translated into significant return on a company's CASE tool investment. Why then do the task-level process requirements of most CASE tools remain as rigid as they are?

The reason is the singular vantage point that many CASE tool designers represent. In such cases, the resultant CASE tool is an embodiment of its creator's approach to application development. While the methodologists that create such tools are often thought to be leaders in their fields, and the CASE tools that embody their approaches therefore have a great deal of merit, they support singular views of development—views that are based on the development paradigm on which the CASE tools were based. The problem is that such CASE tools don't represent a dynamic time compressed view of development, in which the development process changes and evolves as current development technologies and approaches are enhanced, and new technologies and approaches are introduced.

Reuse in a Time Compressed Environment

Developing applications by assembling them from reusable components is a common and sought-after goal that traverses many development technology paradigms, from reuse of modules and subroutines in structured development, to reuse of data, rules, and procedures in IE, to reuse of classes and frameworks in OO development. The reality is that regardless of how ubiquitous reuse is as a goal, achievement of significant reuse—so that its results are seen in terms of measurable business impact—remains an elusive ideal that most development organizations fail to achieve. The major problem underlying the dearth of significant reuse is not the goal or the idea, but its implementation. And the most prevalent problem with its implementation, even in a stable technology environment, is a lack of infrastructure to enable and promote reuse.

Before we explore the differences and complexities of achieving reuse in a time compressed business and technology environment, let's take a look at four key reuse infrastructure basics that are required regardless of the dynamics of the technology or business environments. (See Fig. 9.12.)

The first key, not surprisingly, is a rich library of reusable application components. Although this infrastructure requirement may seem obvious, its achievement requires a significant investment in time and effort. And expending the time and effort to develop a rich library of reusable objects requires an organization that is chartered to do so. That is an organization that has been freed from the day-to-day pressures of delivering applications on a tight schedule, and has the ability to identify reusable component opportunities across functional areas and projects. I've come across very few companies that have organizations chartered to identify, locate, and maintain a library of reusable components. The realities of budget pressures and a lack of

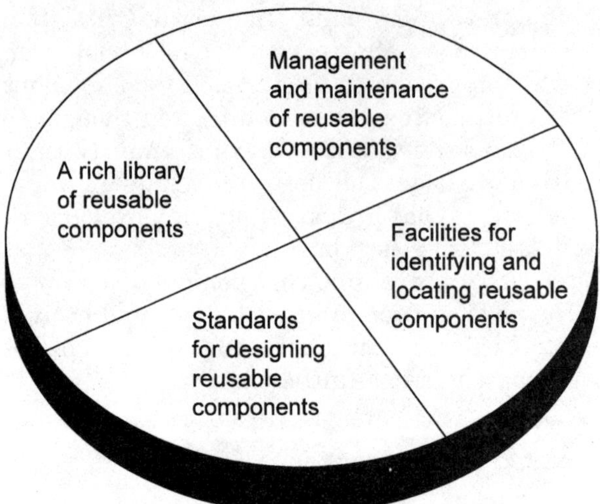

Figure 9.12 Infrastructure components for implementing
reuse in a single-technology environment.

organizations to emulate that have achieved high levels of reuse, get
in the way.

The existence of an organization dedicated to administration and
maintenance of reusable components, although necessary, isn't sufficient. For such an organization to be effective, it must have standards
for developing, maintaining, and certifying the reusable components
that it works with. Regardless of whether the reusable components
are entity types, HPS rules, IEF procedures, C++ classes, or
Smalltalk frameworks, they won't be extensively reused if developers
are under pressure to deliver applications don't have implicit confidence in them. And developers won't have that kind of confidence if
reusable components aren't developed to, and certified against, a
rigidly enforced set of standards. The pervasive problem, and a key
reason why reuse has remained as elusive as it has, is that these
kinds of standards don't exist. As they don't come with commercially
available methodologies and tools, or even with many commercial-
class libraries, the development organizations that can most benefit
from reuse and that want to take advantage of it, are left to develop
their own standards for reusable components.

Fortunately, developing standards for reusable components doesn't
have to be expensive or difficult. In most organizations, what's needed
is a team of seasoned professionals who understand, and are experienced in, the paradigms being utilized for application development,
along with a set of guidelines for developing the required standards.

Although the actual standards will differ from one paradigm to the next, they should almost always include:

- documentation standards for what the component does and how it works,
- exception and error handling,
- expected use,
- testing procedures, including test case results, and
- the environmental requirements that the component will be expected to meet.

Identification of the specific reusable components that will help application developers to deliver better applications more quickly is another obvious requisite for garnering business benefit from reuse. Yet, aside from the basic browsers and keyword search capabilities that accompany many development tools, there is little infrastructure to help us meet this almost universally acknowledged need. What's really needed is a means for locating reusable components that are "close" fits, and "sort of close" fits, for the developers' intended purposes. A C++ function that doesn't meet a need, but could be made to meet the need by adding three lines of code, is a good example of a reusable component that's "close," as is an entity type that's missing an attribute or a use case that requires another alternate course or an additional step. Although I haven't come across any tools that solve this problem, I believe that it could be solved through application of appropriate information technologies, such as artificial intelligence and fuzzy logic.

So much for the basics. Two additional infrastructure extensions are required to achieve significant levels of reuse in a time compressed changing multiple-technology environment. (See Fig. 9.13.) They are:

- facilities for making usable components technology-robust, so that they can be usable in a number of development, approach, and execution technology contexts; and
- a reusable component administration that's conversant with the diversity of development technologies and the paradigms in use at the organizations it serves.

In today's time compressed environments, companies will get little business benefit from reusable application components if the components can't be utilized outside of the technologies that they were

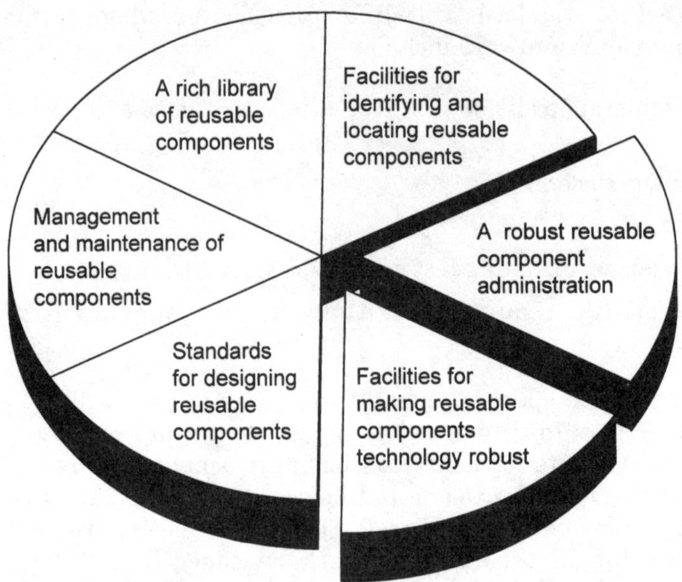

Figure 9.13 Infrastructure extensions for implementing reuse in a multiple-technology environment.

developed in. For a component written in C++ to provide substantial ROI over its useful life, it should be accessible not only by applications written in C++ but also by applications written in C, Smalltalk, or Visual Basic and by developers utilizing tools such as PowerBuilder, HPS, or IEF—the kind of disparate mix of development technologies and paradigms that can be found at many of today's organizations. In other words, for components to be widely used, they must be technology-robust.

This goal can be accomplished by developing, testing, and documenting application components so that they can be accessed through standard ORBs, through standard Application Program Interfaces (APIs), and through data. Components that are accessed through common ORBs [including those based on CORBA and Object Linking and Embedding (OLE)] should be accessible by most OO development applications being developed in Smalltalk and C++. API generators can be employed to develop common APIs that can be used to make applications accessible by non-OO development graphical tools. For data-driven tools, development of relational database interfaces, in which relational tables (or, in some cases, columns) are utilized as input and output queues, represent a viable alternative. Although not all development tools can take advantage of the latest ORBs or APIs, few cannot read and write to a relational database.

The second enhancement to our reuse infrastructure is making the reusable object administration technology-robust, so that it can provide meaningful guidance to development teams in locating and reusing components that were developed in different technologies and paradigms. Reuse mentors, who are equally conversant in Smalltalk and C++, for example, can help a C++ development team to understand and address the constraints imposed by components that are tied to a Smalltalk image. The same thing can happen in reverse, when a Smalltalk development team needs to modify a few lines in a "close" C++ function to turn it into an exact fit. Even where the technologies are identical, it's hard for developers under pressure on a tight project to understand what's available in terms of reusable assets easily and quickly enough to make searching for such components into an attractive proposition.

The idea is to help developers who are experts in their technologies and paradigms to locate and utilize reusable components that were developed in their technologies, as well as in other paradigms and technologies that they don't fully understand or aren't comfortable with. The goals are to equip the company's reusable object administration with the cross-technology expertise that it needs to break down the prejudices and barriers that develop around technologies and paradigms that development teams don't fully understand, so that application components in their time compressed environments can enjoy a wide range of reuse, and to provide this service to the developers in a form that they can quickly and easily use.

References

1. Developers who favor a pure OO approach may take exception to modeling data and data accesses along with use cases and objects. In theory, this view is correct. However, my experiences with large-scale OO business application development is that many of the data that are supposed to be encapsulated within objects actually reside in shared data stores, such as relational databases, that are accessed by a mixture of applications representing a number of OO and non-OO paradigms. In this kind of mixed execution environment, modeling use cases through the objects that are involved in their execution and the data access required to populate those objects, is an essential part of ensuring that the OO application will meet its performance requirements.
2. For a good description of association matrices, along with how they can be applied in a conventional (non-OO) environment, see James Martin, *Strategic Data Planning Methodologies,* Prentice Hall, 1982. Also see James Martin, *Information Engineering* Book II; Prentice Hall, 1990; and Dennis Minium, *A Guide To Information Engineering Using The IEF,* 1st ed., Texas Instruments, App. B, which provides insight into the history of matrix-based clustering along with their implementation in Texas Instruments' IEF CASE tool.
3. This phenomenon, although acknowledged for OO development, actually holds true for all development paradigms. My experience with traditional development paradigms that, although development is *supposed to* proceed as a series of head-to-tail

tasks, it really doesn't. What happens is that, as downstream life cycle phases call for more and more detail, designers and programmers must often seek more and more detailed information—even though formal mechanisms for doing so may no longer exist. The result is frustration for designers and programmers who have trouble getting much of the detailed information they need, and for managers who must pay for downstream changes at 10 to 100 times the cost of getting things right up front.

4. This is a profile of a very successful OO project that was developed using an Objectory-based analysis followed by a design and implementation in Smalltalk.

5. Chris Kemerer "How the Learning Curve Affects CASE Tool Adoption," *IEEE Software,* May 1992.

6. Frederick Brooks, *The Mythical Man-Month,* rev. ed., Addison-Wesley, 1995.

7. This kind of data model is explicitly called for in data-driven development, and in my experience should be called for in all large-scale development. Such a data model can also be of substantial aid in developing OO applications that have to function in tightly integrated shared data environments. As most large-scale OO business systems fall into this category, I'm comfortable with this assumption, even though it violates some theoretical OO tenets.

8. Those who have trouble accepting this premise, might try executing a series of challenging business processes, under tight time pressure, utilizing a number of applications with different interface styles and behavior. As I, along with many others, can personally assure them, the experience can be very persuasive.

9. For additional insight into these methodologies, see: Grady Booch, *Object-Oriented Analysis and Design,* Second Edition, The Benjamin/Cummings Publishing Company, 1994; Ivar Jacobson, *Object-Oriented Software Engineering: A Use Case Driven Approach,* Addison-Wesley, 1993; Rebecca Wirfs-Brock, Brian Wilkerson and Lauren Weiner, *Designing Object-Oriented-Software,* PTR Prentice Hall, 1990; and James Rumbaugh, Michael Blaha, William Premerlani, Fredrick Eddy and William Lorensen, *Object-Oriented Modeling and Design,* Prentice Hall, 1991.

10. See Ivar Jacobson, *Object-Oriented Software Engineering: A Use Case Driven Approach,* Addison-Wesley, 1993; James Rumbaugh, Michael Blaha, William Premerlani, Fredrick Eddy and William Lorensen, *Object-Oriented Modeling and Design,* Prentice Hall, 1991; James Martin, *Information Engineering,* Book II "Planning and Analysis," Prentice Hall, 1990; and James Martin *Strategic Data Planning Methodologies,* Prentice Hall, 1982.

11. To provide significant added value from a combination of diagrams and techniques, a CASE tool must add value via tight coupling to the process it supports and via inter- and intradiagram consistency checks. Changes to a use case model, for example, should be reflected in the tool's object model and interaction diagrams. If entity relationship diagrams are supported, adding high value to the development process will require it to provide traceability from each of the other diagrams (use cases and object models, for example) through to data accesses on the data model, and along with the traceability and object to entity type attribute cross checks. While these kinds of coupling and consistency checks can add significant value to the development process, they can also require surprising amounts of time and effort to develop and test.

10

Development Dependencies and Time Compression Management

Randy gazed into the eyes of each of the people sitting around the oak conference table in his CFO's office, wondering how to react and what he might be able to do or say. During the past 2 years, with the help of the support organization that reported to him, he had spent $14 million of what would have been his company's profits completing a set of sophisticated OO development frameworks, only to find that the functionality they provided was now fully available in a number of inexpensive off-the-shelf commercial products. The managers of the five development organizations that he supported, and who had been developing their applications without the aid of his frameworks, weren't pleased. Without a detailed understanding of the frameworks he would produce, or how they would work, they had gone off in five different directions—developing applications that weren't compatible with his frameworks, or with the commercial products. No one had much to show for his or her efforts, and while the managers weren't totally sure of exactly what had happened, they were completely sure of one point. The development managers had counted on Randy to deliver, and now that he hadn't they weren't going to share the blame.

At the same time, but at a different company 2500 miles to the east, Randy's counterpart found herself, along with her boss (who was also the company's CIO) in the CFO's private conference room. The CIO was both pleased and contrite. At the cost of many difficult meetings and sleepless nights, he had fought his intuition and heeded her advice—postponing development on several critical projects until the requirements for her frameworks had been firmed up, and a search of commercial sources for the needed functionally had been completed.

The search had paid off. A vendor had been selected, a site license negotiated, and the OO frameworks that it produced were being put to good use. The first two development projects to utilize the commercial frameworks were on schedule and slightly under budget. The CFO was pleased, which was very apparent as he heartily congratulated Linda and her CIO on their insights and efforts.

The striking contrast between these two situations, and their impact on those who took part, didn't have anything to do with their companies' application development support needs, or the technologies that were required to fulfill them. These factors were the same for each company. Nor was it a function of the evolving support technologies that were quickly becoming available in the commercial marketplace to fulfill them, or the criticality of their development projects. They too were the same. What was different, and what ultimately led to the vastly different outcomes, was their understanding of critical dependencies in terms of their quickly proliferating and evolving time compressed technology environment, and the strategies that each company employed to deal with them.

In this chapter, we'll examine the four key technology dependencies that plague large-scale business application development efforts in a time compressed environment, along with workable strategies and techniques for managing each one. (See Fig. 10.1.)

Support Layer Dependencies

Let's begin with "support layer dependencies"—the dependencies that exist between the application and support layers that make up many of today's systems, the dependencies that were partly responsible for

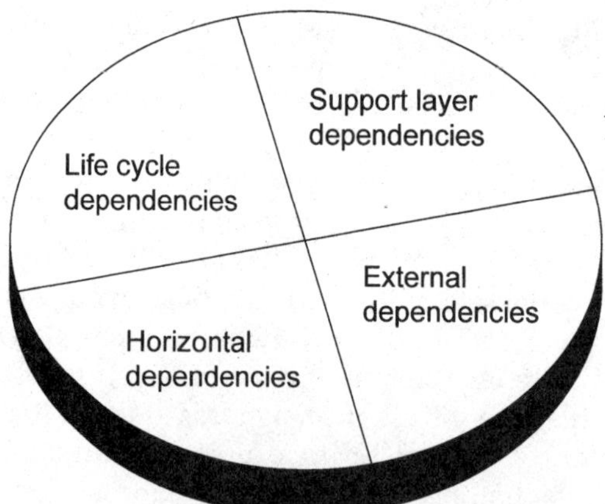

Figure 10.1 Four key dependencies that are made worse by time compressed change.

the differences between Randy's and Linda's experiences. To illustrate what application layer dependencies are, and how they work, consider the layered architecture utilized by many large-scale OO applications.[1] (See Fig. 10.2.) By removing common application behavior, and developing it in the form of a "framework" layer so that it can be leveraged by each application to achieve its unique functionality, very high levels of reuse and productivity can be achieved. Navigation frameworks, for example, can alleviate a company's developers from the time consuming tasks of designing and programming complex navigation software into each system. Embedding user navigation software into a common framework layer can also ensure that each system's navigation will behave in a consistent way, regardless of the application. The same idea holds for other functionality needed by lots of applications, such as access to common databases and integration with commonly accessed legacy systems. Object-oriented frameworks are pretty nifty tools.

But there are problems. The first problem is that frameworks can be complex, often requiring substantial amounts of time and effort to design and develop. And once they are developed they don't provide business users with any direct benefits—all they do is increase the consistency and productivity of the next set of applications. So OO frameworks can be a tough sell for those who want to use them, and in companies with limited development resources, they can be difficult to stay with for enough time to get an acceptable return on their development investments. The second, and more insidious, problem is that there are critical, but often poorly understood, time dependencies between development of frameworks and development of the applications that the frameworks support. (See Fig. 10.3.) When these

Application layer

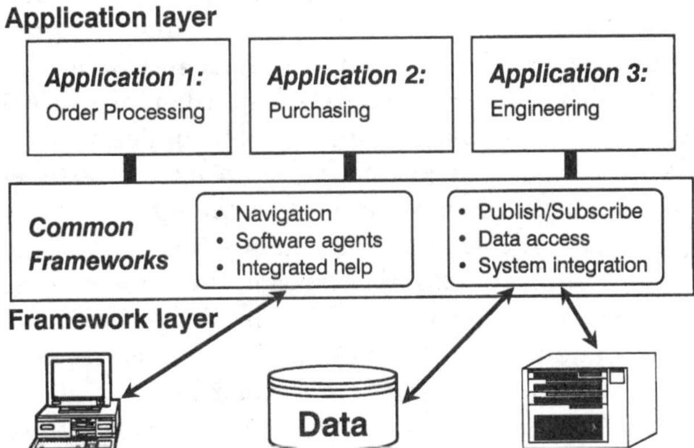

Figure 10.2 Layered object-oriented application architecture utilizing frameworks.

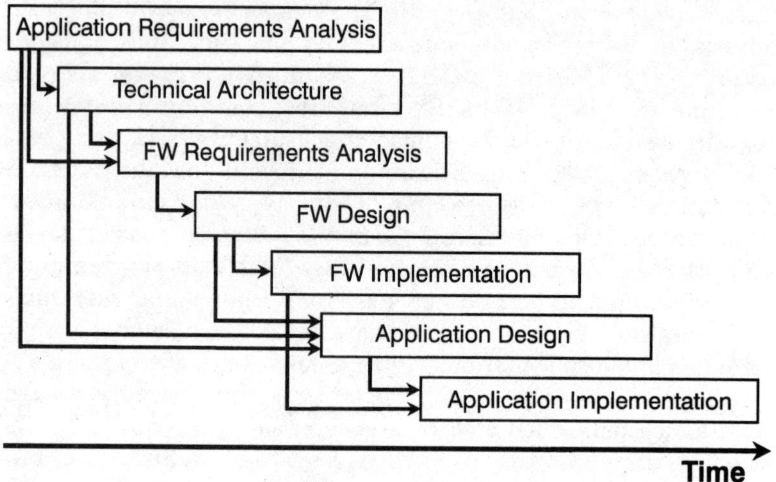

Figure 10.3 Critical dependencies between applications and frameworks. FW-frameworks.

dependencies aren't understood and taken into account, the typical result is development of application and framework layers as parallel, but as separate and disconnected, projects. The predictable consequences of this kind of development are failed projects and useless frameworks.

Fortunately, once support layer interdependencies are acknowledged and understood they aren't difficult to manage. Figure 10.3 illustrates the support layer dependencies between application and framework layers for typical OO development projects. As the figure shows, the interdependencies really occur between application and support layer phases and tasks.

To understand how these dependencies work, it's helpful to view development of the frameworks layer as a full-scale development project—with analysis, design, and implementation phases—just as the application layer has. With this in mind, the a number of critical dependencies for the frameworks analysis phase can be understood:

The first is on the application's requirements, and user interfaces that the frameworks will be expected to support. Although it's rarely necessary to wait until the application's requirements have been fully refined before beginning requirements analysis for the frameworks, it's almost always necessary to postpone their analysis until the major use cases have been defined so that the application and its user interface requirements begin to take shape. My experience is that for large-scale development projects, this typically occurs at about a third to halfway through requirements analysis—the point at which use cases can be developed for the frameworks with the application serving as their "primary actor."

As the OO framework layer is often relied upon to provide specific support functionality, such as persistence, there is a second, but equally critical, dependency on the execution architecture for the layered application. The application's design phase is also dependent on the design of the frameworks. C++ classes, for example, cannot be designed without an understanding of what the framework does and what it will require of the application. The final interdependency is the dependence of the application implementation on the implementation of the frameworks. (See Fig. 10.4.)

There are two additional characteristics of support layer dependencies that deserve mention. The first is that the support layers and the application layers that depend on them often overlap, just as the phases of OO projects do. When this happens, completion of the support layer phase doesn't necessarily gate the beginning of the application layer phases that depend on it. What is gated are the individual application tasks that depend on individual framework tasks, such as the dependence of an application's user interface components on the specific navigation frameworks that are required to support them.

Frameworks that don't take these critical dependencies into account often wreak havoc on the developers, who count on them and must revise their project plans when their frameworks aren't ready. It doesn't take many late projects for entire organizations of people who are

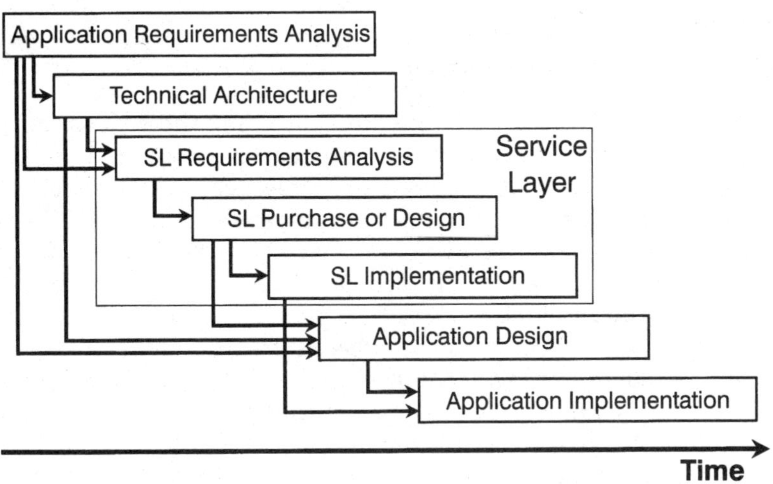

Figure 10.4 Critical dependencies between application and support layers.

measured on timely delivery of applications to sour on this very worthwhile technology. When this happens, the entire company loses out.

Although I've utilized OO frameworks as a convenient example of how support layer dependencies for new technologies interact, the concept holds true for many new development technologies and the infrastructure layers that are often required to support them. By substituting relational database development for development of OO frameworks, similar dependencies quickly surface for SQL-based graphical development, such as Client/Server applications developed using PowerBuilder. By substituting web technology for OO frameworks, similar dependencies become apparent for applications developed using Java applets. Although the service layer can be developed along with the application, or purchased from a vendor, as Figure 10.4 indicates, the dependencies remain substantially the same. The point is that from a management perspective, the support layer dependencies are similar for many of the new technologies that we encounter in our time compressed world, and that once they're identified, and taken into account, they have to be managed.

Although the precise strategies and approaches utilized to manage support layer dependencies will vary with individual technologies and situations, the support layer CSFs include:

- identifying the dependencies and acknowledging them in the plans for development projects,

- promoting communications between teams responsible for developing each layer, and

- including checkpoints within each layer's development process, at which differences between the functionality that's required of, and provided by, each layer can be identified and resolved.

By ensuring that each is achieved, and observing the dependencies outlined in the above figure, there's no reason why management shouldn't be able to keep service layer dependencies under control.

Identifying and acknowledging service layer dependencies starts with management looking for them and suspecting that they might be present in each new development technology and approach. Although this admonition may sound easy and obvious, it can be surprisingly difficult to implement. In time compressed environments, in which promising new development technologies become available at a rate too rapid to absorb, service layer dependencies aren't generally known, and many vendors aren't forthright about potentially expensive support requirements that can offset some of their products' productivity gains. The result is that this CSF isn't often achieved.

A good method for ensuring its achievement is to assign teams of seasoned developers the responsibility for analyzing and reporting on support layer technologies that might be required to make the new technology pay off. If the teams are composed of consistent sets of people, time boxed (for most new technologies, a 3- to 5-day assignment should be sufficient), and are formed as needed on an ad hoc basis, they will become sensitive to these kinds of dependencies, seeking familiar clues and patterns that to others might not be obvious. When contrasted against the tens of months and millions of dollars spent on correcting troubled development projects after unknown support dependencies have been discovered, the few thousand dollars spent on such a study becomes a very prudent investment.

With the support layer dependencies identified, and development (or procurement) of both layers under way, ensuring that the teams responsible for each layer communicate quickly surfaces as the next challenge for multilayered development. There are two main reasons why interteam communication doesn't happen unless management takes measures to actively promote it. The first is that application and support layers are typically developed by very different kinds of developers, who in many companies belong to different organizations and who have very different mindsets. While application layers are developed by application programmers, who are—or should be—close to the business, support layers such as middleware and OO frameworks are often developed by much more technical individuals, who are far more mindful of the technologies themselves than how they might be utilized to facilitate application development. Without a specific mandate to do so, these groups don't typically interact. The second reason is that people who will be measured by their ability to deliver applications on time and within budget typically won't take the extra time, or expend the extra effort, to validate how another team might make use of what they do.

The answer is to foster communication between the two teams through joint team building initiatives, briefings, walkthroughs, usability laboratories, and workshops at which members of each team can try the dependency out. This is one new technology area in which management has lots of good options, once the CSF is understood and the need to manage it is internalized.

For many large-scale development efforts, it's also necessary to take specific measures to ensure that the support layer's analysis and design remain consistent with the application's requirements. This is especially true for technologies, such as OO development, that are based on business models that evolve throughout the project. As the requirements modeling tasks proceed, and more is discovered about what its business users really want, it becomes critically important that the support layer projects track the evolutionary changes and take them into account. The best way that I've found to do this is through checkpoints at critical stages in each project, at which the application and support models are checked and recalibrated against each other. As with the other support layer dependency CSFs, the cost of doing this is small compared to the potential risk.

The problem is far broader and more pervasive than our example might suggest. Similar, and just as insidious, dependencies exist between graphically developed applications (using SQL-based development tools such as PowerBuilder) the databases that they depend on, and the analysis and development efforts that lead to the stable databases on which this kind of development depends. For successful large-scale development in a time compressed environment, the same concepts can and should be applied to interdependencies between applications and non-OO layered application architecture components, such as data models, stored procedures, and templates. The venues and details are different. The basic problems and solutions are essentially the same.

Life Cycle Dependencies

In Chap. 1 we took a quick look at the interactions among development, approach and execution technologies, along with the affects that each of these technologies has on the others. We also explored the impact of development technology maturity on the size of the domain within which they interact. In today's time compressed environment, with each of these technologies evolving and proliferating at an exponential rate, the need to take their interactions into account becomes especially acute, because:

- more of each of these technologies are becoming available for evaluation and use,

- more are involved in our applications' development and execution,

- many of the technologies we use are immature, and therefore don't fully interoperate with the other technologies in our development and execution technology environments, and

- "release propagation" (as we saw in Chap. 6) causes conflicts between different releases of these technologies.

To illustrate the number and diversity of the development technologies and sources that can become involved in today's development projects, consider a large-scale OO business application such as an order processing system or a reservations system. Its development might include:

- a work flow tool for modeling the application's reengineered business environment[2],

- a class library, purchased from a vendor, for the controls that comprise the application's user interface,

- a user interface navigation framework, purchased from another vendor, or perhaps developed internally,

- an analysis CASE tool for developing requirements and design models,

- a C++ compiler and standard template library (STL) for the system's Windows workstations,

- a tool for prototyping the applications user interface,

- a usability laboratory for validating the application's user interface,

- a class library for providing server functionality,

- a CASE tool for modeling the relational data that the application shares with other (non-OO) applications,

- a C++ compiler and STL for the application's UNIX servers,

- testing tools, and

- a tool for configuration management.

The application's execution environment might include:

- three different workstation platforms, perhaps one for entry clerks, another for the company's executives, and a third platform for employees who telecommute,

- a combination of Microsoft NT and UNIX servers for the application's data and web sites,

- mainframe servers for other data that the application must access,

- a number of different databases,

- a middleware product to provide access to the different databases,

- an ORB,

- a web browser,

- a company-standard security system, and

- a help subsystem.

The application's approach technologies might include:

- an OO methodology for requirements analysis and design,
- portions of an IE methodology for modeling the application's data and access paths,
- an approach for facilitated user development sessions,
- an approach to developing a sophisticated human computer interface (HCI),
- a separate testing approach, and
- a project management approach.

If you add them up, you'll find 12 different development technologies, 10 execution technologies and 6 approach technologies—28 separate and distinct technologies in all! If all or even most of these technologies came from a small and bounded number of vendors, were compatible with one another, and didn't change throughout the life of the project, managing their interactions throughout the development life cycle would be straightforward. But this isn't the case. They typically come from a variety of sources, some of which are competitors that have different strategies and agendas, and that have conflicts of interest when it comes to interoperating with each others' products.

The number of products, vendors, and incompatibilities can be managed—when they're chosen together by compatible teams with consistent objectives and that serve a single management. But this optimistic scenario isn't always the case. For most projects in most organizations, many of these technologies are chosen by different teams in different organizations, at different times to serve a different set of objectives—even though they must function together on many of the same development projects. While this might have worked in the past, the increasing numbers of new technologies, the rate at which they evolve, and the increasing scope and complexity of many of our late-1990s applications all but guarantees that it won't work in today's environments.

The solution is to concurrently engineer each of these technologies for our development projects, so that they are addressed at the same time, and conflicting objectives and priorities can be identified and dealt with. (See Fig. 10.5.)

To see how this solution works, let's consider each of the different kinds of development and execution technology support that are required as development teams move through their projects' life cycles and the potentially equal number of approach technologies that are required to utilize them. For large-scale development projects, the presence of multiple development and execution technologies mani-

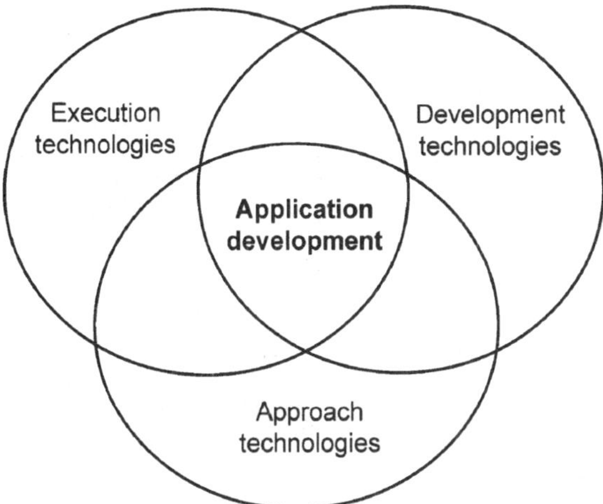

Figure 10.5 Development, approach, and execution technologies should be concurrently addressed.

fests itself as multiple "threads" of minimethodologies (approach technologies) that wind their way through different parts of the system's full development life cycle. (See Fig. 10.6.)

A User Interface thread, for example, might first appear during a project's use case-based requirements analysis, but might follow a submethodology for developing and validating the system's HCI that's closer to the system's business models and to the actual work flow environment than to the rest of development. The same thing can happen with a project's Data thread that concentrates on conversion and shared data issues, and that's driven by entity relationship data models instead of the object models that drive the rest of the system. The same thing happens with other threads, such as an Integration thread or Execution Technology thread. Each thread addresses a different, but necessary, portion of the development process, each is executed by a different set of participants with a different outlook and body of knowledge, and each can be associated with a different set of technologies and approaches.

The different threads also interact. Although few would question dependencies within each thread—for example, the dependency of User Interface Design on Business Models, or User Interface Development on User Interface Design—what most large-scale projects don't attempt to see, and therefore don't take into account, are the dependencies between threads. (See Fig. 10.7.) While User Interface Design is certainly dependent on Business Modeling, it's also dependent on the system's Requirements Analysis and Workstation Design. System Testing may be as dependent on

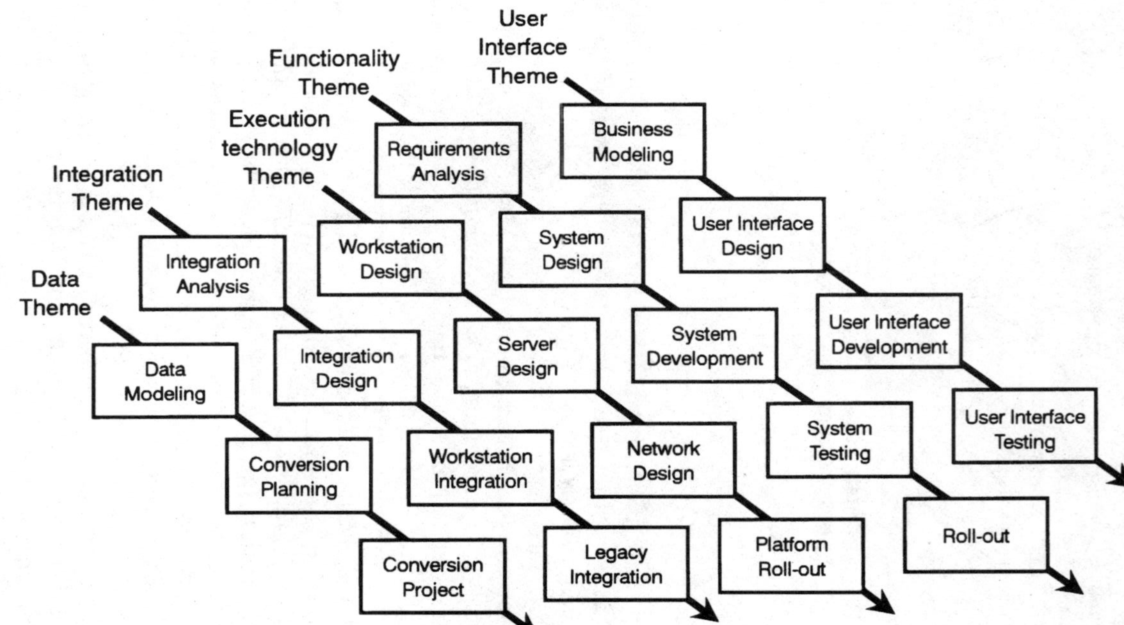

Figure 10.6   Life cycle threads present on many large development projects.

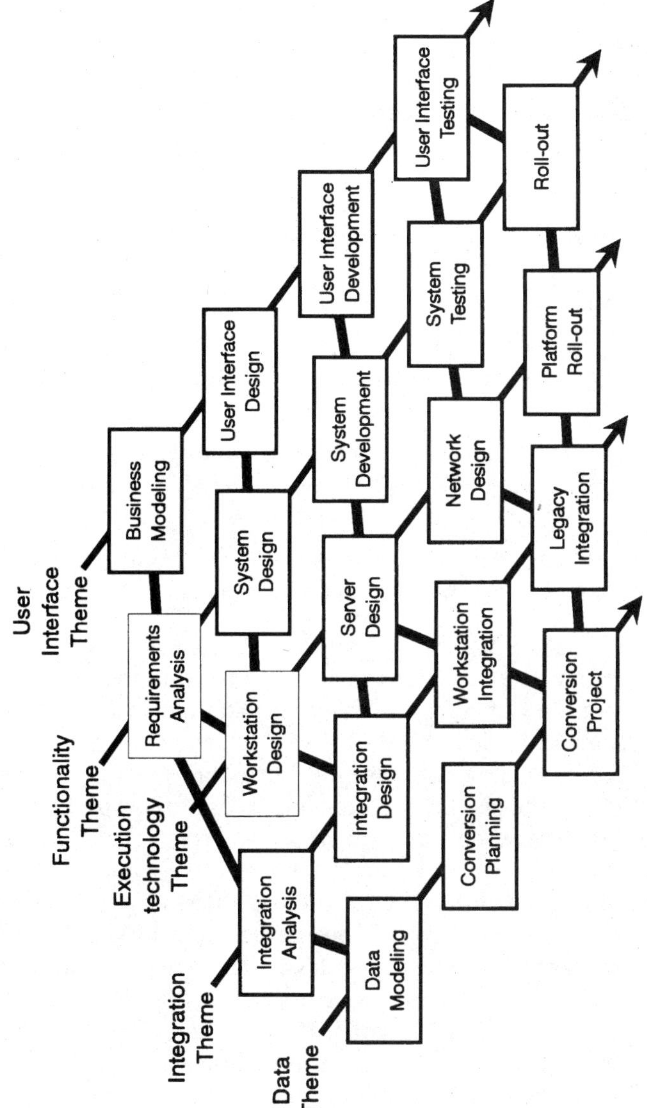

Figure 10.7 Life cycle thread interdependencies.

Execution Technology, User Interface, and Integration threads as it is on Functionality threads. And the System's Roll-out may be dependent on the Platform Roll-out, Legacy Integration, and Conversion threads.

The point isn't the precise dependencies, which will be different from company to company and project to project, but the existence of the dependencies and the need to take them into account. The solution is to concurrently develop the project's life cycle threads. This entails:

- developing requirements for dependent threads at the same time, so that each thread can take its dependent threads' requirements into account,

- including representatives from each thread's developers in technology decision processes, so that decisions for one thread don't place unworkable constraints on the others,

- including representatives from each thread in execution technology decisions, to ensure adequate performance of each of the system's components when they're rolled out, and

- holding calibration meetings at key design points, to ensure that the system's life cycle threads are evolving in consistent directions.

Although conceptually simple, these four points can be unexpectedly difficult to implement. The reason is that, in many companies, the different threads cut across different organizations with different needs and agendas. When this happens, the needs of the different organizations can come into conflict with the needs of development projects. The standards put in place by the organization that's responsible for workstation, server, and network architecture, for example, might address the company's need for stability, reliability, low maintenance, and compatibility with standard office software products. By concentrating on a small set of configurations and vendors, they can guarantee the support and service levels that they're accountable for. So the configurations they support might not include the latest version of the company's standard operating systems, which supports the latest version of C++ and graphical object libraries, that are required by some development projects, but which aren't stable enough to meet the company's service level requirements.

In most companies, the governance domains covered by these kinds of conflicts are too large for those responsible for application development projects to address. They are, however, fully addressable by IT and business management, provided that the following life cycle dependency CSFs have been achieved:

- Information Technology strategy oversight by a cross-functional steering committee, representing a broad cross section of development and execution architecture groups,

- measurement criteria for each group that are broad enough to account for conflicting sets of requirements,

- identification of the life cycle threads represented on major development projects, along with coordination plans to ensure that their interdependencies are taken into account, and

- a cross-functional mechanism for resolving interthread conflicts.

An IT strategy oversight committee composed of major stakeholders in each life cycle thread can be an effective mechanism for ensuring that IT strategies are evaluated in terms of the needs, issues, and constraints associated with each group. With such a committee in place, a strategic direction for application development would be scrutinized not only for development improvements, but also for restrictions that it might impose on network and platform architectures (that are in use, but that it might not support), user interface designs (that the technology can't handle), or interfaces to legacy architectures (that the developers of the technology may not have fully thought through). The two key ideas here are that:

- an IT strategy for improving something—such as development productivity or HCI design—is only as good as its ability to support each of the threads associated with system development, and

- early knowledge of the constraints that come along with a strategic direction is a lot better than finding about them downstream, in the form of missed commitments and failed projects.

This kind of committee need not impose a significant burden on its participants. Quarterly meetings are sufficient for most organizations, as long as the committee can meet on an ad hoc basis to handle exigencies as they come up.

The second CSF addresses the business reality that, no matter how noble the purpose, people tend to behave as they're measured. And where conflicting objectives come into play, as they do when there are many development and execution technologies on a project, striking a balance that's optimal for the business demands that those who are most directly affected be measured according to the desired business result. Although achievement of this CSF is likely to require a combination of top business and IT management, it's well worth the effort in terms of achieving a suite of development and execution information technologies that really support the business.

The third CSF addresses the management reality that unless the life cycle threads are identified and coordination plans to handle their interdependencies are implemented as an integral part of each development project, pressures on development teams to come through on time and within budget will prevent their being taken into account. It's up to IT management, via this CSF, to ensure that coming through on project commitments includes coming through on life cycle thread interdependencies.

The fourth and final CSF is a cross-functional mechanism for resolving life cycle dependency disputes. For small organizations, the strategy oversight committee can serve this purpose. But for companies that are large and geographically dispersed, and in which business units have diverse development needs, small and agile local groups, representing system architects, application developers, development support, and business users can often fulfill this CSF. The important considerations are that the groups are small and agile enough to be convened quickly when and where they're needed, that each affected area is represented (the affected areas will vary depending on the technologies and the disputes), that the groups' mission and objectives are clearly articulated, that the groups are empowered to make decisions, and that their decisions are demonstrably backed by business and IT management.

Horizontal Dependencies

The third class of large-scale application dependencies made worse by time compressed change is "horizontal dependencies"—dependencies among applications—that commonly show up as systems that don't fully interoperate with one another and as systems that have trouble accessing each other's data. This problem has two main origins.

The first is that many new technologies are much more focused on increasing development productivity and reducing maintenance than they are on fitting applications into a business environment polluted by unwanted technologies that are currently in use. From the vantage point of many new technology developers and advocates, older (legacy) technologies (that their technologies replace) represent unfortunate constraints that limit their technologies' effectiveness. They see older technologies as the results of poor decisions (or good decisions made in a poor environment) that they weren't responsible for and that they'd rather not deal with. The same mindset, of course, can apply to new (nonlegacy) technologies when they represent competing philosophies and products.

The second origin (as introduced in Chap. 1) is a result of technology maturity. Companies that develop and publish new technologies can gain a lot more return on incremental investments by introducing new and distinctive products and features than by introducing interoperability with additional older or competing technologies. A rapid prototyping facility for visualizations or software agents—things that have lots of sizzle, and are really interesting and unique—can be a lot more newsworthy than interfacing with legacy applications that were written in COBOL—applications that many companies would rather forget. Vendors of the hottest new technologies don't have time to—and from their perspectives, probably shouldn't—concern themselves with niceties, such as interoperability with technologies from another era[3].

The origins may differ, but the consequences are the same: a continuous stream of new and interesting development and execution technologies, that have lots of whiz-bang features, but that don't always interoperate with—or even recognize—other development and execution technologies that are in use at many companies. The impact on many large organizations is a loss of functionality, as business users are forced to hop from application to application along boundaries based on technologies rather than their needs. The visible result is the continual entry and reentry of the same information into different applications to serve different needs that can be found in many business organizations.

Although the problem is pervasive and the consequences can be severe, there are a number of simple yet effective measures that most application development organizations can implement to minimize their impact on the applications they develop and the business organizations that they support. These organizations can:

- develop architectures around technologies that facilitate interoperability and integration,

- enhance development methodologies and tools so that they fully address interoperability and integration, and

- take market share into account.

The simplest defense that development organizations can deploy against technologies that don't interoperate well with one another is to develop architectures around technologies that facilitate interoperability across wide ranges of technologies. A good mid-1990s example of such a technology is the relational database. Although relational databases aren't superbly suited for all technologies (storing and retrieving objects, or decision support, for example), much of our business data are stored in relational databases and they support an exceptionally wide variety of development, execution, and end user environments. The advantage of relational databases is that applications developed utilizing almost any of today's technologies can access them, and with a little care, can be made to share many of the same data. In this environment, conflicts over data currency, locking, and integrity can often be handled through database triggers or through middleware layers that deflect database calls to programs designed to identify and resolve these conflicts. CORBA-based ORBs are another good example of an increasingly common technology that can be employed to help OO applications (or even individual objects), that have been developed and execute in different technologies, to interoperate with one another. Both of these technologies accomplish the objective. But as we'll see, ORBs are in an earlier part of their life cycle than relational databases, which means that they're a better bet from interoperability and integration perspectives.

An additional measure that can, but often isn't, employed to help ensure that applications developed in different technologies will interoperate with one another is inclusion of interoperability tasks and checkpoints in the form of an integration or interoperability thread in the company's application development methodology. Doing so can help ensure that interoperability considerations, such as utilization of common workstation architectures, OLE links among workstation-based applications, identification of required functionality among reusable components (that are already in production or that are being built as part of another development project), or discrepancies among data or user interface conventions, are addressed.

As most development methodologies, and the tools that support them, are focused on standard approaches to application development, inclusion of an interoperability thread usually means that the methodologies and tools will have to be modified and enhanced. In most organizations, implementing the required modifications and enhancements shouldn't be especially difficult. Methodologies, if they're to be useful, have to be modified and enhanced so that they fit into each organization's culture, needs, and style of development. And they have to be maintained over time, so that they can continue to provide meaningful support to the company's development and execution technologies as they evolve and proliferate under the impact of time compressed change. In most companies, the additional investment associated with adding integration and interoperability tasks—such as checking for common user interface standards, locating common behavior among other applications' class hierarchies, and designing applications based on a common set of frameworks, to a methodology that's already in flux—should be more than offset by business productivity gains that result when applications really interoperate. Although development tools are harder to modify and enhance, my experience is that, where there's good technical justification for the enhancements, and their customer is willing to pay for the required modifications, there are CASE tool vendors that are willing to customize and enhance their products so that they support the functionality needed to achieve good interoperability and integration. This kind of enhancement represents a "win-win" situation, in which the purchasing company gets exactly what it wants, when it needs it, and the CASE tool vendor gets the benefits of the customer's inputs and insights along with a chance to offload some of its development costs.

A final strategy for helping to ensure that applications developed in a time compressed technology environment continue to integrate and interoperate is taking market share into account. By building development and execution technology architectures around technologies that are expected to maintain a substantial and increasing base of new users, the market forces that drive development technology publishers can be leveraged to help ensure that an organization's applications will interoperate.

To understand how this works, consider the concept of a development technology's useful life (introduced in Chap. 4). (See Fig. 10.8.) While technologies in each portion of their useful lives can be successfully leveraged, successful development and execution technologies that are in the early portion of their life cycles (the left part of the curve) will attract the most technology vendors. The reason is that software product development is a time-consuming and capital-intensive business, and to be successful, developers and publishers of development and execution technologies have to bet on the present and the future, not on what may have happened in the past. And in time compressed environments, the future tends to come up very fast! To companies that want to be sure that the technologies they deploy

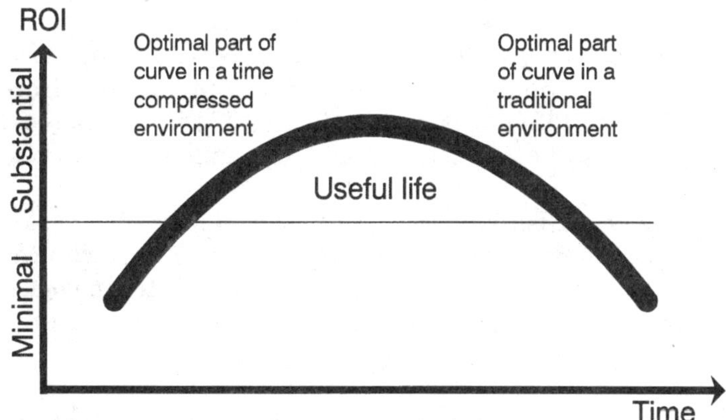

Figure 10.8 How the technology life cycle can be leveraged to help ensure interoperability in a time compressed technology environment.

interoperate, this means that they stand a better chance of success if they go with technologies in the earlier portion of their useful lives—technologies such as CORBA ORBs in the late 1990s—that are finally maturing to the extent that they can be successfully utilized in real business environments, but that also have bright futures.

The interesting thing about this strategy is that it's so different from the strategy that would have been used to achieve the same result in a non-time-compressed environment. In relatively stable environments, such as those that IT organizations enjoyed during the 1970s and much of the 1980s, when development and execution software vendors were able to sell into a stable market, leveraging technologies in the latter portions of their life cycles was the best bet. In today's time compressed environments, it's precisely the opposite.

External Dependencies

External dependencies—technology dependencies between technologies developed in house and those developed by external vendors—represent an interesting set of risks and opportunities for companies developing applications in today's time compressed environment. At the heart of the problem is a "catch 22" situation, in which application development organizations need development and execution technologies that aren't yet available from commercial sources, but which commercial vendors are developing very fast. If they wait for stable and tested commercial products—the kind that can be utilized with confidence for mission-critical applications—to become available, they run the risk of having to develop their applications in older technologies that won't carry their organizations into the future. If they develop the needed technologies on their own, they run the risk of spending substantial sums of their company's bottom line dollars developing technologies only to find that, before they're finished, the same technologies are available from commercial vendors at a fraction of the price. Those that choose correctly, like Linda, are heroes. Those, such as Randy, who are scooped by the commercial market, look like fools.

The difference between becoming a Randy or a Linda is the result of strategy and awareness more than business acumen or technical expertise. In a time compressed environment, in which technologies and vendors come and go at an accelerating pace, taking measures such as:

- staying attuned to what the development technology market is doing,

- establishing checkpoints at which in-house and commercial development efforts are evaluated at short intervals, and

- managing expectations, so that switching back and forth between in house and commercial sources for similar (or even identical) technologies doesn't take anyone by surprise,

can go a long way toward blunting time compression's ravaging effects.

The objectives of an IT research and planning organization, in a time compressed environment, should therefore include close contact with a wide range of technology vendors, so that their strategies and directions, technology initiatives, successes and failures, are understood, and conclusions can be drawn. The idea is to continually monitor, the viability of commercial sources for needed technologies so that the foundation for future development initiatives can be put in place and kept up to date. My experience during the mid-1990s is that monitoring fast-moving technologies (OO CASE tools, CORBA-based ORBs, and Microsoft OLE, for example), on a quarter-by-quarter basis, is sufficient. As we move into the next century, and time compressed change accelerates the pace of technology development, it might easily become necessary to monitor key technologies on a monthly basis!

From a project perspective, the development, approach, and execution technologies that can impact its success should be monitored on an equally frequent basis. Had Randy instituted this simple precaution, he might have been able to predict that some commercial vendors would be successful in bringing the project's key technologies to market. Armed with that information, he might have been able to concentrate his framework development efforts on technologies that wouldn't become available from commercial sources, instead of those that did, saving his company's shareholders several million dollars in the process. Were he sufficiently astute, some of the money he saved might have been channeled into monitoring quickly emerging standards, so that regardless of which direction things took, the development organizations that he supported wouldn't have been caught short.

Education of business peers, to managing their expectations, is also becoming an increasingly important factor in time compressed technology management. Although businesspeople aren't always aware of the accelerating pace at which technologies are emerging, a quick look at our global financial markets reveals that at least some business people are well acquainted with continuous and violent change, the havoc that it can wreak, and hedging strategies for managing it.

Hedging is what concurrent monitoring and development of emerging technologies is all about. By maintaining close contact among vendor and in-house development efforts, monitoring problems and progress, meeting often to assess status and draw conclusions, and taking measures to ensure that key development projects maintain sufficient agility to go both ways, many of the problems associated with external dependencies can be dealt with. As time compressed change increases the rate of key technology evolution and proliferation, the range of intervals may have to be shortened and the range of monitored technologies expanded. The concept, however, should continue to work.

References

1.   The emphasis here is on layering of distributed OO application behavior into application and frameworks layers, without regard to which hardware and system software platforms different portions of each layer might be implemented on. This kind of layered architecture should not be confused with Client/Server architectures, in which part of an application runs on a workstation client, the rest runs on a server, and the critical dependencies are a bit more obvious. In this kind of application, the frameworks layer might be implemented on each workstations, as well as on a number of servers. For a good discussion on this kind of architecture, along with how OO frameworks fit into the big picture, see Robert Orfali, Dan Harkey, and Jeri Edwards, *The Essential Distributed Objects Survival Guide*, Wiley, 1996.
2.   For good discussions of business reengineering, see Michael Hammer and James Champy "Reengineering the Corporation," Harper Business, 1993; and Ivar Jacobson, Maria Ericsson and Agenta Jacobson, "The Object Advantage: Business Process Reengineering with Object Technology," Addison-Wesley, 1994.
3.   For insight into the pressures on vendors of hot new technologies, along with their rationale for not providing the highest possible service levels, see Geoffrey A. Moore, "Inside the Tornado," Harper Business, 1995.

A Life Cycle Approach to Time Compression Management

The entire conference room sat in stunned silence, as Bob—whose twisted face had reached a deep shade of purple—completed the screaming tirade that he had directed at his company's corporate CIO and returned the telephone to its resting place. The outburst, which was neither becoming nor typical of the 10,000-person Sales and Marketing Division's President, underscored the depths that his New Order Management System project had reached, and the importance of the half-million orders that weren't being processed. The custom system, which a well-respected vendor had developed for him, had run into trouble interfacing with the division's Inventory and Credit systems. And instead of offering constructive suggestions and providing much-needed help, the corporate CIO had washed his hands of the entire affair, explaining that C++, the language that the vendor had written the system in, wasn't part of their corporate standard and was therefore beyond his responsibility to support.

The incident, and the firings that resulted from it, didn't have a lot to do with order processing, the vendor, integration with legacy systems, or C++. The issues were empowerment, a division's right to seek the best IT solutions for its business, and the obligation of corporate IT to support its divisions' systems initiatives—regardless of the technologies that might be involved. Behind these issues—and the underlying reason for the problem and the incident—was corporate IT's traditional approach to new technologies, which didn't enable it to support the breadth of technologies that today's applications are developed in, and the advent of time compressed change that brings today's vast array of new technologies about.

In this chapter, we'll examine the management of time compressed change from the perspective of technology life cycles—the processes through which new information technologies enter organizations, are utilized to develop and run applications, and are eventually discarded. We'll see why the traditional life cycle approaches, that worked perfectly well in more stable times, fail in today's world of empowerment, in which business units are free to choose from a wide variety of multiple and evolving technologies that couldn't have been foreseen just a decade earlier. Then we'll look at a more fluid and less synchronous approach to life cycle management that's based on acquisition, communication, management, and connectivity, rather than the well-worn sequential familiarization, acquisition, transition, and implementation phases. (See Fig. 11.1.) And we'll see why the new approach is better suited to support the combination of new technologies and empowerment that comprise our companies' IT landscapes.

Traditional Approaches to Technology Life Cycle Management

Before we dive into our new TCM approach to technology life cycle management, let's take a quick peek at traditional approaches to IT management, so that we can better understand the differences between what most companies do and what they should be doing. Although traditional approaches are as different as the companies they support, most are renditions of a basic process in which development, approach, and execution technologies are identified, selected, and carefully fit into a single, centrally controlled, and highly opti-

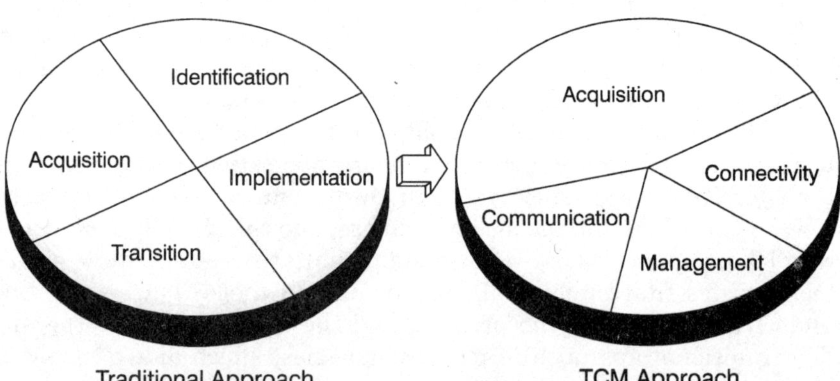

Figure 11.1 Traditional and TCM approaches to life cycle management.

mized environment. The idea was simple, and it had a singular and noble purpose: to make the most of the stable trickle of marginally adequate development, approach, and execution technologies of the day, so that they could be harnessed to support the business.

The process usually began with an "identification" or "familiarization" phase, in which the horizon was scanned for new and emerging information technologies. While some (mostly larger) companies maintained organizations to do this, and a few supplemented what they found by developing new and innovative technologies on their own, most delegated the process to their major IT vendor. Independent technology sources, if they were considered at all, were typically limited to systems integration vendors and consulting firms that also based their offerings on the technologies of the day. The results included controlled and stable evolution of the information technologies deployed by most companies as they moved—often in lockstep—from one offering to the next, with good backward compatibility with older information technologies that were still in use, and a stable of qualified people to staff increasing numbers of development projects. What they didn't include were familiarization with business needs, attainment of an understanding of how the company's evolving suite of information technologies might be harnessed to address them, and an evolving and responsive strategy to providing optimal business support.

Against the preglobalization backdrop of centralized management, stable business needs, controlled evolution of IT, and few strategic applications, it worked. Familiarization with the next incremental evolution of the stable technologies of the day could be accomplished largely through vendor seminars and briefings. As new suites of technologies matured and became widely used, they could be acquired, and with a bit of direction and help from a friendly technology's vendor, successfully transitioned into the company's centrally optimized IT environment.

The small, centrally maintained set of development, approach, and execution technologies of the day made it possible to do this. The sources of new technologies were few, the target was fixed, and for the most part the hurdles that had to be overcome as part of the transition process were stable and well known. As late as the mid-1980s, transition from hierarchical to relational databases quickly became a well-defined, generally understood, and repeatable process. Since many organizations, and the suite of systems that supported them, were architected along centralized autocratic business models, implementing the transitions—switching from IMS and IDMS to DB2, for example—could be executed and monitored as a set of centralized and controlled processes. And when the transition processes were completed, the result was a new, single, long-lived, and centrally maintained environment that was reoptimized for the company's new suite of applications that was evolving at a pace that, by today's time compressed standards, seems calm and lethargic.[1]

But during the same mid-1980s, the well-defined, centrally maintained IT environments and processes were beginning to break. New and innovative development and process technologies—such as IE-based CASE—were proving difficult to transition to and successfully implement.[2] At the same time, new execution technologies—in the form of fast, inexpensive, and ubiquitously available PC-based workstations, servers, and tools—were beginning to make a host of new possibilities available to newly reengineered business units that were empowered and encouraged to take control of their own destinies, and by inference, to become technologically independent.[3] The result was the emergence of a significant gap between the single IT environment that the centrally optimized IT life cycle model produced, and the business needs that it had to serve. This is the gap that, in our opening example, cost two people their jobs, and that comprises one of the fundamental problems behind many of the issues discussed throughout this book.

What's needed is a reengineered life cycle model that's optimized to support the host of quickly evolving empowered business organizations that populate today's companies and the increasing array of ITs that result from the time compressed technology changes that we all have to live with. (See Fig. 11.2.) Let's take a look at the reengineered model so that we can see how it might work.

Critical Assumptions and Objectives for the TCM Life Cycle Approach

To the extent that the TCM life cycle approach is a process with a number of definable states through which new technologies pass, our reengineered model—which consists of acquisition, communication, management, and connectivity components—mirrors the traditional approach. But this view belies differences that are both fundamental and far-reaching in their effect. Two of the most basic differences between the two models are the set of assumptions on which each model is based, and the sets of objectives that the traditional and reengineered models are designed to achieve.

Let's start with critical assumptions—the set of fundamental assumptions that each model makes about the technologies, development environment, and business units that it must be able to support.[4] Whether the critical assumptions are explicitly identified, analyzed, and painstakingly documented, or implicitly made by default,

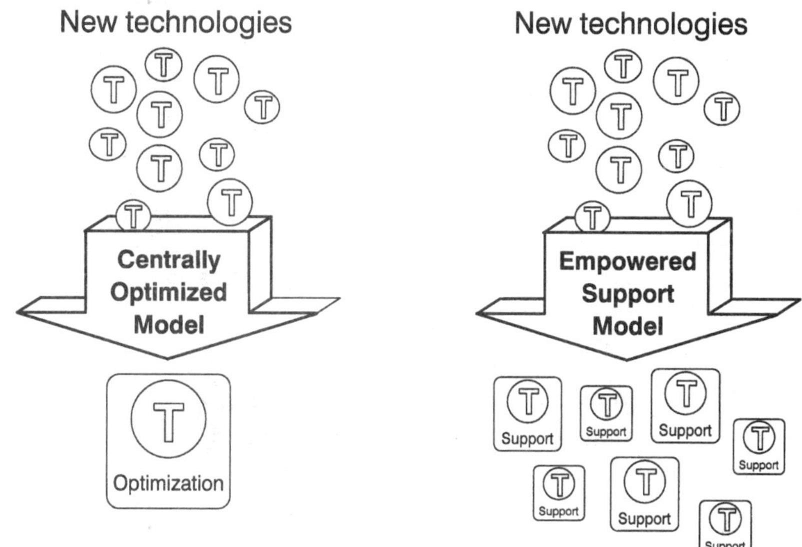

Figure 11.2 New and traditional models for information technology adoption.

they're equally important because they form the basis for each company's technology life cycle approach. And, as we'll see, the differences between the traditional set of critical assumptions and the set of critical assumptions that's appropriate for our turn-of-the-century time compressed environment, could hardly be more pronounced.

The basic set of traditional technology assumptions—the 1970s set of technology assumptions that continue to guide many of our IT organizations—include a stable environment, a bounded suite of ITs, a small number of technology vendors, and a technology environment that's controllable by IT (or more accurately, controllable by a small set of IT vendors and influenceable by IT). Today, and almost certainly into the early part of the next century, this assumption doesn't hold up. The forces of time compressed change provide us with a new, unstable and diverse set of technologies that can change month by month. Technologies—such as ParcPlace Smalltalk, Visual C++, Java, PowerBuilder, Dynasty, and HPS—can come into direct conflict with one another, as they represent vastly different approaches, from a growing array of large and small vendors, to do the same things. A similar set of differences, changes, and conflicts permeates almost every corner of our development and run-time technologies, from middleware standards—such as CORBA versus ActiveX/OLE—to an equally chaotic set of run-time environments in terms of different technologies for databases, web sites, servers, networks, and desktop workstations.

Changes in the critical assumptions that we make about the development environment that our suite of ITs must support are no less dramatic. The host of business units, each with its own set of requirements for IT support—and increasingly often, with its own set of internal- and vendor-based solutions for its needs—represents a significant break from the stable lockstep environment of the past. If our re-engineered technology life cycle is to work, if it is to provide meaningful value to our reengineered business units as they struggle to compete in their evolving global markets, it must do a lot more than simply support a diverse and challenging technology environment. To succeed in our time compressed technology and business environments, our reengineered life cycle must actively support the company's business units, along with the suites of technologies and vendors that they're increasingly empowered to choose for development and execution of their applications.

The underlying critical assumption here is that IT is no longer—and should no longer be—the exclusive provider of ITs to the business community. Today's business users have the ability and the impetus to make their own informed choices when it comes to development, approach, and execution technologies, along with a ready and willing set of external vendors to help them implement the choices that they make. If our business organizations are to successfully compete in tomorrow's time compressed business and technology environments, they must make a fundamental shift from exclusive provider of ITs to the non-exclusive roles of IT provider and facilitator to an increasingly empowered set of customers. And if our reengineered approach to technology life cycle management is to work, it must hold up under each of these critical assumptions. (See Fig. 11.3.)

Given these fundamental shifts in our critical assumptions, let's take a look at what the technology, environment, and business life cycle objectives of our reengineered life cycle should be so that IT can provide appropriate turn-of-the-century business support. While the objectives of the traditional life cycle technology model center around providing indirect business user support in stable and managed business and technology environments, our new set of objectives must address the combination of time compressed change and a community of increasingly empowered, capable, and technology literate business users.

To do this, our technology life cycle objectives must shift from ensuring that a small trickle of new and obsolete technologies don't adversely impact the company's stable and highly optimized development approach and execution technology environments, to a combina-

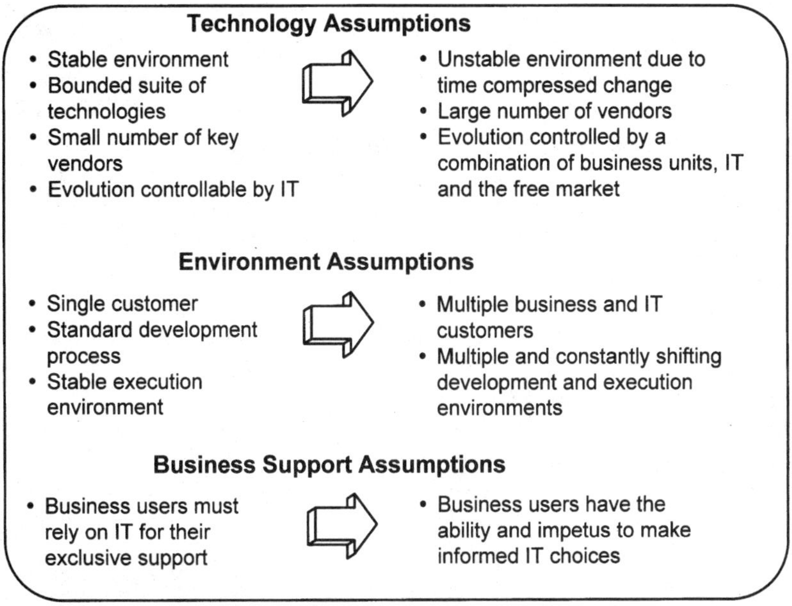

Technology Assumptions

- Stable environment
- Bounded suite of technologies
- Small number of key vendors
- Evolution controllable by IT

- Unstable environment due to time compressed change
- Large number of vendors
- Evolution controlled by a combination of business units, IT and the free market

Environment Assumptions

- Single customer
- Standard development process
- Stable execution environment

- Multiple business and IT customers
- Multiple and constantly shifting development and execution environments

Business Support Assumptions

- Business users must rely on IT for their exclusive support

- Business users have the ability and impetus to make informed IT choices

Figure 11.3 Critical assumptions for traditional and TCM approaches to life cycle management.

tion of coping with time compressed change and leveraging advances in ITs for overall business benefit. A fundamental, and new, technology life cycle objective must therefore be to support business units as they leverage the increasingly diverse array of development, approach, and execution technologies that they're empowered to acquire and use. A second—and at first glance, conflicting—objective must be to ensure that the diverse array of application technologies that results from our first new objective doesn't impair the company's ability to leverage its corporate information assets over multiple business units. In addition to addressing multiple and evolving technology needs of individual business units, our reengineered approach must also address the needs of different business units' IT infrastructures to interoperate with each other, and the needs of the company as a whole, for consistent and reliable access to all of its information.

To do this, our technology life cycle objectives must undergo two fundamental changes. The first is a shift in emphasis away from optimizing the development environment and support for each new or enhanced technology, as it makes its way into—and eventually out of—the company's development and execution environments, toward optimization for the large and diverse suite of technologies that populate the company's business units. The implications of this shift are that specific technologies won't be supported as well as they might have been in more stable times, and that the range of technologies that actually in use will be supported much better.

The second change is also a shift in emphasis—this time from optimization for a stable set of technologies to optimization for the multiple technologies of today that are undergoing rapid, uncontrollable, and accelerating change. The key idea is that the objectives of the technology life cycle must shift away from technology and toward technology change. In mathematical terms, we have to shift our emphasis from development, approach and execution technologies to their first and second derivatives. The implication is that, to achieve this new objective, we'll have to monitor and act on a new and different set of technology life cycle variables. And, as with the first change, the impact will be a lower level of optimization for the hot technologies of the day and a higher level of optimization for suites of technologies over time. (See Fig. 11.4.)

The shift in life cycle objectives for supporting business users must also undergo two changes. The first is a shift away from the traditional support model, in which the needs and prerogatives of business users are buffered by application development and production organizations that are steeped in, and optimized for, fixed sets of technologies, to a new model in which the life cycle provides business users with more direct and immediate support. The second change is that

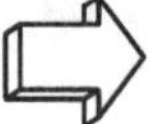

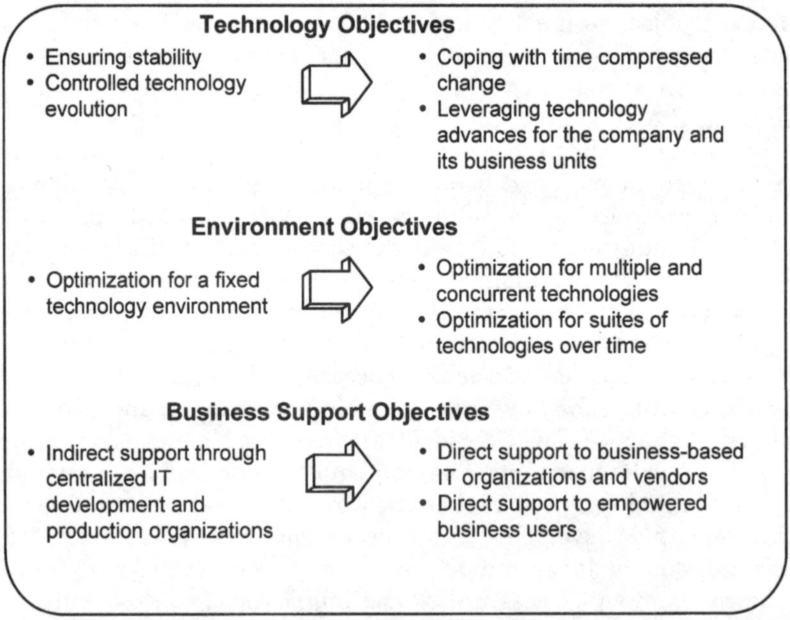

Figure 11.4 Objectives for traditional and TCM approaches to life cycle management.

the business support objectives must be broadened to include, not only the company's business users, but also a combination of traditional business users, technology-literate business users, business unit–based IT organizations, and the technology vendor and systems integration communities that support the companies business users.

TCM Life Cycle Components

Against the backdrop of these far-reaching fundamental changes in critical assumptions and objectives, let's take a look at each of our TCM life cycle components to see how the changes are addressed.

At first glance, the acquisition, communication, management, and connectivity components of the new process resemble the familiarization, acquisition transition, and implementation phases of the traditional approach. But they're as fundamentally different as the critical assumptions and objectives that both processes support. In addition to the tasks and activities that they contain, which we'll examine in the rest of this chapter, there's a key difference that must be understood for the reengineered life cycle process to make sense. The difference is that, while the traditional life cycle model is based on a *synchronous* process, implemented as a series of head-to-tail sequentially executed phases, the new model is based on an *asynchronous* process consisting of concurrently executed components. (See Fig. 11.5.) With the exception of Acquisition, which starts before the other components, the components that make up the new life cycle model execute

Traditional model: Discrete phases

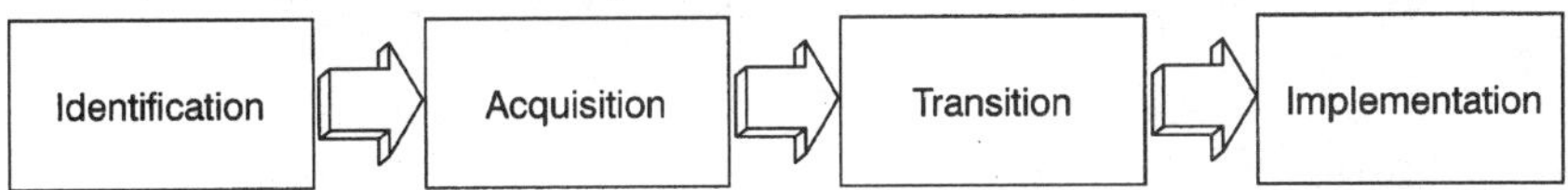

Reengineered model: Concurrent components

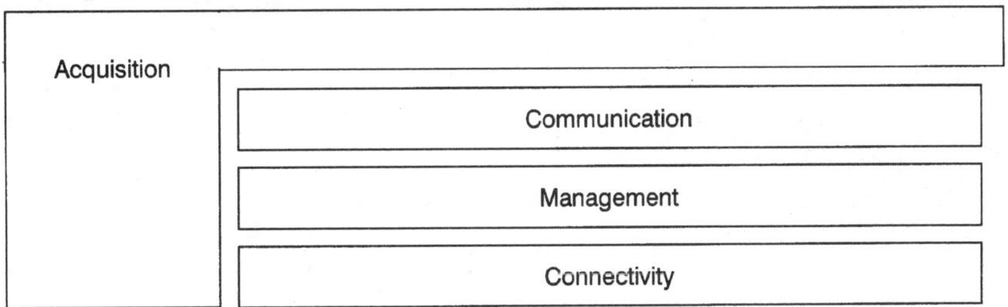

Figure 11.5 Discrete phase versus current component technology life cycle models.

concurrently with each another. Once technologies have been acquired—which, in our reengineered model, can occur through IT, business units, and external vendors—three key processes occur at the same time. These are the processes through which information about the technology is communicated, the technologies are managed, and through which we ensure connectivity between applications developed and executed using the new technology.

In our reengineered model, development, approach, and execution technologies are free to come on the scene, run the course of their useful lives, and be discarded. But it all happens within the context of a technology life cycle framework consisting of acquisition, communication, management, and connectivity components. When viewed from a business perspective, over the abundance of concurrent development, approach, and execution technologies that populate today's IT and business landscapes, the life cycle components are in continuous flux—with different instances of each component dealing with different technologies—as they progress through the phases of their life cycles at varying rates. (See Fig. 11.6.) When viewed at a point in time, such as the time indicated by the vertical line on the figure, different portions of each component are active for different technologies at the same time.

It's important to keep this "big picture" business perspective in mind, so that we understand the new model in the context of the many technologies that populate an entire company. But to understand the new TCM model so that it can be applied in a real-world organization, we'll have to take a closer look so that we can understand how each component of the life cycle model addresses each new technology as it runs its course. Here's how it works.

TCM Acquisition Component

As the concurrent component model implies, the acquisition component plays a unique and pivotal role in our reengineered approach to technology life cycle management. (See Figs. 11.6–11.7.) Its tasks and activities begin before the new technology comes on the scene and before the start of the other life cycle components. The acquisition component continues in parallel with the other components, through the technology's selection and utilization, and it finishes after the other components have finished—after the technology has run its useful life and disappears from the corporate landscape. The acquisition component's tasks include:

- working with a new and expansive set of technology sources,

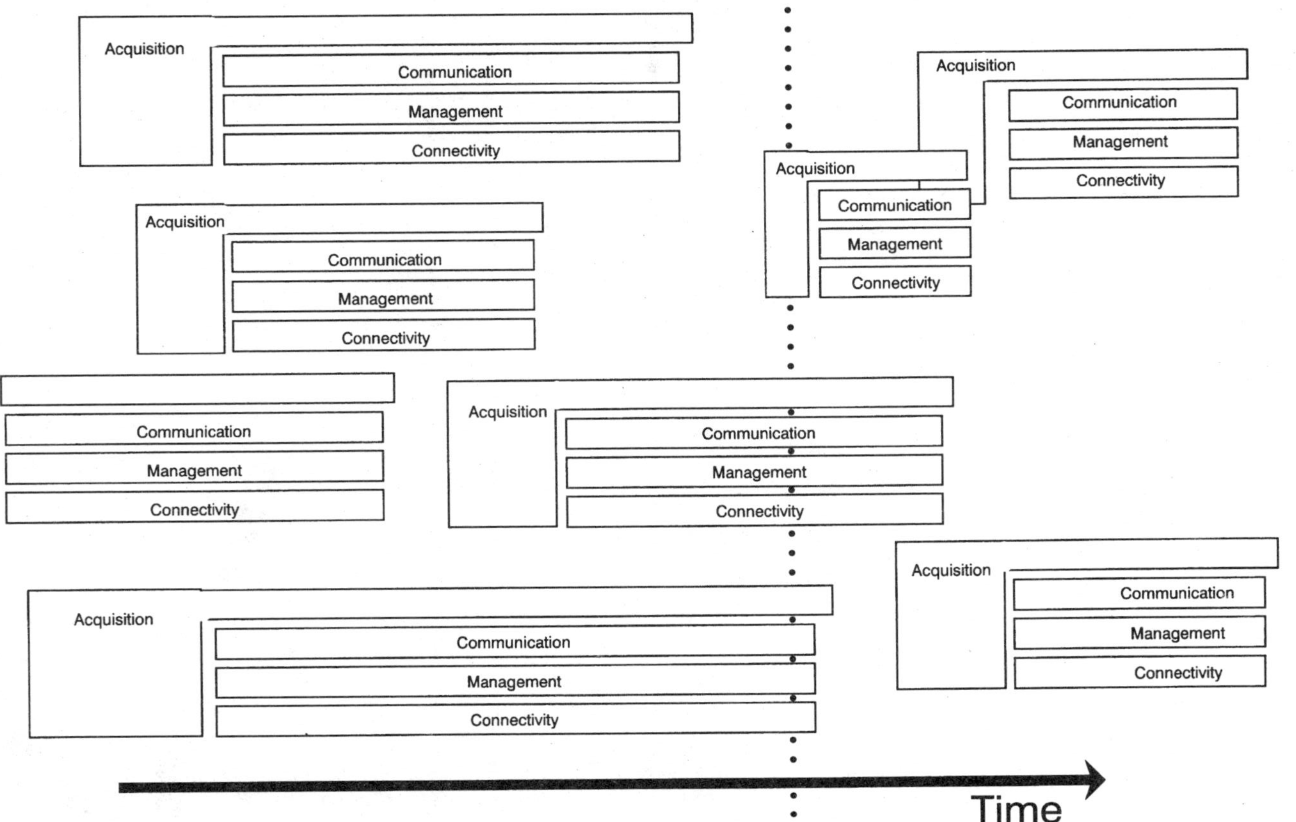

Figure 11.6 Business perspective: many concurrent models covering many different technologies.

- continuous monitoring and assessment of emerging technologies and technology trends,

- continuous monitoring of emerging business models, business needs, and business trends,

- modeling the technology's life cycle, solving for maximum ROI, and

- documenting the options, requirements, and commitments associated with the technology.

To be effective in a time compressed environment, the task involving continuous monitoring and assessment of emerging technologies must include a lot more than the perfunctory new vendor- and product-related activities that many companies currently perform. Its evaluation activities must be broad enough to encompass all of the technologies that the company's empowered business users might reasonably come in contact with for their application development. Technologies that business units can purchase through IT, technologies that they can purchase themselves, technologies that might be used by systems integration and consulting vendors who sell directly to the business units, and technologies that business users read about in magazines should all be addressed. In this model, the sources of the technologies that feed the evaluation process—and to a slightly lesser extent, interactions between those technologies and their sources—are driven by the organization's empowered business units and the free market, not by IT. This is a sharp departure from traditional models, in which technology sources are supposed to be—but in reality, often aren't—centrally driven. It's also a departure that addresses the realities of time compressed change and empowerment.

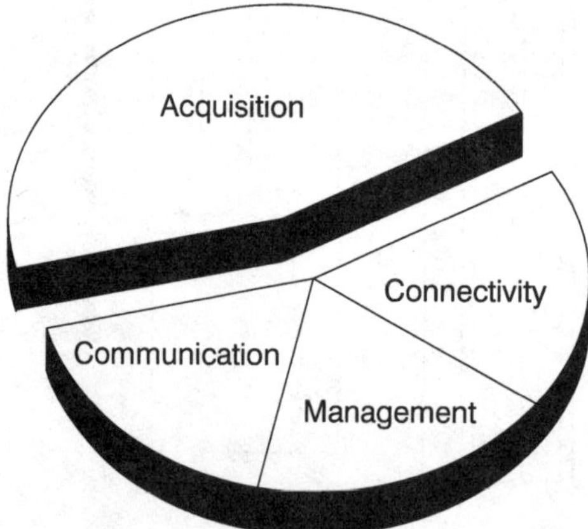

Figure 11.7 TCM acquisition component.

The results of this departure are a more fluid set of technology sources and a broader set of interactions between the technologies that they produce and the increasingly expansive and diverse set of empowered individuals that populate today's flatter and more nimble organizations. To meet the needs of this new and expansive audience, the results of the monitoring and assessment activities must include a combination of business and technical products, such as management seminars, technical white papers, business reports, and hands-on workshops. If the company's technology assessment activities don't address the development, approach, and execution technologies that are available to the its business communities, and if they don't reach—and aren't meaningful to—the company's population of business and technical users who are empowered to make technology decisions, there will be little worthwhile benefit from this important task.

As important as meeting the expansive demands of today's time compressed technology environments—but more often overlooked—is continuous monitoring of business trends and needs, so that the impact of time compressed changes on today's business requirements can be taken into account. Understanding where the company's business, and the environment in which it operates, are headed is a CSF for properly assessing the implications of new technologies in a time compressed environment. Armed with this information, the impact of new technologies—and, more importantly, new combinations of new development, approach, and execution technologies—can be understood and assessed.[5]

Although the time compressed onslaught of new technologies can't be slowed by the need to understand their impact on business and technology strategies and infrastructure, their utilization can be understood in terms of business benefit and the results disseminated to the company's decision makers. A valuable, but almost universally underutilized, tool for tracking, analyzing, and reporting on these interactions is the matrix processor found in many information engineering CASE tools, and more recently in some OO CASE tools as well. By entering associations between combinations of development, approach, and execution technologies, and business and technology strategy and infrastructure parameters, a full picture of these complex impacts can be brought to light. By extending the associations to include business and IT objectives and CSFs, and adding weighting factors to the business parameters and properties to the associations, the nature of each technology impact can be analyzed. The suite of technologies can then be optimized for a best fit to the desired set of business and IT strategy and infrastructure impacts and benefits.

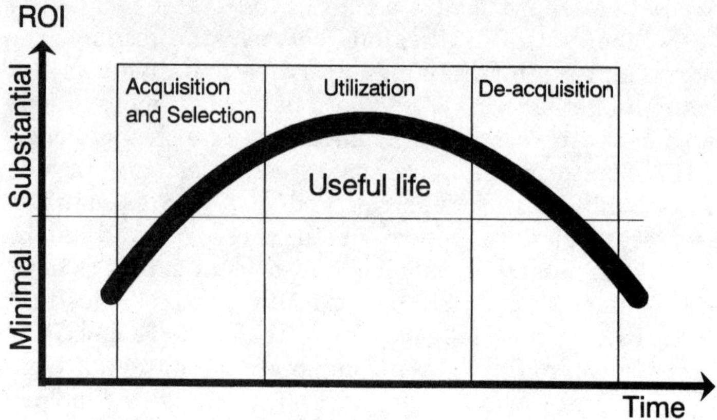

Figure 11.8 Optimization of a technology over its useful life.

The acquisition, utilization, and deacquisition tasks can also be optimized for maximum technology life cycle ROI. (See Fig. 11.8.) Once the interactions among these tasks are understood, these acquisition component tasks can be managed to control the combinations of training, infrastructure development, and cultural change that we explored in Chap. 4, so that the ROI to the business is maximized over the useful life of each technology in a number of different technology combination scenarios.

Armed with this information, the technology suite and scenario that best provides maximum return to the business can be chosen, and each of the technologies in the suite can be managed to its forecasted useful life for the company, its strategy, and its infrastructure. As new application development initiatives surface, the acquisition component tasks for each initiative can—and should—be reoptimized for the current set of business objectives, technology combinations and IT parameters. Although some of the business, technology, and IT optimizations will conflict with each other, an overall "sweet spot"— the operating area in which each of these optimizations is reasonably served—can be achieved.

The key idea here, which is also a technology compression management CSF, is that optimization in time compressed business and technology environments requires that the operating point—the "sweet spot" that represents the best overall compromise—be allowed to shift. A dynamic environment demands an equally dynamic set of optimizations.

When the technology and infrastructure optimization curves, representing a number of initiatives, are combined with life cycle optimization curves, a two-dimensional region of best overall ROI for the suites of technologies in use at any point in time can be developed.

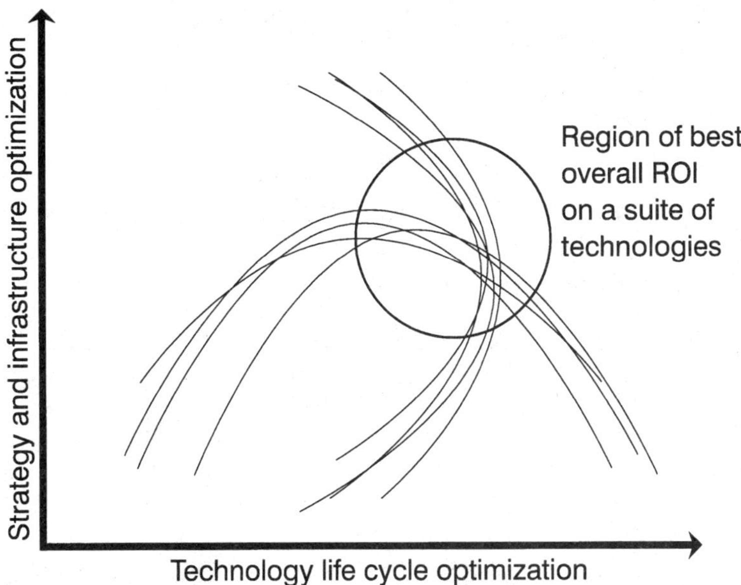

Figure 11.9 Overall optimization along two dimensions.

(See Fig. 11.9.) Although, at first glance this idea might seem a bit complex, this kind of optimization can be achieved with little more than a good matrix processor and an electronic spreadsheet.

The final optimization that should be included in the acquisition component is setting the IT project mix based on the impact of each additional technology on current commitments and downstream constraints. Analyzing and documenting each new technology's requirement, in terms of technology infrastructure, architecture options, culture, skills, and competencies will bring an overall picture of the options and constraints associated with the technology's implementation in its intended environment to light. By repeating the exercise for a number of different technology, staffing, and infrastructure scenarios, an overall view of the relationships between new technology options, their business and IT benefits, and their infrastructure and Human Resources requirements and constraints will become apparent.

With the aid of fast desktop workstations equipped with matrix processors and spreadsheets, these simulations can be conducted in real time, as time compressed technologies and needs come on the scene and must be addressed. The CSFs for making this work is for IT and business management to:

- set technology policy guidelines for the company and its business units, based on the results of the scenario simulations,
- ensure that the simulations are available and easy to run, and
- ensure that technology and business leaders understand, and are measured against, the business's overall objectives.

The idea here is not to totally optimize the technology mix. There are too many technologies and legitimate conflicting interests to do that. Nor is the idea to optimize the development, approach, and execution technology mix for each project. The goal is to utilize this model as a framework for achieving a workable set of compromises between the needs of individual projects and those of the business. Although far-reaching, expensive, and disturbing to some users, I believe that the additional monetary and organizational costs associated with this task are a fraction of the costs of the confusion and chaos that result when there is no overall approach to new technologies in a time compressed environment.

In addition to providing the means for dynamically selecting and optimizing the suite of development, approach, and execution technologies that the company employs on its application development initiatives, there are a number of more mundane selection, utilization, and deacquisition services that also play key roles in helping companies to meet the challenges of our increasingly time compressed environments.

The acquisition component's selection services should include:

- projection of legacy system and technology impacts and options,
- proof-of-concept pilot projects, and
- metrics for forecasting and measuring productivity and performance so that quantitative business cases can be developed for technologies being acquired.

A significant, if sometimes overlooked, impact of our time compressed technology environments, is the exponential proliferation of legacy technologies. As each successful new application goes into production, it adds to the company's legacy technology landscape the set of development, approach, and execution technologies that are required to maintain it, interface to it, interoperate with it, and run it. The result is that legacy technologies proliferate just as quickly as new technologies, with increasingly shorter time intervals between the appearance of new technologies and their reemergence in the form of legacy systems.

The impact on TCM is that the ability of each new development, approach, and execution technology to address the company's current and future legacy environment must be taken into account. As we discussed earlier in this book, there are two main reasons why this process isn't always easy to implement. The first is that the purveyors of many of the newest technologies are focused on the benefits of their creations, and aren't anxious to see those benefits compromised by the constraints of a legacy environment. The second reason is that many new technology vendors and consultants don't understand legacy environments, their issues and needs, or the technologies that they're composed of.

The responsibility for addressing new technologies' legacy environments therefore lies, not with their vendors, but with the companies acquiring the new technologies for developing their applications. The good news is that the key to addressing legacy technology environments can be found in the same place—among the employees and vendors that developed the legacy applications. By setting policy to ensure that new technology development projects are staffed with people representing a mix of new and legacy technology skills, and by extending the organization's development methodology to ensure that project plans for the suite of technologies being selected include tasks that address legacy integration, companies acquiring the new technologies will derive two significant benefits. The first is that the development projects employing the new technologies will reflect the time and effort required for integration. The second benefit is that competencies among the company's technical and business staff will expand to include a wider range of technologies—a desirable and important benefit for companies that have to develop applications in a time compressed environment.

Where new, and largely untried, technologies are involved, the selection process should include proof-of-concept pilot projects, so that the company can develop a stable of hands-on experience with the technology's shortcomings and benefits. By setting up a proof-of-concept laboratory for executing pilot projects in a controlled environment, and setting policies, guidelines, and methodology tasks for when new technologies should be subjected to pilot tests, a good understanding of each technology's requirements and constraints can be developed.

An additional benefit from proof-of-concept pilot projects is that the results can be utilized for developing early productivity and performance metrics. By developing sets of standard technology adoption curves (the kind we explored in Chap. 4), optimizing them for the company's infrastructure and development project environments, and utilizing the results of the pilot projects to calibrate the curves for each technology, a set of early and objective company-specific metrics for each technology can be developed.

The key to making this concept work is continuous improvement. By examining the results of each development project, and applying the lessons learned to the technology adoption curves and refining the factors utilized to calibrate them, significant improvements in their accuracy, and in everyone's understanding of the confidence levels at which they can be used to predict productivity, will result.

The component's suite of utilization services for our time compressed environment should include:

- a single point of contact for vendor-related services—such as negotiations, licensing, and volume discounts,

- configuration services—such as distribution, installation, upgrade management and license enforcement,

- representation of business units in vendor programs—such as customer councils, joint development efforts, custom enhancements and beta tests, and

- testing and certification of new releases.

Although time compressed change doesn't impose requirements on these services that are significantly greater than what they would be in a non–time compressed environment, the business trend toward more flattened and empowered organizations does. The idea behind this suite of services is to free empowered and technology-competent business users from the mundane—but important—acquisition responsibilities associated with dealing with increasing numbers of technologies and vendors, while not constraining their ability to exercise their technology prerogatives. By providing this suite of centralized services, business units can acquire the technologies that make sense from business unit and corporate perspectives, without having to concern themselves with time-consuming and hard to manage vendor- and technology-related services.

The final suite of services in the acquisition component don't address acquisition at all. They handle technology deacquisition, which, in a time compressed environment, must occur a lot more frequently than it did in the past. The purpose of these important but almost universally overlooked services is to help the company and its business units plan and execute their transition out of legacy technologies in a graceful and businesslike manner. At a minimum, deacquisition services should include:

- developing a "release propagation map" so that the new technologys' dependencies on enabling technology releases can be charted for impact during acquisition, utilization, and deacquisition, and

- assessing readiness to transition out of the technology.

We can't make the problems associated with release propagation (that we examined in Chap. 6), disappear. But we can manage them, and an important mechanism for managing them is the release propagation map. A release propagation map is a series of tables, each showing the dependencies of a different class of application and enabling technology on an IT release that's a candidate for acquisition or deacquisition. The columns in each table contain a qualitative measure of the severity of the impact—such as Low, Medium, and High—along with a description of the properties of each dependency. Figure 11.10 illustrates what the structure of a propagation matrix might look like for a large organization with a substantial number of OO applications.

Release propagation maps, which can be developed using a variety of technologies from simple relational and OLAP databases to matrix processors, can then be used to analyze and illustrate the consequences of implementing and deimplementing new technology releases. Although development, population, and maintenance of release

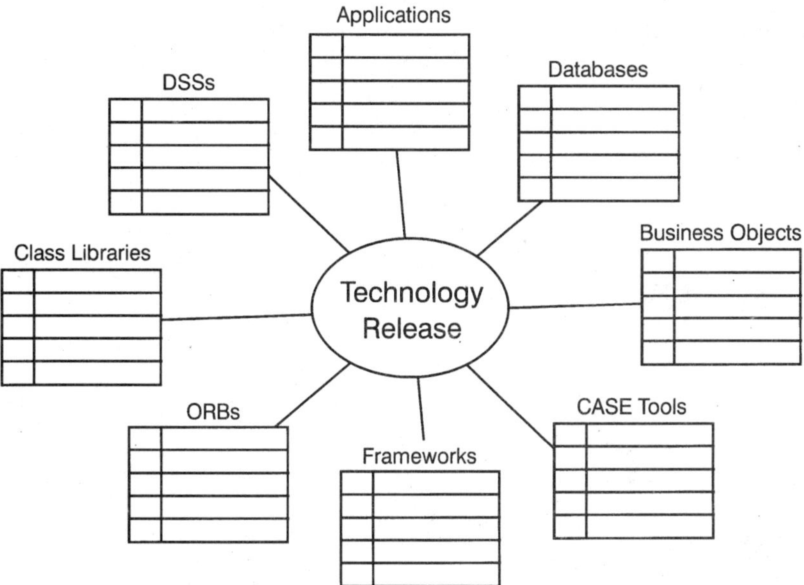

Figure 11.10 Release propagation map.

propagation maps represents additional effort and cost to companies that don't currently track this kind of dependency, I believe that such incremental costs are small compared to the substantial effort and the monetary, business, and political costs of discovering release propagation dependencies when new releases are installed and an unexpected, and seemingly disparate, array of systems suddenly fail.

The combination of release propagation maps and analyses of the skills and infrastructure required to support each technology and release can be combined to form a "readiness footprint" for acquisition and deacquisition of each technology and release. The idea is to develop a holistic understanding of the business case—benefits, impact, and costs—of the acquisition and deacquisition of each new technology. Having done so, the resulting business case model can be used as a basis for rationalizing the acquisition and deacquisition processes. It can also be utilized for ensuring that the changes in skills and infrastructure required for the transition(s) are in place, so that the costs of technology adoption (discussed in Chap. 4) can be minimized.

The Communication Component

Two of the characteristics of new technologies that almost unerringly lead to trouble are the lack of information on the technologies and how to use them, and our inability to communicate and disseminate what little information there is. Our inability to get needed information to teams of developers who are trying to utilize the new technology or approach to deliver their applications results in the same set of blind alleys, mistakes, and lessons learned being repeated over and over again, by team after team, until the information finally makes

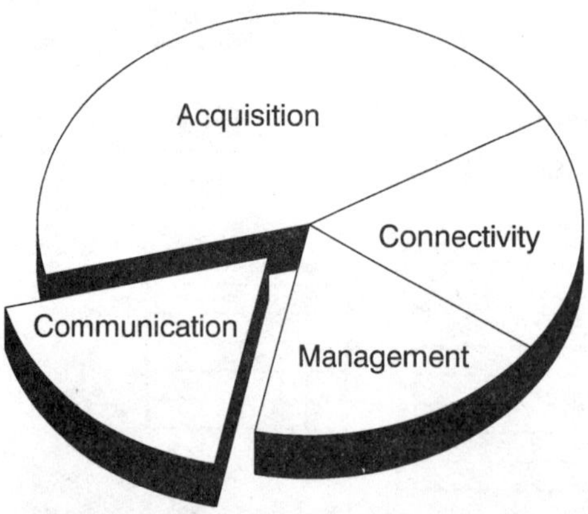

Figure 11.11   TCM communications component.

its way into the common body of our knowledge. The good news is that the information does spread, and developers eventually do learn how to deal with the new technology or technology combination. The bad news is that it can take many months—even years—for this to happen.

The solution, and the principal function of the communications component, is to speed the communications process up so that the information is available to the development teams and support functions that need it when they need it. (See Fig. 11.11.) This goal can be accomplished through a set of four simple, but key, classes of information that the communications component makes available to practitioners: They are:

- technology reviews, taken from the literature, conferences, technical organizations, and the Internet,

- guidelines addressing when and where the technology should—and shouldn't—be applied,

- white papers, covering technology-related issues—such as stability, performance, utilization to solve special problems, and compatibility with other technologies, and

- problems and solutions discovered by developers, within and outside of the company, as they begin to put the new technology to use.

By continually searching the generally available body of knowledge on development, approach, and execution technologies that are in use—or might be in use—at their organizations, a company's corporate IT function can perform an extremely valuable service to business units that are thinking of using the technology. Although this kind of information is generally available, the combination of short staff, persuasive vendors, and business pressure to quickly get something done creates an atmosphere in which the time and effort to search out and compile the needed information isn't expended by those who need the information most. By expending the time and effort as a service that is centrally funded and staffed, and making it available to all who need it in a convenient format, such as web pages on an internal internet, companies can leverage a common need and help their business units to make the most of their technology empowerment.

Just as important, but a lot more specific, is dissemination of guidelines addressing when and where development, approach, and execution technologies should be used and where they shouldn't. Information on which approaches and technologies are appropriate and inappropriate for processing large batches of information, high-speed transactions, advanced user interfaces (such as graphical visualizations and electronic performance support), developing applications that are highly adaptive (for applications that deal with fleet purchase programs or volatile financial instruments), highly integrated user interfaces, fault tolerance, simulation, and decision support can be a valuable asset to a development team in the throes of making technology decisions. When supplemented with the reasons why such decisions are appropriate or inappropriate—so that the business unit teams can assimilate the reasons and exercise their own best judgment—and reference examples of projects that have succeeded and failed—so that members of development teams can contact them, probe their experiences, and develop their own levels of comfort (or discomfort), the disseminated information becomes a valuable business tool as well.

White papers addressing the knotty technical development, approach, and execution technology issues that development teams are likely to encounter can also add substantial value to development projects that are executed in a time compressed environment. In an OO development environment, topics such as developing use cases for applications that will be based on preexisting frameworks, techniques identifying common behavior that can be abstracted into higher-level classes, and high-performance techniques for populating objects with data stored in non-OO data stores, represent a small sampling of common subjects that developers need to know about. These topics aren't found in the general literature, and aren't available from vendors, but can be addressed through directed research. When the information in the white papers is supplemented by examples from proof-of-concept prototypes and real projects, it can become an invaluable asset to teams that have to deal with large numbers of new technologies for which these kinds of issues haven't been fully worked out.

The final class of information that can be extremely valuable to developers in a time compressed technology environment includes experiences of practitioners who encounter problems, and find solutions to problems, as part of their ongoing project work. By setting up and administering groupware facilities, such as internal web sites, a central IT function can provide much-needed help to developers without impinging on their prerogatives and empowerment.

The Management Component

The function of the Management Component is to ensure that, as time compressed technologies progress through the utilization portion of their life cycles, development teams have the support they need to properly leverage the technologies, even though only a fraction of the

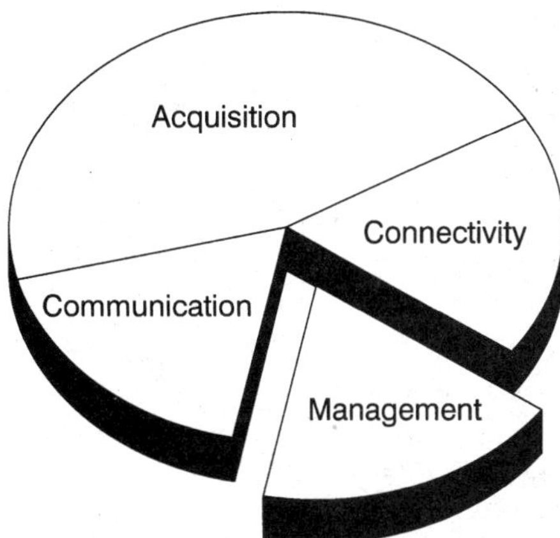

Figure 11.12 TCM management component.

development, approach, and execution technologies that make up their development environment may be stable and mature. (See Fig. 11.12.) The issue addressed by this component is this: as the information age matures, and the technologies that it's based on are becoming more capable and sophisticated, they're also becoming more demanding in terms of infrastructure and support. To borrow a term from electrical engineering, the "Q" of our application development systems is increasing. New development paradigms and technologies can be leveraged to develop better and better applications, more and more quickly. But to do so, they require narrower, and commensurately more focused and sophisticated, support. The resulting problem for companies developing applications in a time compressed environment is that the combination of large numbers of new technologies, the sophistication of their support requirements, and constantly increasing business demands for shorter and shorter development times doesn't provide enough time to develop the support infrastructures required for many of the technologies to work. The typical business result is lots of bottom line dollars thrown at sophisticated and capable new technologies, with little business benefit to show for it.

The Management Component helps companies to address this problem by providing four of the most cost-effective areas of infrastructure and support, and by funding them centrally, so that the substantial support burden that they represent can be amortized over many projects utilizing a wide spectrum of technologies instead of by single projects. The key support areas addressed by this component are:

- internal user group management,
- inclusion in methodology,

- mentoring and training services, and

- enhancing the services offered by the company's development support organizations so that they cover the new and multiple technologies that are likely to be in use.

Internal user groups can be an inexpensive, yet surprisingly effective, tool for identifying and analyzing common problems, solutions, resources, and requirements with technologies in a time compressed environment. They can be started, as new technologies transition into their life cycle's utilization phase, and ended, as the technologies are deacquisitioned. And they're great forums for facilitating face-to-face contact between different groups and business units that are using— or contemplating using—new technologies. By helping to keep multiple business units in close touch with each other, internal user groups can also become mechanisms for helping good technologies and combinations of technologies spread within the organization. Perhaps the nicest thing about internal user groups are that they're fluid, inexpensive to set up and administer, and they can be organized around the dynamic needs of the company and its business units.

Including new and multiple technologies in the company's development methodology, so that the roles and needs specific to each technology can be addressed, is critical to managing technology utilization in a time compressed environment. Fortunately, there are two good approaches that when taken together help companies accomplish this goal.

The first approach builds on a theme introduced in Chap. 9: the development of metamethodology route maps that address the needs of technologies and technology combinations. If the company's application development methodology isn't too steeped in a single development paradigm, a metamethodology is the best choice. The development of such a metamethodology can usually be accomplished without an undue amount of effort. The benefit of this approach is that it provides a mechanism through which developers can tailor their methodology to the needs of the suite of new and multiple technologies on each of their projects. Its drawback is that, in a time compressed environment, such an approach can result in lots of route maps.

The second approach is to provide help to project teams in selecting the correct route map out many potential route maps available. This can be done through a rules-based selection process that can be incorporated into the company's process management tool or methodology delivery mechanism. Although I currently know of only one process management tool vendor offering this kind of support (and the implementation the vendor offers is too primitive to effectively address this issue), the direction is correct, and I believe that a number of process management tool vendors will come out with some viable rules-based offerings in the near future. For those who can't wait, this is a good example of an expert system that shouldn't be very difficult to develop.

Mentoring and training represent good management component support functions, as they're critical to each technology's success and are expensive to develop. When centrally run, mentoring and training services have two key advantages over their commercial counterparts. The first is that they can be tailored to the company's business and its needs. Order entry and video rental store examples make a lot of sense from the perspective of training vendors, as they're universally applicable across a wide base of clients, but they're not relevant to companies that have to address a host of specific and nettlesome problems associated with integrated supply chain logistics, tracking airline reservations, or trading financial instruments. By contrast, centrally maintained examples that are tailored to an organization's needs, can be very relevant. The second advantage is that mentoring and training facilities can be developed and supplied on a just-in-time basis. As new technologies come into use, the people who evaluated them, participated in their proof-of-concept pilot projects, worked on infrastructure support, and developed the methodology route maps that address the technology can be pressed into service as mentors while formal training courseware is being developed. In addition to making mentoring services by knowledgeable internal people available when and where they are needed, this strategy provides valuable and immediate feedback to those who developed their support. The result is that they develop a better understanding of what it's like to utilize their product on real development projects, so that they can incorporate their lessons learned into subsequent releases of their products.

The two ideas here are to get help to practitioners in timeframes commensurate with the onslaught of new technologies in a time compressed environment, and to set up a mechanism through which infrastructure developers get good and immediate feedback so that they can revise their support services in time to help those who need them most.

The final element in our management component suite involves enhancing the offerings of the organization's development support services (security, network, software asset management, data administration, database administration, production, quality assurance, to name a few) so that the needs of the suites of new and multiple technologies are addressed. This can be accomplished by adopting a meta-model-based approach—similar to the metamethodology approach discussed above—in which services in each of these categories are broken down into elements that can be combined to fit the disparate needs of a number of different new multiple technology projects. Although the reengineering of a company's fixed support infrastructure into a metamodel-based support infrastructure can be expensive to implement, it need only be done once. After the company's support infrastructure is reengineered into a metamodel-based approach, new technologies and combinations of technologies need only affect the specific elements, and combinations of elements, that are required to support them. The other elements can be left untouched.

By tying the metasupport combinations to metamethodology route maps, the company will be able to garner substantial savings, as a single expert system can be utilized to manage both. In this way, a single expert system route map selector can be utilized to optimize methodology and support environments for the combination of new and older technologies utilized on each project. (See Fig. 11.13.)

The Connectivity Component

Connectivity among development projects and the applications—their ability to communicate, interface, and interoperate with each other—takes on added importance in time compressed environments. (See Fig. 11.14.) In most traditional development environments, data

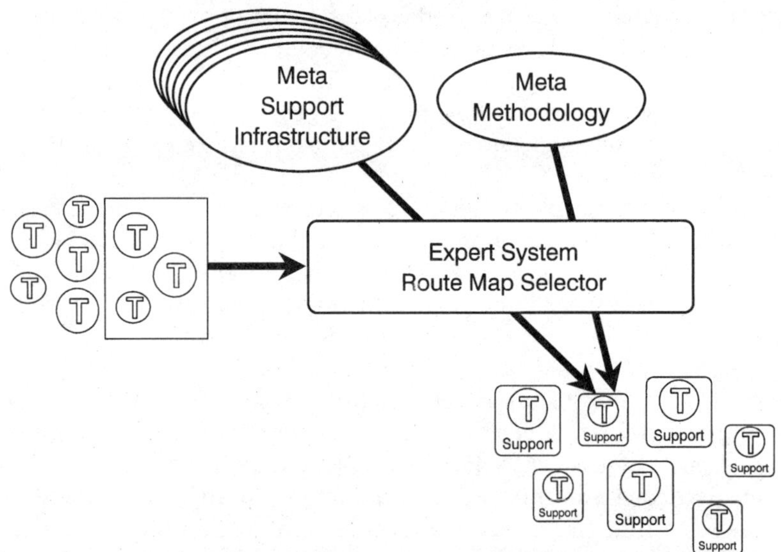

Figure 11.13 Expert system route map selector utilized to optimize methodology and infrastructure to support the suite of new and multiple technologies on each project.

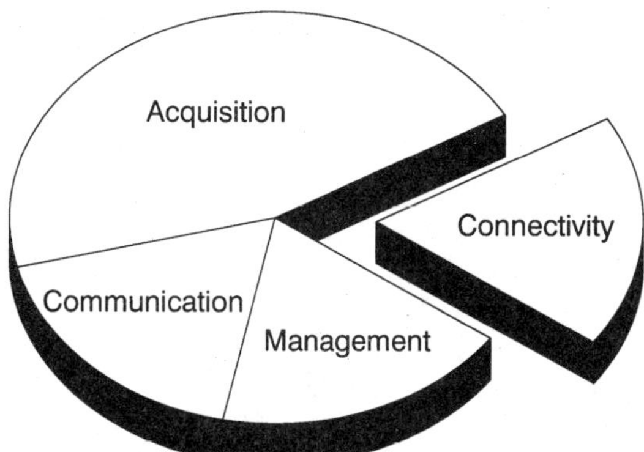

Figure 11.14 TCM connectivity component.

administration and database administration functions were sufficient to ensure that each project and system addressed the company's data in an appropriate and consistent way. The narrow technology base, centralized development and execution models, and small number of development projects made it easy to ensure that each project utilized narrow set of tools and technologies in a correct and consistent way, and that the systems that resulted would integrate and interoperate. As long as everyone played by the same set of centrally maintained and enforced rules, connectivity was a foregone conclusion. There was little need to give it a second thought.

In today's time compressed environment, with many disparate development projects, each managed under local governance and able to leverage a unique set of development, approach, and execution technologies and paradigms, the connectivity issues are a lot more complex. There's no straightforward way, for example, of assuring that an OO sales support application developed in Smalltalk will interoperate with an order processing application developed using HPS, an accounts receivable system developed in COBOL, or that any of them will interoperate with an Internet-based product information system that was developed using HTML and Java. In addition to not being able to access the same data, these systems may not even have been based on a consistent set of requirements models.

This is a tough problem. The reality of the late 1990s and early 2000s is that the onslaught of new, and not fully compatible, paradigms and technologies can't be stemmed, and the increasing numbers of empowered business units leveraging them to develop their applications can't be controlled. As with the other time compression related problems discussed in this book, the solution is not to make the problems go away. Rather we must address them head-on by altering our processes and infrastructure so that they're friendly to change, instead of being antagonistic to it. The connectivity component includes three elements that leverage this concept. They are:

- neutral data servers,

- neutral application servers, and

- common configuration management.

Taken together, these three elements can be employed to help ensure that the development projects are consistent, that applications can be migrated from one technology to the next, and that the applications that they produce will integrate and interoperate. Although these components aren't available yet, I don't believe that they would be especially difficult to develop by the organizations that need them, or by enterprising entrepreneurial companies looking to tap an emerging market. Here's how this goal might be accomplished.

Neutral data servers are middleware programs that provide consistent and current data to development projects and applications, regardless of the technologies that they execute in or that were used in their development. (See Fig. 11.15.) They're centrally maintained and have access to all of the company's data, regardless of the technology used to store the data. As new development technologies are

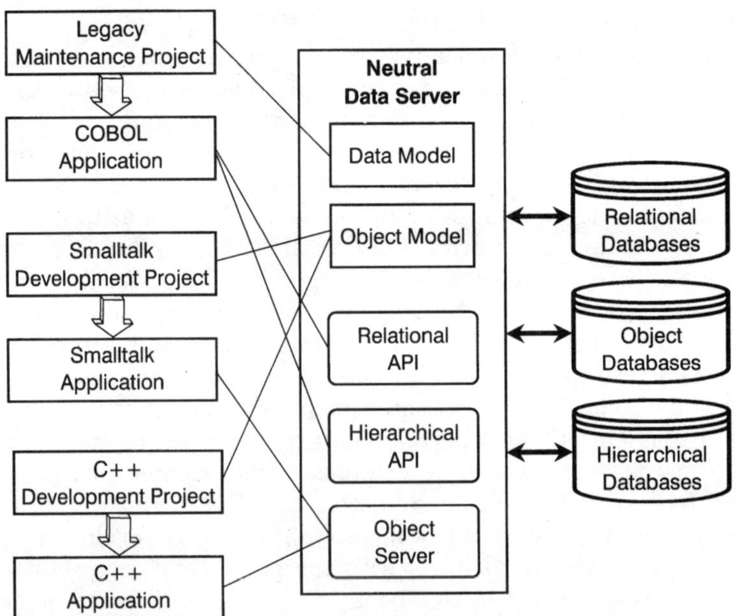

Figure 11.15 How a neutral data server supports three development paradigms.

acquisitioned, the company's information assets are mapped onto models (such as object models for Smalltalk or data models for HPS) that are appropriate for the new technology. As applications are developed, they provide data APIs in a form that's suitable for the application's execution. For legacy COBOL applications, this might be a hierarchical API that emulates IMS, while for applications developed using PowerBuilder, IEF, or HPS an ODBC-style relational interface might be most appropriate. For applications developed in C++ or Smalltalk, an object server that responds to messages from the application—or its ORB—would be appropriate.

The neutral data server resolves inconsistencies and maintains currency across applications that access the data. There are a number of very enabling technologies (such as polling, database triggers, and event notification), that can be leveraged to do this. As development and execution technologies, data stores, and data run the course of their useful lives and are eventually deacquisitioned, the company's neutral data servers can be maintained to reflect this course of events.

The salient ideas therefore are to centralize the burden of managing the data technology diversity that accompanies time compressed change, and to do so in such a way that development projects and the applications they produce don't have to know—or care—about the underlying technologies utilized to store the data or to maintain them in consistent states.

Neutral application servers would perform the same kind of function as neutral data servers, but with two differences. The first is that they perform their functions for applications instead of data; the second is that our quarry is technology-independent integration and interoperability. The idea is to utilize application servers to transform the disparate set of application interfaces associated with a large and growing diversity of execution technologies into a bounded number of standard and ubiquitous application program interfaces.

Although the composition of the APIs will migrate over time, as technologies are acquisitioned and deacquisitioned and as common standards come and go, holding the number to a small set should do the trick. Providing, documenting, and maintaining CORBA, OLE, and relational APIs for each new and legacy application, for example, would substantially reduce the impact of time compressed change on most development projects' ability to achieve interoperability and integration.[7] The idea here is to ensure that the functionality provided by the company's applications is accessible to any other applications having the proper authorization and that can interoperate with CORBA or OLE (the two currently emerging standards) or that can simply read from and write to a relational database. For companies with large numbers of legacy applications that cannot access relational data, an API based on nonrelational data stores can be substituted for the relational API.

An additional advantage to providing multiple and common APIs to all applications is that, when combined with neutral data servers, they form a technology-neutral migration path for the company's legacy applications. Once all applications can access the same data (via the neutral data server's multiple APIs) and can interoperate with each (via the same set of APIs) applications can be migrated at will from legacy technologies to current technologies without running into data problems or losing interoperability.

The final element in our connectivity component addresses the problem of software configuration management (SCM), which is substantially more challenging in a time compressed environment. The reason is that, in addition to managing application artifacts vertically—from business models through production code—time compressed multiple-technology environments require that these artifacts must be managed horizontally—across technologies—as well. There are several reasons for this.

The first reason is that in today's time compressed environments, the sets of business objectives, value propositions, transformation levers, CSFs, and information needs are often satisfied through a number of different applications and information technologies. The implication, and the SCM impact, is that it's no longer sufficient to trace objectives or information needs through requirements analysis artifacts such as subject areas, processes, and entity types. In today's environments, they must also be traced through object models, use cases, applets, and web sites—to name just a few. The second reason is that each of these requirements analysis artifacts can be implemented in a number of different technologies. The implication here is that an analysis object may be implemented as, and therefore must be traced through, a number of C++ and Smalltalk classes, class libraries, and frameworks. The third complicating factor is that many of the classes, class libraries, and frameworks are distributed—and sometimes also replicated—over large-scale networks. If consistent configurations are to be maintained, the same set of business requirements artifacts must be traceable all the way through to multiple distributed network-embedded objects.

Configuration management in this kind of environment requires SCM tools that go beyond the commercial technology-, environment-, and paradigm-specific products that are available today. The purpose of this is to ensure that updates to system components can be executed without showing up as surprises in applications where one would least expect them, and that function versus cost scenarios can be accurately run on applications. I don't have a satisfactory solution for this problem. But I do know that if we are to succeed in developing and operating the large-scale, multiple-technology network-embedded applications that are on the horizon, it will have to be solved. I'm confident that, given the severity of the problem and the amounts expenditures that will be impacted by it, the problem will be addressed and someone will make a lot of money solving it.

References

1. For a good discussion of development, approach, and execution technology transitions, along some of the factors that have promoted and inhibited them in the past, see Robert Fichman and Chris Kemerer, "Adoption Of Software Engineering Process Innovations: The Case Of Object Orientation," *Sloan Management Review* 34(2), Winter 1993.
2. John Stone, *Inside ADW and IEF: The Promise and Reality of CASE*, McGraw-Hill, 1993.
3. Vaughan Merlyn and John Parkinson, *Development Effectiveness*, Wiley 1994; and Michael Hammer, *Reengineering The Corporation*, Harper Business, 1993.
4. For good discussions of critical assumptions, although in a different context, see John C. Henderson and Jay G. Cooprider, "Dimensions Of I/S Planning And Design Technology," Massachusetts Institute Of Technology CISR Working Paper No. 191, September 1990; and James Martin, *Information Engineering* Book II, Prentice Hall, 1990.
5. For an in-depth treatment of how business and technology strategy and infrastructure interact, see Beverly Goldberg and John Sifonis, Dynamic Planning, Oxford University Press, 1994; Also see John C. Henderson and N. Venkatraman, "Strategic Alignment: A Framework For Strategic Information Technology Management," Massachusetts Institute Of Technology CISR Working Paper No. 190, August 1989.
6. In Electrical Engineering, the term "Q" refers to the "Quality" of a circuit. "High Q" circuits provide substantial advantage over a narrow frequency spectrum. "Low Q" circuits provide smaller advantage, but they provide it over a wider spectrum of frequencies.
7. CORBA and OLE standards are well documented. The relational API need consist of nothing more than a set of relational database tables—some for input queues, other for output queues—that are set up for accessing an application's functionality.

12

Conclusions

In the past 11 chapters we explored time compressed technology change—the accelerating pace at which application development is changing—in terms of the technologies we utilize to develop applications, the approaches we employ for development, the technologies required to execute our applications once they're developed, and the increasingly short (compressed) amounts of time that we have to deal with the change that it brings. Today's application developers are caught in a vortex between an onslaught of new and more powerful technologies, accelerating business autonomy, expectations, and demands, and a relatively stagnant culture and infrastructure. We examined the reasons why many of the new and powerful technologies that should be making things better, actually make them worse.

In the second part of the book, we also explored TCM, a framework of workable strategies and techniques for managing time compressed change so that we can harness the powerful technologies that it brings for developing better applications instead of being hurt by them.

In Part 1 of the book, we examined each of the driving factors of time compressed change, not only in terms of the accelerating pace at which information technologies are evolving and proliferating, but also in terms of equally potent business drivers, such as:

- globalization, business reengineering, heightened competition, and the increased importance that these factors place on application development,
- lower cost, increased accessibility, and easier approachability of new information technologies, and

- the resulting willingness of today's empowered business users to leverage the new technologies that time compression brings to satisfy their increasing appetite for new application and faster development.

We examined each of the CSFs for large-scale business application development, along with the impact that time compressed change has on each. We also explored the jagged interface between the fast pace of time compressed change and our slow-moving business, management, and IT infrastructure and cultures.

A number of basic conclusions can be drawn from our investigation. Although some of these conclusions are disturbing and run counter to conventional wisdom, what the industry pundits say, and what we read in the press, I believe that it's important to set them down so that we can understand what's really happening to application development. If we can't understand the reasons why—despite significant and rapid advances in the technologies we use—we still can't quickly and reliably deliver working applications that support our businesses, we won't be able to address these issues, and we won't be able to make things much better than they are. (See Fig. 12.1.) Our conclusions about time compressed change and how it impacts application development may be summarized thus:

- *Inevitability.* The evolution and proliferation of development, approach, and execution technologies that defines time compressed change is real—these forces are accelerating, and can't be slowed down or stopped.

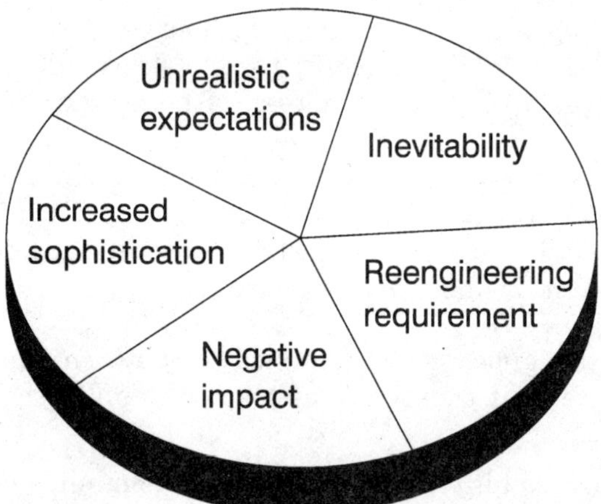

Figure 12.1   Basic conclusions about time compressed change and application development.

- *Unrealistic Expectations.* Our expectations for the new technologies that time compressed change brings are inconsistent with the realities of how technology change is adopted and how it's assimilated into our culture and processes.

- *Negative Impact.* Time compressed change negatively impacts the people, processes, and infrastructure that we employ for our application development.

- *Increased Sophistication.* Many of the technologies that time compressed change brings are more sophisticated than those that existed before them. These new technologies require more sophisticated processes and infrastructure to be productive and to pay their users back.

- *Reengineering Requirement.* The policies, culture, infrastructure, and processes that served us in the past have trouble coping with time compressed change. If we are to succeed, they must be reengineered so that they address the realities of development in the late 1990s and early part of the twenty-first century.

The inevitability of time compressed change is the result not only of the many new development, approach, and execution technologies that we constantly find at our doorsteps, but also of the myriad of channels through which such new technologies affect application development. In Chap. 6 we saw that of the 10 principal ways in which this comes about, 5 aren't even functions of technology. They're related to business. Regardless of the policies, initiatives, procedures, or mandates that IT organizations employ to try and stem the tide, the combination of mergers and acquisitions, software packages, business communications, extreme requirements, decentralization, and empowerment act to ensure that time compressed technology change is a turn of the century reality that we all have to deal with.

Our ability to deal effectively with time compressed change requires that we understand something about it, the technologies it brings, and what we need to do in order to leverage them. Addressing time compressed change must begin with realistic expectations in terms of the substantial time that it takes to successfully adopt many the technologies that it brings, and the equally substantial short-term investments that are required to make them pay off.

What gets in our way is the combination of technology vendors making unrealistic claims so that their products gain visibility in our crowded and noisy markets, industry pundits who make their livings touting the latest and greatest, our collective faith in technologies, and sophisticated user interfaces that gloss over the underlying complexity. Such factors cloud our views, making realistic expectations difficult to set and manage. The typical result is that even when things go right, and the technologies brought by time compressed change are successfully adopted for application development and put to good use, the successes that result can be perceived as disasters.

Another part of the problem is that time compressed change brings technologies that are a lot more sophisticated than anything we had before. They require new approaches that are more business oriented, more constrained, and more abstract. New and different infrastructure components are needed, and development projects that utilize them produce sets of new and confusing signals that make it difficult for management to discern which projects are doing well and which need help. And like many high-tech innovations, a goodly number of the advances that time compressed change brings are applicable over narrower ranges of problems and for shorter periods of time. But our corporate cultures, IT organizations, and application development environments are legacies from past eras, and have been carefully optimized around ITs that were far more stable and a lot less numerous than those available today.

The result is that when many of these new technologies are brought into traditional application development environments they can do more harm than good. As we saw in Chap. 2, time compressed change can negatively impact each of the CSFs required for large-scale business application development, wreaking chaos and havoc on good development organizations that have performed well in the past.

The underlying problem, and a major theme of this book, is that the organizations, processes, culture, and infrastructure that served our needs in the past are becoming a lot less viable and appropriate than they once were. The paradigm in which a single IT organization, infrastructure, staff, and culture could be carefully optimized around a bounded suite of development technologies and business needs—the paradigm that served our needs for almost three decades—doesn't hold up in today's time compressed world. What's needed is a reengineered application development capability in which the processes, culture, and infrastructure are optimized, not for the stable trickle of marginally adequate development, approach, and execution technologies of the past, but for the global business pressures, empowered organizations, and time compressed technology change that our companies will confront as we close out the twentieth century and push into a new millennium.

However, reengineering of this magnitude would be too wrenching and far-reaching for most companies to tackle, and it would involve a lot more risk than most responsible and prudent managers would be willing to take. What's needed is a simple, holistic approach to help managers successfully address the multitude of problems associated with the time compressed changes that mark today's application development. This approach must be a practical one, composed of strategies and techniques that can be implemented as needed, with incremental investment and risk, and incremental ROI for the business. The TCM approach presented in the second part of this book is an example of this kind of approach.

Index

ABOUT THE AUTHOR

John A. Stone is Chief Technology Officer of Bowne &
Company, the world's largest financial printer. He regularly
writes and speaks on the many business, technical, and cultural issues encountered while transitioning to new technologies such as OO and Internet with emphasis on productivity, risk, performance, quality, culture, organization,
infrastructure, and return on investment. He has lectured
at numerous professional societies, corporations, academic
institutions, and conferences that include TRW, Chase
Manhattan Bank, Colgate University, OOPSLA, and the
MIT Sloan School of Management. He is also the author of
Inside ADW and *IEF: The Promise and Reality of CASE*,
published by McGraw-Hill. He can be contacted at (718)
858-6710 or Stone 130 @aol.com.